DATE DUE		
DEC 0 3 1997			

Nothing to Fear

Nothing to Fear

Risks and Hazards
in American Society

EDITED BY ANDREW KIRBY

The University of Arizona Press   Tucson

The University of Arizona Press

Copyright © 1990
The Arizona Board of Regents
All Rights Reserved

This book was set in Linotron 202 Sabon
⊗ This book is printed on acid-free, archival-quality paper.
Manufactured in the United States of America.

95 94 92 91 90 5 4 3 2 1

Library of Congress Cataloging-in-Publication Data

Nothing to fear : risks and hazards in American society / edited by
    Andrew Kirby.
        p.   cm.
    Includes index.
    ISBN 0-8165-1185-3 (alk. paper)
        1. Disasters—Social aspects—United States—Congresses.
    2. Technology—Social aspects—United States—Congresses.
    I. Kirby, Andrew.
    HV555.U6N68   1990
    363.3'4'0973—dc20   90-11011
                                                            CIP

British Library Cataloguing in Publication data are available.

CONTENTS

v

Contents

FIGURES AND TABLES

CONTRIBUTING AUTHORS

JoAnne Brown is a graduate of Yale and Wisconsin-Madison, and is currently assistant professor of history at Johns Hopkins University. Her research has focused broadly on intellectual history, and she has worked at the Smithsonian Institution in Washington on a display dealing with the creation of cleanliness as a concept within American society. As part of this interest, she has also written on professional uses of language, and in particular, on what she calls "the words that succeed." Her work has appeared inter alia in the *Radical History Review*, and she is working on books to appear with Harvard and Johns Hopkins University Presses.

Clayton P. Gillette has been professor in the School of Law at Boston University since 1984. He specializes in law, urban development, and municipal debt. He has published in the *Michigan Law Review*, the *Boston University Law Review*, the *Minnesota Law Review*, and the *Harvard Law Review*, and is a contributing editor to the *Municipal Finance Journal*.

Douglas MacLean is professor in the Department of Philosophy and Public Policy at the University of Maryland. He has published extensively on the relations between social values and social actions. Recent edited books include *The Security Gamble: Deterrence Dilemmas in the Nuclear Age*, and *Values at Risk*, published by Rowman and Littlefield. He is director of the Center for Philosophy and Public Policy.

Claudia Mills is also at the University of Maryland, where she is editor of *QQ*, the report from the Center for Philosophy and Public Policy. She has co-edited *The Moral Foundations of Civil Rights*, and, with Douglas MacLean, *Liberalism Reconsidered*.

JAMES K. MITCHELL, professor and chair of the Department of Geography at Rutgers University, has received university awards for excellence and distinguished public service. His extensive experience with both natural and technological hazards has been tapped by the National Academy of Sciences, congressional committees, domestic and international commissions, and planning teams investigating disaster prevention. Mitchell has also served as a consultant to the National Research Council, the United Nations, and the U.S. General Accounting Office. Aside from extensive publications in the geographical literature, his work has appeared in various National Research Council reports, and in collections of essays published by the University of Chicago and the University of Minnesota. He currently serves on the editorial boards of *Geographical Review* and *Applied Geography*.

ROY S. POPKIN was for many years the director of the American Red Cross, in which capacity he was responsible for emergency relief programs throughout the United States. Based in Silver Spring, Maryland, he continues to employ his extensive practical insights as an author and private consultant.

JOHN H. SORENSEN is a graduate of the University of Colorado, and is currently a scientist at the Oak Ridge National Laboratory, Tennessee. He has published extensively in the broad field of technological hazards, producing numerous laboratory reports and articles in professional journals. He has also appeared as an expert witness in several important legal cases dealing with nuclear power throughout the United States.

JOEL A. TARR is presently acting dean of the Carnegie Mellon Social and Historical Studies faculty, where he is also professor of history and public policy. Tarr is the author and editor of numerous books on technological change and urban politics, published by the Illinois, Temple, and Carnegie Mellon University Presses. His articles addressing public sector response to environmental problems have appeared in over a dozen edited volumes and in journals such as *Environmental Engineering, Technological Forecasting and Social Change, Social History*, and the *American Journal of Public Health*. His research has been funded by multiple grants from the National Science Foundation, National Oceanic and Atmospheric Administration, and the Exxon, Sperry-Hutchinson, General Electric, and Mellon foundations.

PHILLIP K. TOMPKINS is professor of communication at the University of Colorado and former associate dean at Purdue University. He is an expert in organizational analysis and worked for NASA during its formative years as a communication consultant. He is a past president of the International Communication Association and has published widely in the discipline and elsewhere; his most recent book *Organizational Communication*, was published by Sage in 1985.

WILLIAM A. WALLACE is professor and chair of the Department of Decision Sciences and Engineering Systems at the Rensselear Polytechnic Institute in New York. He has worked in the fields of public administration and operations research and has a long list of publications in the technical and user journals. His current research concentrates on the response phase of crisis management at the operational and strategic levels.

PREFACE

This book has a relatively long and complex history, only some of which is relevant to the reader. Its origins lie in the first instance in a collaborative interchange between individuals associated with the Natural Hazards Research and Applications Information Center at the University of Colorado in Boulder, and representatives of the Center for Environment, Technology, and Development at Clark University in Worcester, Massachusetts. Implicit in these exchanges was a concern for some dialogue between researchers more focused upon so-called natural hazards, and those concentrating upon technological dangers, and beneath that concern lay a realization that the two fields were developing along rather different intellectual axes, despite their concern for a single broad phenomenon—that is, risk and the human response. For a number of reasons, this collaboration has remained unfinished, but it did result in a submission to the National Science Foundation in 1985 by the editor and colleague Bill Riebsame, which was funded in 1986 as NSF grant ECE 8516152.[1] The purpose of this funding was to organize a colloquium that would bring together a number of researchers who work in the broad fields that together inform the risk community. Some of the persons invited were unfortunately unable to attend (Charles Perrow, for example), but after much correspondence we created the group represented in this volume.

In choosing our group of discussants, we paid attention to research links between the natural world and the technological realm. In addition, we also sought consciously for individuals who offered perspectives beyond the usual discourse of risk and hazards. We invited Phillip Tompkins (to take but one example), a communication specialist who would not regard himself as a hazards researcher, but whose work on organizations has explicitly used examples from the space industry, both before and after the Challenger disaster. Conversely, we did not include one of the more established and vital conduits of criticism to be found within the risk community. We did not seek out an individual to offer a Marxist analysis, because we felt, rightly or wrongly, that other points of departure were in more pressing need of adumbration; nor should this be taken as evidence that the extensive fruits of such analysis are rejected or ignored in what follows.[2]

Our meeting took place in Boulder during August 1987. Participants presented their written papers to the group over a period of three days, and their efforts were discussed by their colleagues. The papers were rewritten in subsequent months to take into account those comments, and the responses of the organizers. In pulling the chapters together, I have been very conscious of the varied problems that face the creation of an edited volume. In many ways it is like a detective story—written with some deductive premises in mind, but read inductively. This is of course the attraction of the latter genre, for the reader pays to be confused and to be kept waiting until the end for some denouement. The reader or reviewer of the edited collection is, though, less forgiving. It is normal for book reviewers to complain of inconsistency between essays, their variable quality, and a lack of direction. In part, this reflects the irritation of the busy reader who has to assimilate all the chapters, rather than simply dip into the text of a single-author book. In larger part too, it reflects the debasement of the publishing currency, for it seems that no group of scholars can meet these days without recording their events for posterity.

This volume does not add to the demise of the multiauthor volume. The deductive premise is straightforward: to indicate how the scholarly discourse on risk issues can be enriched by taking account of a broad range of disciplinary research. That said, we have not opted for eclecticism— some sort of postmodern stew. As the Prologue indicates, the chapters have a restricted number of common themes, which are developed in a limited number of directions. The book possesses a simple punch line (which could be inferred by the reader) revealed both here and in chapter 1; namely, that risk issues are to be understood only historically and situationally—that is, in the social setting within which they rest—and that responses to hazards must be developed as part of a collective interchange that also pays attention to the varied contexts of both risks and social groups.

In writing for a specific audience, the authors have addressed themselves in the first instance to the academic community. This reflects a view that, for the most part, the present risk and hazards literature is pragmatic and constrained by its orientation toward the short-term goals of public policy. That said, this book's contents do not remain at the level of abstraction that is typical of so much of contemporary social theory: the chapters are grounded in specific narratives, and some also address the policy realm head-on. Nonetheless, and to repeat, our concerns here rest with the development of broad ideas, and not policies per se.

NOTES

1. One of the most salient reasons for this hiatus is that, of the original participants in the discussions concerning collaboration, only two still remain within the respective institutions—at Boulder and Clark.

2. See, e.g., some of the powerful contributions to Hewitt 1983. Of particular importance is Watts' chapter: 231–62.

REFERENCES

Hewitt, Kenneth, ed.
    1983   *Interpretations of Calamity*. Boston: Allen and Unwin.
Watts, M.
    1983   "On the Poverty of Theory: Natural Hazards Research in Context."
            In *Interpretations of Calamity*, Kenneth Hewitt ed., 231–62.

ACKNOWLEDGMENTS

A book such as this, developed over a relatively long period of time, depends on a large number of individuals and institutions for their support. Initially, I must thank the participants in this enterprise, who did a fine job in bringing their ideas to fruition, with the exception of only one chapter that disappeared en route. In addition, I should like to thank Bill Riebsame, who put a lot into this project and who refused to take anything out.

The author of chapter 5, Roy Popkin, and the editor thank Peter May for his kind permission to reproduce material from his book *Recovering from Catastrophes*, which constitutes Tables 5.1–5.4.

Many others deserve credit. The staff of the Institute of Behavioral Science at the University of Colorado did a marvelous job of support and succor: Debby Ash, Mary Axe, Illana Gallon, Fay Tracy, and Jean Umbreit have all left their mark here. Jerry Jacob put things together at the outset, and helped us spend the National Science Foundation's money, without which this would not have gone ahead. Anonymous referees provided helpful commentary, as did Marvin Waterstone and Terry Connolly, and the University of Arizona Press was very supportive. Finally, and crucially, I should like to acknowledge the help of David Butler, who did an enormous amount to turn a pile of paper into a manuscript. Thank you all.

ANDREW KIRBY

Nothing to Fear

On Social Representations of Risk

Andrew Kirby

"INCAPABLE OF TAKING A RISK"

A recent British newspaper article asks gloatingly whether Americans are becoming "yellow":

> America the brave, the land of the free, has developed a thick yellow streak. . . . Americans, who are better nurtured, protected, safer than at any time in their history, have become cowardly, whingeing and incapable of taking a risk.[1]

The commentator traces this trend back to Ralph Nader in the 1960s, who, it will be remembered, led a campaign against the Corvair automobile on the grounds that it was "unsafe at any speed." For his next example the journalist draws on Joseph Heller's novel *Catch-22*, which was written about the Second World War but has a timeless quality that allowed it to become too a metaphor for the Vietnam conflict. Its hero, Yossarian, was fond of observing that there were "catastrophes lurking everywhere, too numerous to count. When he contemplated the many diseases and potential accidents threatening him, he was positively astounded that he had managed to survive in good health as long as he had."[2]

This alleged new pathos within America—dubbed the "land of the wimp"—is manifested in an obsession with dietary regimes, with the avoidance of sexually transmitted diseases, and with the harmful effects, rather than the pleasures, of alcohol and tobacco. Many of these obsessions have resulted in new items of legislation designed to reduce the factor of risk within everyday life, such as bans on smoking in public places and the compulsory wearing of seatbelts in automobiles.

Embedded in this astonishing article are some interesting insights concerning the nature of risk and its place within our society.[3] Of particular importance here is the assumption that risk-taking is an integral part of the human psyche and an impulse to be lauded rather than restricted; it is the incentive that has driven explorers, astronauts, scientists, and capitalists toward their various goals. By this measure, we are, as a society, open to criticism: the author sadly contrasts NASA's response in the 1960s to the deaths of three astronauts in an Apollo spacecraft, to the deaths in the Challenger explosion of 1986. In 1967 the reaction was to push ahead with the space program; in 1986 it was to ground the space shuttle for three years.

In short, America can be seen to have shifted in its collective mood. In 1933 Roosevelt could uplift a nation with the cry that "the only thing we have to fear is fear itself." To some outsiders, it appears that this has changed: everything is now a hazard and everyone a potential victim.[4]

RISKS AND SOCIAL CONSTRUCTIONS

While provocative, the notion of cowardice as a collective characteristic is a problematic sociological insight. In the first instance, we could just as easily identify situations in which Americans perceive themselves to be leading more risky lives than they did forty or fifty years ago. A moment's thought suggests the following list of putative events, any number of which might contribute to a sense of dread, or what MacLean and Mills describe below as a conservatism toward risk:

1. death by irradiation in a nuclear war, perhaps caused accidentally, perhaps caused via a third-party conflict;
2. incapacitation and, ultimately, death via transmission of the HIV virus, sexually or via transfusion;
3. injury or death following midair collision or terrorist attack on an airplane;
4. death or injury following a shooting incident;

5. dependence upon drugs or alcohol, increasing the possibility of overdose;
6. illness and possible demise due to tropospheric ozone contamination of urban areas, producing long-term smog conditions and respiratory difficulties;
7. long-term alteration of the global environment, leading to higher rates of skin cancer.

This litany of risks, many of which are beyond the control of any single individual (or even of a lone government), can be interpreted in two ways. On the one hand, we might say dismissively that "things fall apart," and that therefore there is no need to pay attention to the overall risk calculus (this outlook is explored further in chapter 1). As usual, there is a cliché (a T-shirt slogan, a hit record) that summarizes this tendency: "don't worry, be happy."

The alternative is the one under scrutiny here. That is to say, as overall risk levels are assumed to rise, so individuals search for some substitutions in order to bring down again the totality of risk that faces them. Realistically, it does not make any sense to try to balance out the potential threat of being killed by a gunman on a shooting spree via the introduction of a ban on smoking in public places; the first threat remains untouched by the second action. Nonetheless, individuals may feel that they, and their political representatives, are at least taking control over some portion of their lives. This interpretation is consistent with the general perspective being developed in this book, namely, that the risks that surround us become part of our everyday existence. Just as we construct our collective ideas about the neighborhood school or local politics, so we evaluate hazards as large, small, or nonexistent threats; and as we may change our combined evaluations about a high school or a politician, so we can change our estimates of risk at will.[5]

Douglas and Wildavsky are therefore right to ask a counterposed question: "are the dangers really increasing, or are we more afraid?"[6] Certainly, the two phenomena—the level of danger and the level of fear—do not need to be proportionally linked; but we do need to go further in order to identify the various processes at work in determining danger and producing fear. Why, to echo them once more, has "confidence about the physical world turned into doubt?"[7]

THE PROCESSES AT WORK

In trying to penetrate a social construction, we address not only the events of everyday life, but the ontology of risk also. Put another way, we need to examine both the components of our lives that contribute to risk, and in addition the discourses that surround them; the perceived dangers of drug-taking cannot really be separated, for example, from the intense political debate that surrounds drug use in this country. In beginning this investigation, we can distinguish a number of contexts; it is the changes taking place within these settings that together contribute both to the current level of risk and to our interpretations.

The world order. As Paul Kennedy has argued, we are witnessing the eclipse of the hegemony of the United States as a world power.[8] Vietnam was perhaps the first indication of this process; hostages in Iran and Lebanon more recent ones. The process is not solely political, nor even military; it rests upon profound economic shifts also. In consequence, it is reasonable for American citizens to have doubts about the future—and by logical extension, the present too. Such doubts are not conducive to confidence about smaller issues.

The nation and the state apparatus. As the world order changes, so do its component parts. Individual nations are becoming less powerful—sovereignty within the European Community will be different from sovereignty as it has been codified after centuries of warfare in Europe. In the United States, economic links to Canada and Mexico are also eroding the borders to the north and south, despite the rhetoric against aliens and foreigners. As sovereignty wavers, state institutions attempt to maintain a hold upon the operation and performance of key sectors; political debate about the directions and amounts of public intervention becomes clamorous.

Everyday life. The region of day-to-day life—the locality—becomes more important to the individual as other phenomena change in form. The locality is increasingly the place where debate about economic development or social issues takes place; levels of prosperity and the quality of life are questions that residents expect to dispute and to take action upon.[9]

The home. This too is undergoing metamorphosis, as roles within the family—and even the nature of the family itself—change. The notion of the home as a refuge, a place that is by definition safe, has been destroyed by the economic and demographic changes occurring within both metropolitan areas and suburbs, such as the breakup of families, and the new roles being played out by males and females, parents and children, young and elderly.

In putting these contexts together, we can begin to address the nation's supposed yellow streak—which is of course something other than a paralyzing state of dread. At the very least, it is a reflection of the changes that have taken place within the conditions that encompass American society. As I have suggested, these include a different standing for the nation within the world order, with all that this implies for collective confidence. In consequence, there has emerged a different discourse regarding the responsibilities of the state apparatus, and a changing set of public expectations within the community.[10]

Perhaps the most provocative contextual shift rests on the different meaning given to the home on a day-to-day basis. This represents two developments, with the first being the change that has taken place in the spatial context of the home. For many, the cozy shelter of the suburban, *Leave-it-to-Beaver* house represented either the dream or the actuality of the flight from cities that were seen as malignant and unhealthy edifices (a point discussed at greater length in the Epilogue). At the end of the twentieth century, that flight has been revealed as a wasted journey; there is no sanctuary from reality, if the latter be measured in terms of stress, congestion, crime, and divorce.[11] In addition, the home itself has metamorphosed. It no longer conforms to Rockwell's sentimental images, with a clear role for Ma, Pa, and the two kids. The home is now many things: an office space and communications center, a long-term food processing space, a locus of complex electronic equipment, even a refuge from a potential nuclear war. For an increasing number of families, it is also a social experiment in single parenting. As a result of these changes, I see very different interpretations of risk. There is no insulation from the "out there"; the world flows through the home, courtesy of the electronic media of communication.[12] Changed gender roles dictate that there is no forced or voluntary cloistering for women in the home; there is in fact diminishing workplace-homeplace separation, as the personal computer and the facsimile machine instantly connect dwelling and office. In consequence, the process of assessing risk is being undertaken by a growing number of persons who spend less and less time within the home and more time in metaphorical daily combat—on the streets, in the subway, on the roads.[13]

RISK AND RESPONSE WITHIN EVERYDAY LIFE

Having glanced at some of the large-scale changes taking place in and around American society, it remains to be seen just how these contribute to our collective sense of (in)security. The identification of risk in a complex world is much more difficult than many novels or movies would have us believe.[14] For most of us, urban society is neither out of control, nor even a postmodern dystopia, to use Margaret Fitzsimmon's fine phrase. We learn to accommodate risk because it is, to a large degree, both formalized and institutionalized. A decade ago, Julian Wolpert wrote of the "dignity of risk," and in so doing he challenged many of our assumptions concerning the hazardousness of everyday life.[15] He pointed out that the relation between an individual and some hazard is not a direct one; there are also many intervening variables involved, such as those institutions that undertake to structure different aspects of our existence. Real estate interests and planning commissions, to name but two examples, act to mask the "real" nature of risk. Developers build homes close to—or even on—flood plains, and planning ordinances may reify such choices as acceptable. In such situations, the resident is left to evaluate the risk associated with a residential location decision through a dual filter—the first linked to the market, the second to the public realm. It is an unusual consumer who can sidestep one or the other filter, in order to make an "objective" interpretation of the hazardousness of a place.

Wolpert's work was thus an early example of the recognition that individuals are rarely able to explain the world around them in a way that is independent of the views and actions of others. Once we have this interpretation before us, we can go on to confront two interesting phenomena. The first is related to the ways in which individuals respond to risks that they face and have faced; the second is to do with the ways in which institutions undertake the same task.

Returning to the transatlantic interpretation of America's yellow streak for a moment, journalist Blundy observes that "a litigious lunacy has gripped America."[16] For him, this too represents a timidity, insofar as most corporations and public agencies surround themselves with insurance—at crippling cost—just in case they are sued. But this completely misses the point of litigation of this sort—which claims that a product caused some harm or that some action inflicted emotional distress. It is, in fact, one of the few ways in which the individual can influence the way in which society's risk calculus is resolved. In large measure, that calculus is determined in a formal way. The science of risk analysis has been developed by professionals—those who manage risk on our behalf—and has aimed to place its study on a firm footing, somewhat in the way that professional gamblers work out the possibilities of winning in the casino. There are, though, differences. Just as the sun is likely to rise tomorrow, so too the roulette wheel is likely to turn in much the same way, and the odds of winning and losing are likely to remain essentially the same. This, however, is not true of accidents in nuclear power stations, highway accidents involving nuclear waste or military materiel, or accidents involving biotechnological products. We cannot predict across an infinite future using accident data taken from a finite past. We cannot make any assumptions about the next twenty thousand years in the life of a spent radionuclide from a nuclear power station—to use a salient example—because the degrees of freedom are just too large; in that period of time, the climate may change, forms of governments are unlikely to stay the same, language will alter—all of which makes the storage of radioactive products extremely problematic, and the calculation of accurate risk probabilities an impossibility (see also MacLean and Mills, this volume).

As a result of these challenges, some risk analyses have gained an ill reputation. Risk managers have devised their strategies using best estimates of the possible dangers, but have in many instances erred in their calculations. Confounding Blundy's observations, there is in fact a great deal of risk-taking within American society, and inevitably some risks rebound. The stock market dive of 1987 reminds us that our financial system is of course built on speculative foundations, as are very many technologies. It is simply too costly to design every structure—be it an aircraft or a nuclear power plant—for total safety: even with computer assistance, some systems may be on the margins of being too complex for expert management (see also Wallace's discussions of computerization-as-hazard in chapter 10). Equally, there are profit motives underlying many scientific experiments, which creates a tension between the goal of safety and that of revenue (see, in addition, chapter 3). Perrow has pointed to the way in which extreme caution in the field of biotechnology has been replaced by virtual recklessness, in proportion to the visibility of earnings. He observes that "in our rush for scientific fame or private profit we may be preparing the ultimate accident; indeed, it may already have occurred." [17]

In short, America is far from timid. Much of its corporate activity is based on risk-taking, which then brings us back to litigation. Consumers are usually unaware of what risks are being taken around them; when they purchase a home, they expect it to be safe and to be in a safe location, although it is in fact built only to certain minimum standards and may very well be located in a flood plain or on an earthquake fault line. The risk calculus is exposed only when things fall apart, and at that moment the only recourse for the consumer is litigation. In summary, the determination of risk is a process in which many institutions are involved, and they serve to negotiate between the individual and the source of danger. Much of the time, the calculations are satisfactory, but often things go awry. At that point, litigation and legislation may occur. To the relation between the individual and the corporation we must therefore also add the tension that exists between the individual and the state (see also chapter 9).

THE PUBLIC REALM

The complexity of contemporary society is obvious; it manifests itself in terms of technological challenges, postmodern reappraisals of culture, and new forms of political conflict as old ideologies of politics and economics are transformed. The response of the state apparatus is usually predictable; in order to maintain bureaucratic control, it must penetrate further into private affairs, into the school, the workplace, and the home. In some societies, the growth of the state has proceeded virtually without resistance.[18] Elsewhere, there remains opposition to such growth, and events within the United States must be understood from that point of view. Just as we see an expansion of centralized power, and a constant process of legislation and control, we also see opposition, in the form of political struggles that begin in communities and eventually pass their way through the legal and political system until they reach the exalted levels of congressional and supreme court debate. Questions of personal liberty—which frequently, as in the case of gun ownership, constitute hazards to others— are continually thrown from the highest to the lowest levels of the legal system in search of definition.[19]

The links to the question of risk are clear ones. In many countries, state institutions have intervened in two ways: first, to regulate risk, and second, to control those phenomena that are by definition both risky and necessary. The first case is well documented, for when we consider risk, we are to a significant degree addressing the historical growth of the bureaucratic state. Efforts to clear up urban epidemics, to regulate technologies, and to deal with the aftermath of disaster were poignant challenges to city, State, and federal governments in the nineteenth century (see in particular chapters 4 and 5), and there were other examples of finding accommodations with risk; the history of banking legislation in the United States is a story of balancing speculative risk and financial stability, for example.

The second case is more complicated, for it involves risks over which components of the state maintain much tighter control; examples of such supervision would be the generation of nuclear power, various forms of the "technology of violence"—such as armaments—and civil defense.[20] The complications that surround these issues are manifold. In the field of nuclear power, for example, we are dealing with a dangerous technology, which may place residents at risk. There are, though, numerous other questions to be considered—such as the implications of terrorist attack, the storage of irradiated materials, the transport of waste nuclides through population centers, and so on. With respect to military materiel, we are considering an equally large number of questions: the siting of bases or home ports, the storage of nuclear or toxic products, and the transport of new and spent weapons. We are also dealing with research and development of definitionally dangerous products and the testing of arms and ammunition in simulated combat.

Even assuming that nuclear power and national defense are on balance beneficial, we can see that there are many reasons for state control; for example, the means of violence should not be generally available, and private armies are in consequence undesirable. Dangerous substances—nuclides, toxic gases—need to be regulated, not least because there is widespread disquiet among those who live near the plants, storage areas, or transport corridors.[21] The state is thus placed in a situation of trying to balance national and local interests, which can be achieved in different ways: by providing payoffs to State and local governments (as happened in the case of the high-level nuclear waste repository in Nevada), or by legislative preemption, when communities try to remove dangerous cargoes from their streets.

In these ways, the state is explicitly involved in the collective assessment of risk (a point discussed again in the Epilogue). Given a choice between riding roughshod over objections and garnering political support, an elected government will always seek the latter course. In consequence, public officials are frequently placed in the position of minimizing the risks attached to various technologies (or counterintuitively, even new weapons). As a Department of Energy official once observed about the transport of high-level nuclear waste from Three Mile Island, "if I had a saddle, I'd ride that SOB across the country."[22] The upshot of this partiality is that it is sometimes hard to see government and the courts as independent arbiters in the struggle between lay persons' views and professional interpretations of what constitutes "acceptable risk."[23] Equally, there are reasons to be skeptical that the marketplace can resolve such a definition, for the reasons noted above.

STRUCTURE OF THE VOLUME

These prolegomena have touched on the salience of three factors: first, the ways in which a public discourse about risk is generated; second, the historical evolution of the broad factors that encompass risk; and third, the links between risk and the operation of the public realm. The chapters in this book have been partitioned to reflect this structure, and the reader is offered a brief tour of the three sections.

The first part contains three chapters that broadly address the social construction of danger. Chapter 1, written by the editor, deals with risks and hazards in their social setting, drawing heavily on the example of AIDS. Chapter 2, by JoAnne Brown, is a historical examination of the ways in which the language and metaphors of risk are inextricably connected. Chapter 3, written by philosophers Douglas MacLean and Claudia Mills, explores some of the links between culture and the way that we place a value upon life.

The second section is explicitly historical. Chapter 4, by Joel Tarr, explores some comparisons between natural and technological hazards, and shows how the threats of such phenomena recur from generation to generation. The next chapter, by Roy Popkin, traces the parallel case— namely, the way the politics of hazard management have evolved in past decades. And in chapter 6 Kenneth Mitchell focuses on what we might call here the third estate—namely, the evolution of hazards research within the academy.

The third section emphasizes the control of risk in the public domain, and the four chapters are all focused on specific cases. Chapter 7, by Clayton Gillette, deals with biases in the legal system's risk assessments. In chapter 8, Phillip Tompkins explores the connected questions of risk communication and organizational structure, examining as a specific case the Aviation Safety Reporting System. Chapter 9, by John Sorensen, under-

takes an examination of the emergency planning process. Chapter 10, by
W. Al Wallace, looks at the role of decision aid technologies in disaster
management.

This book thus contains very different perspectives, and as was noted
in the Preface, a cross-disciplinary interchange has all along been one of
the intentions of this enterprise. The aim is not to provide a simplistic set
of remedies for the ills of this country; indeed, it is central to the work
reported here that risk is embedded within our society, and may indeed
possess some dignity, in Wolpert's phrase. If we are fully to understand
the relation between risk and society, we shall need to sharpen the skills
demonstrated in the following chapters; history, anthropology, geography, communication, law, and operations research have all informed the
arguments below. And if we are to move toward some mitigation of the
worst hazards, if we are to find levels of "acceptable risk," then again we
will require some knowledge of these divergent traditions, and the insights
they provide.

The reader should not expect, in this early phase, that the wisdom
collected here points in one narrow direction. The organization of the
chapters reflects my own interpretations, and a different editor (and, perhaps, some of the contributors themselves), would highlight the material
below somewhat differently. In consequence, much is asked of the reader,
in terms of moving beyond the familiar—the worn, near-clichés of much
risk analysis—toward a position that echoes the complexity of the reality
under scrutiny. Such scholarship, which we might provocatively call the
new risk analysis, will move beyond a simple behavioralism, toward analysis that is socially grounded, historically attuned, and contextual. It is the
aim of this collection to show how such a new project might look.

NOTES

1. Blundy 1989.
2. Heller 1961.
3. Astonishing, of course, until one places it in the perspective of a British
audience that enjoys reading about the foibles of foreigners.
4. We should not take this argument too far, of course. It is still usual to
applaud those who have gambled and won—such as Donald Trump—much more
than those who gambled and lost—such as, perhaps, George Custer. Those with
a penchant for taking great risks and falling flat on their faces have never been

popular in the U.S.A., in the way that, say, the inept polar explorer Captain Robert Scott has remained a heroic symbol in Great Britain.

5. For an elaboration of these ideas, the 1967 book by Berger and Luckmann, *The Social Construction of Reality*, still has enormous insight.

6. Douglas and Wildavsky 1982.

7. Ibid.

8. See, e.g., Paul Kennedy 1987. It should not be assumed that this is an abstruse academic argument; Kennedy's book, *The Rise and Fall of the Empire*, has been, at the time of this writing, on the bestseller lists for many months.

9. See, e.g., Clarke and Kirby 1990.

10. For instance, the neoconservative attack on public spending is based largely on pragmatic assumptions that we cannot afford ineffective programs; see, e.g., Murray 1984, and Clarke, Kirby, and McNown 1987.

11. A recent study in *Psychology Today* employs these measures, in order to rank American urban areas (November 1988, pp. 52–58). Small college towns and remote urban areas rank as least stressful.

12. This is argued cogently by Meyrowitz in his book *No Sense of Place*; see also Kirby 1989b.

13. We know of course that many accidents take place within the home; but they are, I would argue, rarely perceived in the same way as accidents that occur in the public realm.

14. I am thinking here of the endless vigilante movies in which armed individuals roam the city streets exacting retribution for violent crimes, and even those cyberpunk creations in which urban chaos finally tips into anarchy.

15. Wolpert 1980: 391. I use "everyday life" in the way it is outlined by *Annaliste* historians such as Braudel.

16. Blundy 1989.

17. Perrow 1984: 303.

18. In some theocracies, like Iran, all the axes of control have been yielded to religious authorities. In others—events in China during 1989 suggest themselves—the monopolistic control of violence has been reaffirmed. In a majority of the world's nations, in fact, concepts of the vote and the election have withered as power is passed from dictator to dictator and from junta to junta.

19. I address these developments in "State, Local State, Context, and Spatiality" in Caporaso 1989. Currently, many communities are attempting to minimize the risks of handguns by passing local ordinances, as federal legislation has been resisted by national lobbies such as the National Rifle Association.

20. As Zimmerman (1988) notes, atomic energy control was preempted by congress in 1946, without opposition, as the national interest seemed so clear.

21. See Kirby 1988; Jacob and Kirby 1990.

22. Quoted in Jacob and Kirby 1990.

23. Fischoff et al. 1981.

REFERENCES

Berger, Peter L., and Luckmann, Thomas
    1967   *The Social Construction of Reality*. Garden City, N.Y.: Anchor.
Blundy, David
    1989   "The Yellowing of America." *Sunday Telegraph*, London. April.
Clarke, Susan E., Kirby, Andrew M., and McNown, Robert
    1987   "Losing Ground—or Losing Credibility; an Examination of a Recent Policy Debate in the United States." *Environment and Planning A* 19: 1015–25.
Clarke, Susan E., and Kirby, Andrew M.
    1990   "In Search of the Corpse: The Mysterious Case of Local Politics." *Urban Affairs Quarterly* 25(3): 389–412.
Douglas, Mary, and Wildavsky, Aaron
    1982   *Risk and Culture*. Berkeley and Los Angeles: University of California Press.
Fischoff, Baruch, Lichtenstein, S., Slovic, P., Derby, S. L., and Keeney, R. L.
    1981   *Acceptable Risk*. Cambridge: Cambridge University Press.
Heller, Joseph
    1961   *Catch 22*. New York: Simon and Schuster.
Jacob, Gerald R., and Kirby, Andrew M.
    1990   "On the Road to Ruin: The Transportation of Deadly Cargoes," in *Hidden Dangers: The Environmental Consequences of Preparing for War*, Anne Ehrlich and John Birks, eds. San Francisco: Sierra Club.
Kennedy, Paul
    1988   *The Rise and Fall of Empire*. New Haven: Yale University Press.
Kirby, Andrew M.
    1988   "High Level Nuclear Waste Transportation: Weak Link in the Nuclear Fuel Cycle" *Government and Policy* 6(3): 311–22.
    1989a   "State, Local State, Context, and Spatiality: A Re-appraisal of State Theory," in *The Elusive State*, James Caporaso, ed., 204–26. Newbury Park, Calif.: Sage.
    1989b   "A Sense of Place." *Critical Studies in Mass Communication* 6(3): 322–26
Meyrowitz, J.
    1985   *No Sense of Place*. New York: Oxford University Press.
Murray, Charles
    1984   *Losing Ground*. New York: Basic Books.
Perrow, Charles
    1984   *Normal Accidents*. New York: Basic Books.

Wolpert, Julian
    1980   "The Dignity of Risk." *Transactions* of the Institute of British Geographers, ns 5(4): 391–401.

Zimmerman, Joseph F.
    1988   "Regulating Atomic Energy in the American Federal System." *Publius* 18: 51–65.

PART I

The Terrain of Risk

CHAPTER 1

Things Fall Apart

Risks and Hazards in
Their Social Setting

Andrew Kirby

This chapter deals with the ways in which society's institutions address the risks seen to threaten them. By way of example, it explores individual and collective responses to AIDS, showing that the social construction of the disease has much in common with the responses to leprosy in the medieval era. One major difference is the way in which there now exist competing discourses about disease and its treatment, a conflict that has important political and social implications; one example of such conflict, in San Francisco, is surveyed in detail.

INTRODUCTION

Things fall apart—the phrase stands as an epitaph for the 1920s. Yeats saw the world's nations stagger to the end of the Great War, which began as a formal, imperial tournament, but ended as a mudbath that was followed closely by the collapse of monarchies, massive social upheaval, and a deadly influenza epidemic (Yeats 1921).[1] In *The Second Coming*, published in 1921, he reflected that the center could not hold: "mere anarchy is loosed upon the world." Yeats represents an expression of modernity, an early twentieth-century recognition of the flux and chaos inherent in the world, and we can trace a direct parallel between the realization that "things fall apart" and a number of other philosophical reactions of this and subsequent periods (see Hollinger 1987). The existential critique, for one, identifies explicitly the entropy inherent within the universe—or the "irrational silence," as Camus (1942) put it.

It is unsurprising that this view of the world has persisted. While it is obviously beyond the scope of this essay to account for the collapse of religious belief within Western societies, there is little question that we do not, in the main, assume an ordered universe overseen by a deity (Hewitt 1983: 16–17). Catastrophe is no longer the divine punishment that punctuates the order of the world—rather, it is universal chaos thrown into even sharper relief. But this is not to argue that an existential sense predominates. As long as there is evidence that the world is likely to be plunged into warfare, riddled with disease, or racked by disasters of various kinds, human society is under great pressure to seek rational strategies with which to deal with such events. As we have moved away from an assumption that events are "acts of God"—that is, beyond control or prediction—so there has been a greater emphasis upon the possibility, and even the importance, of acting rationally in an irrational universe.[2] This shift is of course not unconnected with the ways in which the insights of psychology and psychoanalysis have penetrated the popular imagination, to the extent that we possess an inchoate sense of the unconscious, the determinants of human responses, and the goal of rational behavior.[3]

As a consequence of these shifts in our self-image, from being flotsam of the universe to participants, we can trace a number of other outcomes. We have sought, most importantly, to map our own rationality back onto society, and from there even to the natural realm. In moving—at least in the Western world—from the attribution of events to a God who is beyond prediction, we now seek to assign the regularity of events, the identification of cycles and patterns, to economic, political, and geophysical affairs.[4] But for all this search for rationality, there is no evidence that the world is any less entropic in the 1980s than it was sixty years earlier. While there has not been a world war in four decades, there has not in that time been a year passed without a conflict somewhere in the world, and some struggles have persisted for decades. We have seen economic downturns, physical disasters, technological catastrophes. The appearance of AIDS has been heralded as the return of the "plague years." The world, we can assert, is the same as it ever was—only our expectations have altered.

PLAGUES AND MORAL PANICS

The onset of AIDS is instructive—one is tempted to follow Susan Sontag and say that it represents a metaphor for this argument. The facts are straightforward. AIDS is a collapse of the body's immune system that results from a viral infection. The virus—HIV—is transmitted through exchange of bodily fluids such as sperm or blood. The collapse of the immune system is followed typically by infection, such as pneumonia, cancers of various types, and the degeneration and collapse of the body's major organs. There is nothing inherently unusual about viral infections—indeed, in comparison with diseases of other historical periods, AIDS has not yet become a major killer. At the end of 1987, fewer Americans had died of the disease than were killed in the Vietnam war, or one year's tally of U.S. traffic fatalities.

What is of course unusual is the way in which AIDS has, in the first instance, been concentrated heavily in three populations: hemophiliacs, intravenous users of recreational drugs, and sexually active homosexual males.[5] Had the disease been restricted to the first of these groups, it would not, in all probability, have received a great deal of media attention. The size of the potential hemophiliac-recipient population is small, but more importantly, the contraction of AIDS has not resulted from individuals' behavior, but rather as a result of managerial failure. That is to say, hemophiliacs have suffered as a result of negligence within the medical profession, which failed to detect the virus in blood transfusions until infections had occurred. The profession is, however, adept at maintaining its image despite such lapses, as histories such as the thalidomide case indicate (see, for instance, Starr 1982).

A very different argument is typically applied to drug users and homosexuals. Although representatives of all the three major groups who have tested seropositive for the HIV virus have been subject to abuse including dismissal from school or work, the weight of prejudice has been reserved for the latter groups.[6] This is a result of the way in which these individuals are perceived as willing actors in their own demise. They have participated in acts of drug abuse or nonprocreative sex, and are held by many to be responsible for their own illnesses. In short, the victim is blamed.

It is hard to separate the contemporary situation from preceding generations of homophobia or drug paranoia, but one premise seems clear: addicts and gays are to be punished by the fates (and failing that, their neighbors), for their lifestyles. Despite the fact that it took from approximately 1969 until 1984 to first address, and then isolate, the HIV virus, there seems to be an inchoate assumption that homosexuals in particular should have "seen this coming" and behaved in moderation. They should have undertaken—we should not, presumably, use the verb "enjoy"—safe sex, despite the fact that vast numbers of heterosexuals in the United States and elsewhere do not routinely take the same, now requisite precautions.

This paradox reveals quite sharply the contradiction between our collective search for rationality and the manner in which we respond to external threats. The reaction to AIDS is in reality little different from the way in which medieval societies responded to some forms of catastrophic illness. As the following section shows, we can throw the case of AIDS into sharp relief by moving back and examining the similarities and dissimilarities with a number of other endemic, epidemic, and pandemic diseases, in both the recent, and the more distant, past.

DISEASES OF THE SOUL

One of the most striking comparisons that we can find for AIDS is with leprosy. The similarities between the diseases are numerous. Both take a number of years to manifest themselves; both may involve singular and unsightly skin lesions that mark the sufferer in a conspicuous manner; both lead to progressive debilitation, bodily collapse, and death.[7] Most importantly, both diseases can lead to the individual's becoming a social outcast—indeed the leper is a metaphor for the outcast who wanders the streets without human contact.

Because leprosy has had such an impact upon the human imagination, in both a metaphorical and a literal sense, we have copious documentation of the disease and attitudes to it. It is mentioned at several points within the Bible, typically as a shorthand for retribution visited upon a people (see Leviticus 13, for example), and it occurs again consistently, as in Chaucer's *Canterbury Tales*.

A number of themes reappear from the Bible, through the medieval period, and even to contemporary writing. The first of these is the dread and horror with which leprosy is viewed—a process underlined by the myths that surround the disease. As Brody observes, this was understandable, given its terminal nature and the state of medicine in medieval times and before. As he continues to note, it is less comprehensible when these myths are recycled in contemporary literature. He uses the example of Mitchener's novel *Hawaii*, in which lepers' limbs "fall away." This image of physical degeneration is common, but in reality highly misleading—the extremities may suffer malformation, shrinkage, and decay, but they do not snap off. The core of the myth of leprosy has less to do with its effects, and all to do with its mode of contraction and the subsequent behavior of the recipient.

Since biblical times, leprosy has been viewed as a venereal disease that leads to further sexual depravity. Brody charts this relation in a number of works surviving from the medieval period; the link between lust and leprosy recurs in Henryson's *Testament of Cresseid* (15th century), Eilhart's *Tristram and Isalde* (12th century), and Shakespeare's *Timon of Athens* and *Henry V*. In these cases, and indeed in general usage, leprosy represented a physical expression for moral decay, with characters being either portrayed as lepers, or disguising themselves as lepers as they undertake immoral acts. The venereal dimension to leprosy can be viewed as both causal and contingent. It is common both to link the onset of the disease with sexual immorality, and to portray the aftermath of the disease as heightened lust and depravity. This remains a common metaphor even in contemporary writing; in Michener's *Hawaii*, once again, lepers are portrayed as "wind[ing] up . . . in some public place, naked and lustful, there to indulge themselves with one another."

As a consequence of the gravity of the disease, and the subsequent repercussions for the leper (which extended from banishment to death), it was normal in medieval Europe to submit the patient to examination by panels of "experts"—although their expertise was as likely to be moral as physiological. Their task was to identify lepers and then to isolate them. This was necessary not solely because the disease was contagious, but because it was assumed that lepers normally attempted to revenge themselves, and satisfy their abnormal lusts, by engaging in sexual acts with nonsufferers, who would in turn be diseased—a myth that was retold in a book on leprosy written in the 1930s (Zappa 1933).

DISCIPLINE AND PUNISHMENT

The links between leprosy and AIDS are varied, and each is instructive in terms of the similarity of the social response to the disease, despite the very different social formations under scrutiny. The first linkage has already been discussed—namely, the emphasis placed upon the sexually transmitted nature of the disease, despite the multiplicity of ways in which transmission actually occurs. In other words, there is a concern for the (im)morality of the patient.

The second connection follows directly from this insight, and relates to the practices employed to deal with lepers and those testing positive for the HIV virus. As Foucault (1979) has shown in great detail, discipline has a central role within the maintenance of social structures. In the medieval period, it was normal for lepers to be scrutinized by panels made up of elites within the community. These were rarely physicians, and were much more usually clerics who were required to examine both the moral and the physical attributes of sufferers. If the panel judged them to be lepers, they were required to undergo a prescribed religious ceremony, which sometimes took place in church, or occasionally with the leper standing in an open grave. To all intents, individuals were pronounced dead to the world, and their souls were consigned to the care of God. The leper was then banished from human society, and often removed to a primitive asylum, which was, typically, isolated spatially from the rest of the community.

The connections between these practices and those being applied to persons-with-AIDS (PWAs) are clear. There have been repeated calls to screen various types of workers (notably those in federal employment). An immigrant who seeks to enter or stay in the United States and who is shown to carry the HIV virus can be deported. This is an extreme example of banishment, but there have also been attempts to re-create the sanitoriums of the tuberculosis era, by setting up hospitals devoted solely to AIDS cases.

The third similarity between the two diseases and the social response they occasion is the creation of a "revenge myth." As we have seen, part of the reason for isolating the leprous was the strong belief that their sexual urges, plus their self-loathing, would occasion them to try to pass on their disease to others, by lawful intercourse, or where that was impossible, by rape. There is no evidence that leprosy leads to heightened sexual urges, and we may assume that this is an example of what has come more recently to be called an "urban myth"—that is, a widely circulated rumor that involves variations on a theme of horror, violence, and rapine. Such myths have already passed into the lore of AIDS; one tells of those who have tested positive for the virus who continue to have sexual relations because of an enhanced sense of excitement; the other tells of a nurse taking a blood sample from an AIDS patient, who then stabs her with the infected needle as an explicit act of revenge.

Let us begin to summarize these arguments. In the first instance, I am suggesting that it is usual—and has been so for a long period of time—to place an onus of guilt upon those who have certain diseases seen to threaten other persons. Both leprosy and AIDS have an association with sexual activity, and both have resulted in the circulation of denigratory myths and stringent practices applied to sufferers. In the example of leprosy in the Middle Ages, the deity was assumed to play a role in the proliferation of the disease. This is less often invoked in the contemporary situation of AIDS, although fundamentalists have certainly seen the wrath of God being directed against sodomy.

The point that I infer from these examples is that society responds in a punitive way against those who take risks in particularly taboo spheres of life. Diseases like leprosy become metaphors for the ways in which personal behavior is circumscribed socially, in order to protect the majority. We should also note at this point that the relationship between the real risks involved, and the extent of the social response, is anything but linear; this point will be developed further.

The inference to be stressed here is that the social reaction to external threats is complex, a conclusion that is highlighted further if we contrast the response to leprosy with that associated with other diseases. Consider for a moment the example of the European plagues, again of the medieval period. In quantitative terms, these were much more threatening than leprosy: millions died of the Black Death in Europe in the fourteenth and fifteenth centuries. Yet despite the gravity of the disease, a typical social response was to retreat to a life of hedonism. Boccaccio's *Decameron* is set during just such a plague year, and his is by no means the only report of the collapse of sexual mores and rigid class relations (a long discussion is offered in Deaux 1969). Lest we assume that this was a response confined to the medieval period, similar accounts can be found in Samuel Pepys's diaries, written during the plague of London in the seventeenth century. The disease could be transmitted sexually; it seemed to encourage subsequent sexual activity. However, the sheer speed of the epidemics, and the rapidity with which sufferers were dispatched, made it impossible to exert social controls over suspected persons—although the plague was used frequently as an excuse to undertake pogroms against Jews throughout Europe.

In short, abhorrent diseases did not, in all situations, result in a formal and complex social response. The tendency to punish the patient has become even less usual as we have moved closer to the present. The brief influenza epidemic (or more properly, "pandemic") of 1918–19 killed over twenty million individuals, making it the single most deadly attack in human history. And yet, as Crosby (1976) points out, it is the forgotten epidemic. Unlike the Great War, it figured in no poems, no plays, no novels. It had no impact on medical methods or public health organization. The disease came—and went. Because there were no ways of dealing with it, the pandemic was rapidly obliterated from the collective memory. The only social response of interest is the name that was given to it— Spanish influenza. In an age when it was no longer possible to blame God, it became necessary to blame someone else for originating a disease; in this instance, Spain was a satisfactory, if unlikely, scapegoat.[8]

RISKS FOR INDIVIDUALS AND COLLECTIVES

Leprosy and the bubonic plague are, for the most part, no longer present in advanced societies. It is, however, instructive that they both continue to exist metaphorically. Camus used the plague as a central device in his 1947 novel *La Peste*; the 1980s, as noted, have been heralded as "the plague years." The message is clear; although the diseases themselves may now be forgotten in Europe and the United States, they represent a continuing tradition of social response to the risks of certain types of disease. This explains our lengthy excursion into the etiology of medieval epidemics— namely, the exploration of the relation between human actions and social responses. One conclusion is clear; attitudes to disease, and the risks that they hold, are mediated through the community; they are not calculated anew by the individual.

This long detour is necessary, though, because it is quite usual for social science to examine issues that involve risk in terms of some model of personal rationality. In one sense this is unsurprising, for it is a logical outcome of the penetration of behavioral research into the rest of the academic community. In another sense, it is astonishing that this work has persisted in the form that it continues to adopt. Consider the following critique by Michael Watts, for example; his emphasis is upon work in the so-called natural hazards paradigm, but the general tenor of the remarks could be applied to much else:

> These field studies were ahistoric, insensitive to culturally-varied indige-
> nous adaptive strategies, largely ignorant of the huge body of relevant
> work on disaster theory in sociology and anthropology, flawed by the
> absence of any discussion of the political-economic context of hazard

occurrence and genesis, and in the final analysis having little credibility in light of the frequent banality and triviality of many of the research findings. [Watts 1983]

Watts's argument is not the first, nor the only, indictment of the individual-as-decision-maker view of risk research; but it may be the most succinct. Nor is he the only critic to call for a broader mode of research, which places the individual within a political-economic setting, which itself is slotted into a more robust understanding of the links between society and nature (a point discussed further in the Epilogue).

This critique falls squarely into one of the essential dualisms within social science, that of broad structures and individual actors. As Giddens and others have noted, it is normal to set up these levels as dichotomous, and exclusive, opposites (Giddens 1979). In consequence, the critique offered by Watts and others does not offer any dialogue with individualistic research; rather it attempts to sidestep it and to set up a complex antithesis, which revolves about broad categories such as *people* and *environment*. Given the close affinity between American behavioral science in general (and the work undertaken on risks in particular) with the basics of psychology (note the rising importance of public choice theory, for example), this critique-of-opposites is unlikely to be influential in changing the prevailing discourse. What is required is some alternative interpretation that itself transcends the assumptions of a dualism between agency and structure. In consequence, the next section explores an alternative model of social psychology.

PERSONAL AND SOCIAL BEING

Harré offers us a particular view of the relation between the individual and his or her counterparts. As he argues in his book *Personal Being*, a person is not a natural object but a cultural artifact—a view that is of course very different from the dominant idea maintained within cognitive psychology, which holds that the individual is an automaton, a complex machine with universal patterns of behavior (Harré 1984:20). Moving through Harré's logic opens up a number of important perspectives that have central importance for our thinking on risks. The first is that the individual must be addressed in a setting, for all human development is linked to a public discourse. This setting is essentially local, insofar as the basic medium of connection between the personal and the collective is conversation, which is of course most typically undertaken on a face-to-face basis. Second, we must reconsider how we evaluate certain acts of behavior. As Harré emphasizes, when we consider an individual's *rationality*, we are directing ourselves toward *public* acts, not the *private* evaluations of reality: "To say that someone is rational is not to congratulate them on their private cognitive process but to praise them for their contributions to the *collective discourse*. . . . to be rational is to meet, publicly, the relevant standards of the local collective (Harré 1984:119; emphasis added).

As Harré continues to note—and this becomes of central importance—the links between the public and private elaborations of rationality may be tenuous in the extreme: "contributions which are rational relative to the flow of the public discourse may issue from private discourses which, if they were made public, would unhesitatingly be judged irrational" (Harré 1984:120). This insight explodes the myths that it is possible—or even of any great interest—to examine what has been termed the *risk calculus* of the individual, when trying to evaluate behavior. And indeed the history of the thousands of efforts to explore individual identifications of, and responses to, risks is a story of the attempt to deal with the gulf between the ways in which persons say that they *view* the world and the ways in which they *act*. Devices such as Starr's distinction between voluntary and involuntary risks are no more than heuristic devices that have allowed researchers to fudge the dissonance between what we say and what we do.[9]

As Harré points out, this dissonance disappears if we explore the public/private relation, and it is relatively easy to generate a couple of examples that do this. Let us start with the example of commercial aviation. Most individuals regard flying as dangerous, yet many of us do it, and some of us do it frequently. To Starr this is because the risks are voluntary. A more satisfactory way to interpret the contradiction is to examine the collective discourse associated with flying. Aircraft are perhaps the only form of transport in which the passenger is explicitly warned at the outset—by flight attendants—that there may be dangers. Indeed, the nomenclature is itself instructive—the former term "airhostess," close in terminology to someone working in a bar, has been replaced steadily by the more utilitarian job description. So there are disquieted passengers, who have, in Erika Jong's phrase, a fear of flying. The collective discourse is one of risk, the possibility of cabin depressurization, the chances of landing on water. At this point the passengers should leap to their feet and attempt to flee. What they do is, though, instructive. They bridge the gap between the public and private discourse by *ignoring* the safety message. Look around the aircraft as the attendant acts out the safety information—*no one watches*. Everyone studiously ignores the message. No one examines the safety information card, despite the fact that different aircraft have different spatial configurations and safety features. This passive behavior allows passengers to integrate private and public discourses; by ignoring the latter, by refusing to participate, they can pass the onus of safety back onto the aircraft's crew; in so doing, they do not have to confront their own disquiet by having to calculate escape routes and other strategies.[10]

Contrast flying with traveling in an automobile. Most of us would, typically, leave the airport, breathe a sigh of relief that we were safe, and get into a car. An irrational response, of course. If there was ever an aspect of life in which things fall apart, it is the highway, where the chances of being involved in an accident sometime in one's life are extremely high. Again, it is the relation between the public and private discourses that accounts for this dissonance. Having left the airport, we are now on the freeway, where cars are traveling at or beyond the speed limit. The private discourse here is that driving is normal and safe. We preserve this fiction by attempting to maintain an entirely private discourse; even though each driver's safety depends explicitly on the skill of those in the vicinity, each attempts to behave as if alone, unconnected to a public discourse. For this reason, there exist elaborate rituals whereby the public discourse is emphasized, albeit intermittently; for example, vehicles are stopped periodically by police patrols, and the passengers act as symbolic victims. In order to underscore the public nature of this act, the patrol car employs a battery of lights, which succeed in making the maximum possible display (far in excess of what would be required for the safety of the parked vehicles) for the maximum period of time.

In contrasting these two examples, we see that they are paradoxical insofar as the private risk calculus is all wrong; flying and driving are inverted in terms of the dangers they pose. The manner in which we explain these contradictions is by contrasting personal and collective rationality. Airline passengers deal with their fears by absolving themselves of responsibility for their behavior, and by succumbing to the collective rationality. Drivers maintain their delusions about their invincibility by ignoring the collective rationality, and by refusing to acknowledge that they are extremely vulnerable to others' behavior while driving, particularly at speed.

There are several important implications of employing Harré's interpretations. By stressing the empirical reality of conversation, rather than individuals' views and opinions, we open a door to the study of risks and hazards as revealed by actions, not some inferred risk calculus, and we understand these actions with respect to the collective discourse on risks. Second, we comprehend the collective discourse in a specific setting; it is not a free-floating construct, but a reality of human interaction. In consequence, the collective discourse is to be understood *situationally*—that is, we investigate each setting or context without regard for the necessity of some universal reality (Farr 1985). Third, the existence of a collective discourse suggests that there are no a priori limits to the types of risk that can be examined in such a manner. Traditional research distinctions noted above, in which natural hazards have received primacy, to be followed at some remove by technological hazards, may make no sense if the collective discourse extends to both fields. Fourth, in easing some of the problems of risk research, we reveal inevitably a new and pressing problem—namely, how to understand the process of creating a collective discourse.

PUBLIC AND PRIVATE DISCOURSE

In attempting to think about the ways in which individuals interact, we face one of the fundamental issues of social science. As already noted, theorists such as Giddens have devoted a massive research output to this basic issue—namely, What is the relationship between individuals and their creation of structures, by which society is mediated? Clearly enough, persons do not interact freely, one with another; indeed, they are to a large degree governed by the weight of the past, which is reified in institutions, norms, language, and other forms of cultural, legal, and political practice. And yet persons do make a difference: human agents can shape events, both positively and negatively (Giddens 1984).

In thinking, then, about the creation of a public discourse, we are in large measure thinking about the functioning of society. The collective discourse is, in many instances, a local thing, carried on by conversation, which can include what is taught in schools, and what is discussed on local radio and television stations.[11] By focusing upon the locality, we may simplify some issues (language and ethnicity might remain constant in some cases), but we are still trying to grapple with a complex reality. It has been argued recently by Shotter that in order to comprehend the links between the individual and collectivities, we need to understand the development of *sensus communis*, which can be translated literally as a *common* sense (Shotter 1986). He argues that for individuals to interact one with another, they have had need of a common discourse. Such commonality is rooted, necessarily, in the everyday world of the locality, and "sensory topics" involve the giving of a shared sense to an already shared circumstance (Shotter 1986: 206).

This argument, which follows Vico, provides an interesting account of the bases of human knowledge and awareness, and the starting point for a number of conjectures on the manner in which human interaction develops. Most important of these is the restatement of the idea that there is some intrinsic relationship between persons and their environment— not in a deterministic manner, but rather in the archeological sense emphasized by Foucault. That is, each locality evolves a particular set of coping mechanisms that permit an accommodation to the complexities of life, and these are laid down over long periods of time. In this way, what Geertz has termed *local knowledge* becomes sedimented (Geertz 1983).

These coping strategies are numerous and varied: even when we contemplate the recent past, where such generic processes as capitalism and industrialism predominate, we find that a multitude of strategies has emerged. In other words, the industrial experience of, say, the Massachusetts mill towns was subtly different from the ways in which the same industrial process was organized elsewhere within the United States: ethnic friction, labor organization, worker-manager relations, and political outcomes all developed in a singular way. Some of these dissimilarities, of one locality to the next, reflected contingencies of time and place, but others reflected preexisting social, cultural, and economic relations (Marston and Kirby 1988). In each instance, though, the singularities have in turn become part of the sedimented local knowledge that can be identified today. Although this process has been examined most critically in terms of the manner in which economic relations are worked out, it is also true of the ways in which a multitude of other relationships is resolved. It is the case with language, with religious practice, with gender relations, law, and cultural activities such as music. Literature too is frequently rooted in specific localities, insofar as place becomes a shorthand for a mysterious yet understood set of behaviors (see, for instance, Clark 1985; Pred 1986; Lutwack 1984).

One element of the coping process is, of course, dealing with risk. In the historical sense, the greatest risk is environmental, and many cultural practices evolve around such threats. But in more complex societies, two things happen. First, the natural order is disregarded; and second, more complex risks assume predominance. Put another way, the process of urbanization insulates us from an awareness of nature and the hazards that are embedded within it. Concurrently, the proliferation of industrial processes, and the everyday activities of urban residents, generate numerous procedures, substances and wastes, large proportions of which are hazardous in some form (see, for example, Kirby 1986; Liverman 1986).

The shift from a concern for natural hazards toward one for technological products has some important implications: we recognize that they both share one common characteristic—that is, they are covered by public discourse. By reminding ourselves of this central tenet, we get to the heart of a dilemma that reappears again and again within work on natural hazards—namely, Why do persons place themselves in situations of risk from earthquakes, tornadoes, floods, and the like? In terms of *private* rationality, many households live in parlous locations: cities such as San Francisco, where the long-expected major earthquake occurred in 1989; in trailer parks on the edge of midwestern towns prone to tornado attacks; in flood plains in areas where occasional surges are possible.

In terms of *public* discourse, these locations are thought rational. In a city like San Francisco, a complex coping strategy has evolved in the decades since the major earthquake of 1906. In part, this has involved a subterfuge in terms of language: for many years, 1906 was referred to as the "San Francisco fire," not an earthquake. Building codes have, nonetheless, been revised progressively, schools and emergency centers have been moved away from fault lines, earthquake safety literature is ubiquitous. But overlying these precautions is a more powerful veneer, which involves massive real estate expansion, and beyond that, a very basic assumption that whenever there is another major seismic event, then the federal government will be able to provide emergency assistance, and more important, some form of insurance payout to restart the next property boom (Palm et al. 1983). In short, the *common* sense in the city is that there is nothing to fear.

COMMON SENSE AND *COMMON* SENSE

Let us stay with the case of San Francisco, and return to our previous example of AIDS, a connection that does not, in all probability, require explanation. Above, we examined the nature of the immediate social response to the disease; in this section, we can look at the complications of creating a public discourse concerning risk. As various studies have indicated, San Francisco represents an interesting example of a social experiment in coping, as tens of thousands of gay men, and a smaller number of gay women, have migrated to the city since World War II. Their aim—much like the waves of ethnic immigrants who preceded them—was to create a space for themselves, to then move into the labor market, and in turn the political arena.[12] At the time that City Supervisor Harvey Milk was assassinated in 1978, the gay community had reached a peak of political influence; not long after, the AIDS epidemic began to hit the city. By 1984, of a national total of 5,394 cases, 634 were recorded in San Francisco.[13]

Given the conventional wisdom concerning AIDS—as measured perhaps by the pronouncements of the Surgeon General—we can see that gay men were, in the early years of the decade, extremely vulnerable to the disease. This is a function of the frequency with which some gays change partners, a significant level of recreational drug use, and the nature of gay sex itself, involving as it may some risky practices. We would expect therefore that the private discourse on risk would have been one of concern among gay men; and second, that the collective public discourse would be one of risk avoidance.

In reality, there were by 1984 *two* separate collective discourses concerning AIDS in San Francisco—one within the straight community, and another in the gay community. In the majority population, there was a basic assumption that gay males were at risk, but that the chances of heterosexuals' contacting the disease via casual contact was low. In the gay neighborhoods, the collective discourse was much more complex. First of all, there was a strong concern that a disease that only attacked gay males was implausible, unless it was being spread deliberately—perhaps by agencies such as the CIA (Fitzgerald 1986: 98). Second, some reasoned that to put a spotlight on the disease would harm gay rights legislation being debated in the California legislature. Third, some argued that to admit a problem would hurt the lucrative tourist trade that brought thousands of gays to the city each year. In contrast, the Kaposi's Sarcoma Foundation was already active in emphasizing safe sex guidelines. In consequence, as the *common* sense was fractured, so the private discourse regarding AIDS was also confused. Studies showed that not all gay men were taking elaborate precautions in their personal sex lives—neither common sense nor *common* sense were being developed.

This relationship between discourses was revealed most sharply over the bathhouses in the city. These constituted one of several foci for gay social life, together with bars and bookstores.[14] As locations for recreational sex, the bathhouses became early targets for public health activity at City Hall. This was resisted strenuously by some leaders in the gay community, who saw any attempt to interfere with hard-won personal freedoms as an attack on the gay movement—attempts to close the baths were described as "genocidal" by the chair of the Gay Freedom Day Parade, for example (Fitzgerald 1986:92). In other words, the common-sense strategy (at least as viewed by the straight population) of policing or closing the baths could not become part of a gay collective discourse that endorsed their existence, and as this public discourse hardened, so the private discourse remained open to less safe sexual acts.

This conflict concluded in the fall of 1984, as the city took steps to close the baths. But the conclusion of the fight rested more on the fact that the gay community—after much internal debate—no longer supported the bathhouses as symbolic spaces. Indeed, the furor over the baths resulted ultimately in a wholesale change in the public discourse within the gay community, which shifted from resistance over civil liberties to greater emphasis upon radical education about AIDS and for public health action (Cohen and Elder 1988). And as the collective discourses began to overlap, so the private discourse on risk within the homosexual community also changed: studies showed that sexual practices changed rapidly between 1983 and 1985.

This example demonstrates with enormous poignancy just how complex the understanding of risk can be. To the outsider, the threat of AIDS is such that the private discourse must reject all forms of unsafe sex—perhaps all forms of sexual activity in entirety. And yet for a prolonged period, the private discourse was ruled by a collective discourse that understandably rejected not sex, but rather any attempts to limit personal freedoms. In such a situation, efforts to emphasize health education messages passed to the individual were not totally successful; it was only by forcing a change in the collective discourse that individual attitudes were reshaped.

TOWARD A CONCLUSION

We must, inevitably, be wary of building too much on this one story; and in the same way, we must be careful not to set up the public and private discourses as antinomies. The collective discourse may be governed by political institutions—as was the case in the gay community—and the latter may be exclusive and elite-oriented. Business interests may predominate; ethnic tensions may exclude certain groups. For all this, Harré's ideas give us an important insight into the dynamics of dealing with risks and hazards. In searching for *individual* rationality, we are likely to ignore the conventions of local practice. By appealing to the individual to act in a commonsense way, we ignore the constraints of collective action—the more pervasive *common* sense. At this point, one additional factor must be reemphasized.

We should not assume that it is easy to move from a consideration of the private to a public discourse—that is to say, that the same assumptions of behavioralism that have dominated in past studies of risk can be reapplied. Such an attempt would try to reduce the collective discourse to little more than an aggregation of its members, which would be futile. As we saw at the outset, this chapter has opted for a very different interpretation, one that assumes that it is the norm for the world to appear anarchic.[15] In short, it is usual, rather than the exception, for things to go wrong. This is an explicit recognition that the collective discourse is beset by numerous influences, both secular and idealistic. In consequence, decisions that are made do not often coincide with the ways that we might act in the psychologist's or the economist's laboratory.[16] In searching to understand the realm of risks and hazards, we must turn our backs on short-run interpretations of personal behavior, and place our research into the evolving study of collective behavior within the locality—the ways in which we cope. Without this shift, we can continue to note only, with a sense of bewilderment, that things fall apart.

NOTES

I reached the title of this piece via circuitous means, which led from my colleague Mike Ward, to Chinua Achebe, and back to Yeats. Thanks are particularly due to Mike Ward for his help, encouragement, and example over the years.

1. My former colleague David Butler has pointed out that Yeats was also influenced powerfully by events in Eire, where the country was—literally—being dismembered.

2. It is easy to forget how exactly the phrase "act of God" should be taken. As recently as 1832, an Englishman, Robert Ayvery, wrote of the contemporaneous cholera epidemic: "it appears to me that the Lord is scourging us as a nation for our multiplied sins." It is, however, noteworthy that he was also able to blame

the sufferers for their moral decay: "it ravages more especially the drunkards and sabbath breakers" (quoted in Durey 1979).

3. J. B. Watson's research on conditioning in infants was, for instance, published in magazines like *Cosmopolitan* in 1927 and 1928 (Harris 1979).

4. There are journals devoted solely to the identification of cycles (e.g., *The Journal of Interdisciplinary Cycle Research*), although they are somewhat less than entirely successful in demonstrating causality. For a more successful account, see Modelski 1987.

5. The focus in this chapter is upon American society, although as recent studies have indicated, AIDS is most strongly represented in nondeveloped regions such as Africa. Indeed, the argument being developed here could be extended easily to the international situation, for homophobia has tended to draw attention away from the serious problems being faced by countries like Kenya or Haiti. The World Health Organization, for example, had no formal structure to focus on AIDS until February 1987 (see Heise 1988).

6. The outbreak of social hysteria is anything but uncommon—a point developed by Cohen 1980. For more recent data on the distribution of AIDS cases in the USA, see Cohen and Elder 1988; Kirby 1990.

7. Much of the information in this section is taken from Brody 1974.

8. In reality, the so-called Spanish flu originated in the United States, and spread to Europe with the movement of U.S. troops (Crosby 1976). This was not a usual history (see, e.g., Patterson 1986).

9. It is not my intention here to mount a step-by-step critique of the practices of risk analysis, a field that now possesses its own eponymous journal. For reference to Starr's work, and other important contributions, see inter alia Hohenemser and Kasperson 1982, and Mitchell, this volume.

10. This can even be attempted during an inflight emergency: "Steve Willuwit, 46, seated in row 16, went back to reading a science fiction novel: 'I didn't want to think about anything except getting up and walking off the plane'" (*Time* report on DC-10 crash, Iowa, July 1989).

11. Much of the following section is based on Kirby 1988.

12. This history is discussed by Castells 1983.

13. Data from Fitzgerald 1986: 85. Much of the information used here is taken from this account; I recognize that there is no single version of history, and I am indebted to Walt Westman for his interpretive help, without in any way implicating him in this narrative.

14. The complex social rituals associated with gay life in San Francisco have been documented by Armistead Maupin in his series *Tales of the City*. For a more powerful study of New York, see David Feinberg's *Eighty-Sixed*.

15. It was my original intention to call this chapter, in step with the T-shirt slogan, "shit happens." This remains my favorite aphorism for this argument, although "things fall apart" is perhaps more literary and almost as succinct.

16. One is left to ask, in an entirely rhetorical way, what could be more point-

less than the developing field of experimental economics, in which individuals are given notional sums of monopoly money, and asked how much they would spend on insurance or hazardous waste cleanups—without regard to any prevailing collective discourse?

REFERENCES

Brody, S. N.
    1974   *The Disease of the Soul*. Ithaca: Cornell University Press.
Camus, Albert
    1942   *Le Myth de Sisyphe*. Paris.
Castells, Manuel
    1983   *The City and the Grassroots*. Berkeley: University of California Press.
Clark, Gordon L.
    1985   *The Cities and the Judges*. Chicago: Chicago University Press.
Cohen, Ira, and Elder, Ann
    1988   "Major Cities and Disease Crises." *Social Science History* 13(1): 25–63.
Cohen, Stan
    1980   *Folk Devils and Moral Panics*. Oxford: Martin Robertson.
Crosby, A. W.
    1976   *Epidemic and Peace, 1918*. Westport, Conn.: Greenwood.
Deaux, G.
    1969   *The Black Death*. New York: Weybright and Talley.
Durey M.
    1979   *The Return of the Plague*. London: Gill and Macmillan.
Farr, James
    1985   "Situational Analysis: Explanation in Political Science." *Journal of Politics* 47: 1085–1105.
Feinberg, David
    1989   *Eighty-Sixed*. New York: Viking.
Fitzgerald, Frances
    1986   *Cities on a Hill*. New York: Simon and Schuster.
Foucault, Michel
    1979   *Discipline and Punish*. Harmondsworth: Penguin.
Geertz, Clifford
    1983   *Local Knowledge*. New York: Basic Books.
Giddens, Anthony
    1979   *Central Problems of Social Theory*. London: Macmillan.
    1984   *The Constitution of Society*. Cambridge: Polity.

Harré, Rom

  1984   *Personal Being: A Theory for Individual Psychology.* Cambridge: Harvard University Press.

Harris, B.

  1979   "Whatever Happened to Little Albert." *American Psychologist* 34(2): 151–60.

Heise, L.

  1988   "AIDS: New Threat to the Third World." *World Watch* 1 (1): 19–27.

Hewitt, Kenneth

  1983   *Interpretations of Calamity.* London: Allen and Unwin.

Hohenemser, Christoph

  1987   "Public Distrust and Hazard Management Success at the Rocky Flats Nuclear Weapons Plant." *Risk Analysis* 7(2): 243–50.

Hohenemser, Christoph, and Kasperson, Jeanne

  1982   *Risk in the Technological Society.* Boulder: Westview.

Hollinger, David A.

  1987   "The Knower and the Artificer." *American Quarterly* 39 (1): 37–55.

Kirby, Andrew

  1986   "Introduction to Special Issue Dealing with Risks in Urban Areas." *Cities* 4: 137–64.

  1988   "Context, *Common* Sense, and the Reality of Place." *Journal for the Theory of Social Behavior* 18: 239–50.

  1990   "And the Bandwagon Moved On: Geographers and the AIDS Pandemic." *Focus.*

Liverman, Diana M.

  1986   "The Vulnerability of Urban Areas to Technological Risks." *Cities* 4: 142–47.

Lutwack, L.

  1984   *The Role of Place in Literature.* Syracuse: Syracuse University Press.

Marston, Sallie A., and Kirby, Andrew M.

  1988   "Urbanization, Industrialization, and the Social Creation of a Space Economy." *Urban Geography* 9(4): 358–75.

Modelski, George

  1987   *Long Cycles in World Politics.* Seattle: University of Washington Press.

Palm, Risa I., Marston, S.A., Kellner, P., Smith, D., and Budetti, M.

  1983   *Home Mortgage Lenders, Real Property Appraisers, and Earthquake Hazards.* Monograph #38. Boulder: University of Colorado, Institute of Behavioral Science.

Patterson, K. D.

  1986   *Pandemic Influenza, 1700–1900.* Totowa, N.J.: Rowman and Littlefield.

Pred, Allen

  1986   *Place, Practice, and Structure*. New York: Barnes and Noble.

Shotter, John

  1986   "A Sense of Place: Vico and the Social Creation of Social Realities."
          British Journal of Social Psychology 25: 199–211.

Starr, Paul

  1982   *The Social Transformation of American Medicine*. New York: Basic
          Books.

Ward, Michael D.

  1987   "Things Fall Apart: Or, Logical Analysis of the Transition from
          Peace to War." *International Interactions* 15(2): 65–79.

Watts, Michael

  1983   "On the Poverty of Theory: Natural Hazards Research in Context,"
          in *Interpretations of Calamity*, Kenneth Hewitt, ed.

Yeats, William Butler

  1921   *The Second Coming*. London.

Zappa, P.

  1933   *Unclean! Unclean!* London.

CHAPTER 2

The Social Construction of Invisible Danger

Two Historical Examples

JoAnne Brown

Palpable dangers to human life can present themselves to our understanding in concrete ways that limit, to some extent, our cultural understanding of these events. The wind and rain of a tropical storm have specific material effects that may carry different social meaning to different persons, but that nevertheless pose life-threatening physical dangers readily understood with some degree of consistency by different persons. Floods are wet. Fires are hot. Victims, relief workers, and even social scientists can agree on these physical effects, though they may begin to differ when evaluating what such effects mean to people: what is an acceptable degree of risk, and to whom.[1]

Yet some of the most fearsome hazards of modern life are not as palpable as some ancient threats. Two examples from recent American history demonstrate the social processes by which two invisible hazards came to be understood, within specific historical periods, by a broad segment of the American populace. The acceptance of germ theories of disease and the popularization of benign concepts of atomic energy both demonstrate the utility of ordinary language analysis in the social and historical study of hazards. As Arendt observes, "the impact of factual reality, like all other human experiences, needs speech if it is to survive the moment of experience, needs talk and communication if it is to remain sure of itself" (1958: 25). Any notion on the part of policy-makers of "actual" danger must be considered in light of the cultural arrangements that determine how such dangers are perceived. Prevailing metaphors are one kind of such cultural arrangement, and while these are not fixed over time or place, neither are they entirely escapable. Moreover they are amenable to critical reflection.

METAPHOR AND THE POPULARIZATION OF
GERM THEORIES OF DISEASE

The twin ideas that crime is disease, and disease is crime, permeate the history of criminology, public health, and personal hygiene in the United States from the 1870s to the present.[2] This particular metaphor emerged (or, more exactly, reemerged) historically when the theories, practices, and institutions of one enterprise—epidemiology—became intertwined with those of another—criminology.[3] In America these two domains reinforced one another, so that the popularization of germ theories in public health strengthened analogous ideas in criminology, and vice versa.

After the turn of the twentieth century, ideas about germs reached the public not only through the offices of regular medicine and the new public health, but also through advertising. Public health journals, school text-books, home medical guides, popular magazines, and, later, motion pictures, radio, and television all contributed to the popular image of germs as criminals. Images and narrative fragments from these diverse sources are elements with which Americans in the twentieth century understand sickness and health. This imagery, set in the contexts of law enforcement, civil order, and military struggle, has cultural significance beyond the bounds of epidemiology. Because it illustrates the historical processes whereby an invisible threat becomes real, the development of the public image of germs and germ-caused disease contains lessons for those concerned with the cultural and social aspects of hazards policy. The process is particularly relevant to the problems of nuclear radiation and many forms of environmental pollution whose physical effects are neither immediate nor sensible.

During the late nineteenth century, American medicine was a conservative enterprise, faced with sectarian challenges and antiprofessional populist health movements, and considered inferior to its European counterpart in scientific expertise. American physicians were slower than the

Europeans to accept new "germ" theories of disease when laboratory evidence began to substantiate these theories in the 1870s. Instead, American physicians tended to link illness to general environmental and hereditary factors: sewer gas, miasmas, parental intemperance, and organic poisons (Rosenberg 1976: 33). The idea of specific diseases caused by living "germs" or microbes was a radical one, and as commonplace as the concept of specificity is today, it then marked a major change in the understanding of disease etiology—a change not altogether welcomed by the traditional medical community. This new theory was for many doctors simply unacceptable, for it dictated "antisocial" medical policies, including old-fashioned quarantine, and required that physicians, who strove to appear objectively scientific and learned, profess a belief in invisible creatures (Rosenberg 1962: 77–78). In 1882, the year of Robert Koch's great discovery of the tuberculosis bacillus, prominent New York physician Alfred Loomis protested, "People say there are bacteria in the air, but I cannot see them" (Yew 1980: 490).

If the American medical profession was reluctant to accept the validity and implications of the new germ theories, popular scientific writers, amateur scientists, and patent-medicine merchants responded with greater enthusiasm (Warner 1982). Such amateur scientists wrote popular articles about the looking-glass world of microbes, publishing their discoveries in journals like *The Popular Science Monthly* and *Scientific American*. For twenty years, the medical establishment paid little heed to these amateurs—their prejudice possibly reinforced by the unprofessional nature of the outsiders' microscopy (Belfield 1884).

By the early 1880s, however, a decade before germ theory was fully accepted within the medical profession, some commercial advertisers adopted and began using the popular, "amateur" belief in microbes over professional skepticism, nonetheless attaching a medical imprimatur to these avant-garde theories. An 1885 advertisement for Procter and Gamble Company's new Ivory Soap, featured a testimonial from one Dr. R. Ogden Doremus, M.D., L.L.D., attesting to the soap's purity: "I subjected various samples of the Ivory Soap to rigid microscopical examination. I find it to be free from any forms of animalcular or vegetable germ life, so cordially commend the Ivory Soap for its unsurpassed detergent properties and purity."[4]

Another entrepreneur, Texas-born patent-medicine dealer William Radam, produced a universal "Microbe Killer" made from large amounts of water, tinged with red wine, hydrochloric acid, and sulfuric acid. By

1890, when the American medical profession was just coming to accept fully the existence of "microbes," seventeen factories were producing bottles of Radam's Microbe Killer (Young 1961: 167–70; Starr 1982: 128).[5]

Not every advertiser of hygienic formulas chose to promulgate hygiene in terms of the new germ theory, yet many popular advertisements reinforced an emerging association of disease with both criminality and foreignness. One of the most successful advertising campaigns of the new century was not mounted in magazines or newspapers but in streetcars. This campaign capitalized on widespread distaste for contact with strangers, and nowhere were city dwellers more likely to "rub elbows" with strangers than on a streetcar. The makers of Sapolio soap created an imaginary "Spotless Town" full of hygienic heroes, and "Dingeytown" teeming with filthy would-be emigrés, whose escapades appeared serially on city streetcars—the original "soaps." Over the six years of the advertising campaign, real towns voted to become "Spotless Towns" and schoolchildren rehearsed for "spotless" school plays. The campaign has become a classic in advertising literature.[6] The hero in the "Spotless Town" drama was the policeman, who enforced cleanliness. The Spotless Town policeman prevented immigrant "Dingeys" from coming across the border to commit their dirty crimes. A frightening tale in fourteen parts was set to verse:

> Listen, my children, whilst I relate
> The harrowing, hideous, horrible fate
> When an inky flood over Shining State
> The fair land threatened to inundate. . . .
>
> With their dark forces routed, in shame and in fear,
> The filthy host fled to their hovels so drear;
> Nor ventured again to this town to draw near,
> Except when clean-living and light to revere. . . .
>
> My children, you know, that you all want to grow,
> To fight grime and dirt as we did long ago;
> But of weapons you use, I want you to know,
> There's none that will aid like SAPOLIO.[7]

In service of selling soap, this allegory of unrestricted immigration capitalized on the widespread nativist sentiments prevalent at the turn of the century. Such advertising also fostered perceptions of immigrants and blacks as malicious, perverse lawbreakers and degraded criminals, and reinforced culturally based psychological connections linking immigration, filth, crime, and disease. Conversely, these advertisements, and many others based on the same plot, identified native-born white Americans with the force of law and with physical and moral cleanliness. The "weapons" or "ammunition" of this battle, of course, were the products advertised. By linking a new concept—the germ theory of disease—with an established and particularly topical set of beliefs—nativism—advertisers, medical educators, and others sought to both exploit and make comprehensible a difficult new concept.

Regrettably, while this association helped mobilize the public and policy-makers alike to stiffen public health measures against the spread of disease, it also unfairly identified certain ethnic groups not only with disease but also with crime. In some instances, this association was deliberate; in others, simply opportune. Regardless of intent, the effects on the stigmatized groups were the same: the association undoubtedly added to the discrimination endured by these groups.

The United States Public Health Service also played a central role in establishing the popular imagery associated with germ theories of disease. As the uniformed avant-garde in America's fight against contagion, the Public Health Service, a branch of the military, created a literal association between the uniformed officer and the eradication of disease. In its role as hygienic gatekeeper at Ellis Island, the service further reinforced the connection between disease and immigration, and, ultimately, between immigration and crime.

The medical inspection of immigrants became part of the U.S. Public Health Service's mandate in 1893 as an extension of the service's quarantine responsibilities. Many would-be immigrants *did* suffer from disease and were deported as a result. Immigrants allowed entry into the United States, in the nineteenth century as now, had to meet a certain health standard, to which, of course, native-born Americans were not subjected. The photographs and writings of the Public Health Service contributed to popular associations of specific ethnic groups with the threat of disease germs. Dr. Alfred C. Reed, an officer at Ellis Island (where more than two-thirds of all immigrants came ashore) wrote on "the medical side of immigration" in 1912: "It can truthfully be said that the dregs and off-scourings of foreign lands, the undesirables of whom their own nations are only too eager to purge themselves, come in hosts to our shores" (Reed 1912: 392).

This scholarly discussion in (what was at the time) a scholarly journal,

Popular Science Monthly, echoed the language of the Sapolio streetcar ads, subtly dehumanizing immigrants with terms like "dregs," "off-scourings," "purge," and "hosts." While there is not a clear *causal* connection between the two discourses in advertising and in public health literature, both share the primary metaphor of filth: one dramatizes filth with an immigration story, while the other dramatizes immigration with a filth story. In one case soap is being sold, in another, immigration restriction. In both, the representative of a solution to the problem is a uniformed officer: of the Spotless Town police force or the U.S. Public Health Service. As Dr. Reed explained in an article in *Popular Science Monthly*, illustrated with a photograph of five uniformed health officers, "The medical inspection of immigrants is the first, most comprehensive, and most effectual line of defense against the introduction of disease or taint from without" (Reed 1913: 317). Mental defects likewise were linked both to physical defects and to moral degeneracy, and all came under the mandate of the uniformed public health officer. "Insanity and mental defectiveness [among immigrants] are of grave concern from the standpoint of public health," Reed stated. "The individual victim is predisposed toward crime" (Reed 1913: 325; 1912: 389).[8] Jews in particular, because "the Hebrew race is essentially oriental," were to be excluded on "public health"—that is, eugenic—grounds (Reed 1912).

The American Medical Associations's popular health magazine *Hygeia* also contributed to the popular images of germs as criminals. The "archcriminal Jimmy Germ" was a recurring character in *Hygeia*'s cartoons. A stubbled, skinny, hook-nosed creature, Jimmy Germ bore a remarkable resemblance to contemporaneous caricatures of Jewish immigrants, Italian immigrants, and "the criminal type." Jimmy took perverse pleasure in victimizing those foolish, dark-haired children who neglected to wash and failed to brush their teeth. The archcriminal was thwarted by the fair-haired child who obeyed the "laws" of health (*Hygeia* 1923). During the first three decades of this century, the problem of disease was thoroughly intertwined with the problems of crime, degeneracy, and "race hygiene." Hygiene became the prevailing metaphor in the popular eugenics movement (Kevles 1985).[9] In a wide variety of representations in many different sources, immigrants having dark complexions, large facial features, and small stature were portrayed as carriers of dangerous germ plasm as well as dangerous germs; they harbored bodily parasites and were soon to become social parasites.

Thus, the historically specific institutional contexts in which immigrants entered the United States gave weight to analogies between immigration and disease, and between disease and criminality. In turn, these perceptions brought about a merging of criminology and public health enforcement, and lent force to each enterprise. During the first third of this century, numerous laws were established based on this analogy. Wisconsin abolished the common drinking cup; New Jersey passed sterilization laws against the feebleminded; the Federal Bureau of Investigation established a forensic medical laboratory; and immigrants underwent medical inspections by uniformed officers. Again, each measure reflects and reinforces the relation between hygiene and law enforcement, between crime and disease, between immigration and contamination.

Thus the new "germ theory" of disease was popularized and incorporated into the American vocabulary and culture according to a criminological model—a model that still frames discussions of public health policy. Of course, no conspiracy occurred, but there were victims; the logical necessity of making sense of the new germ theory in terms of older cultural categories, and the coincidence of developments in bacteriology, migration, and criminology created metaphors and analogies—models for policy that worked, that made sense, for experts in these fields who shared certain cultural assumptions, and against those who were cast as perpetrators.[10]

METAPHOR AND THE DOMESTICATION OF ATOMIC RADIATION

A particularly vivid and propitious metaphor can magnify and animate an invisible danger and, in so doing, foster specific policy goals aimed at mobilizing public reaction. The following second historical case study explores the ways in which another metaphor, also timely and vivid, minimized and tamed another danger and furthered other policy goals, this time aimed at quelling public reaction.

When atomic energy exploded upon world consciousness in the summer of 1945, its destructive power almost defied analogy. In announcing the annihilation of Hiroshima, President Truman explained, "It is an atomic bomb. It is a harnessing of the basic powers of the universe. The force from which the sun draws its powers has been loosed against those who brought war to the Far East" (*New York Times* 1945).

Truman was not the first to suggest the solar analogy, however; an eye-witness to the Trinity test earlier that summer recounted, "Suddenly and without any sound, the hills were bathed in brilliant light, as if somebody had turned the sun on with a switch." General Leslie Groves officially reported the Trinity explosion as "equal to several suns at midday" (Williams and Cantelon 1984: 46, 48).

Yet the solar metaphor in reference to radioactivity predates the atomic bomb; it appeared in reference to radium, in 1904, when W. J. Morton introduced his elixir "Liquid Sunshine," formulated to "bathe a patient's entire interior in violet or ultraviolet light." In 1909 physicist and chemist Frederick Soddy wrote of radium in a more scholarly, poetic way, employing Morton's metaphor to weightier effect: "It seems to claim lineage with the worlds beyond us, fed with the same inexhaustible fires, urged by the same uncontrollable mechanism which keeps the great suns alight in the heavens over endless periods of time" (*Scientific American* 1904).

The solar metaphor expressed dramatically a sense of wonder among the researchers who used it—awe not only at the sheer force and mystery of nature, but at human capacity to govern it. Over the course of the century, and particularly after 1945, it was the latter that prevailed. During the critical five years 1945 to 1950, Atomic Energy Commission officials stressed the benign aspect of the solar analogy. "Harnessed" replaced "uncontrollable" as the agency sought to diffuse public apprehension. Drawing on older images of the life-giving promise of radium, this semantic transformation paralleled and reinforced a more complex process by which the domestic uses of atomic energy became as familiar to the American public as the military uses for which it was unleashed against the Japanese.[11]

A key person in this transformation was the chairman of the Atomic Energy Commission, David Lilienthal. As former head of the Tennessee Valley Authority, he was a widely respected and well-known public figure. In late 1947 he traveled to his hometown, Crawfordsville, Indiana, to deliver a radio address to the nation on the subject, "Atomic Energy is Your Business" (*Bulletin of the Atomic Scientists* 1947: 335–38). In this address, which became a touchstone for subsequent policy pronouncements on atomic energy, Lilienthal acknowledged that the atom had been compared to other great natural forces: to electricity, to gravity itself. But the greatest and most beneficent of nature's forces was the sun:

> I suppose there is nothing of a physical nature that is more friendly to man, or more necessary to his well being than the sun. From the

sun you and I get every bit of our energy . . . the energy that gives life and sustains life, the energy that builds skyscrapers and churches, that writes poems and symphonies. The sun is the friend of man. In its rays is the magic stuff of life itself.

It was this comparison that Lilienthal deemed most apt:

The life-giving sun is itself a huge atomic energy plant. The sun, I repeat, is an atomic energy plant. [*Bulletin of the Atomic Scientists* 1947]

In this semantic context, much of the threat of the atomic bomb was dissipated, subtly transformed into a benign domestic influence. To fear nuclear radiation was to fear life itself.

Why was this metaphor plausible, in light of the terrible image that resulted from the bombing of Hiroshima and Nagasaki? What, other than fulsome rhetoric, counterbalanced the acknowledged dangers of radiation, as publicized in the 1928 case of the radium watch-dial painters?[12] To understand fully the impact of this metaphor on postwar audiences, it is important to recognize that in 1947 the sun and its effects on human health were thought to be much more benign than they are thought to be today. From the turn of the century, the disinfectant power of the sun in destroying the newly discovered germ of tuberculosis had transformed the sun, in medical and popular understanding, from a destroyer of gentlewomen's complexions to a symbol of healthful, progressive living. Apart from influencing the clinical treatment of consumption, this discovery spelled the end of the dark, ornate home furnishings that characterized the Victorian style. Windows and doors were flung open to light and air, veils went out of fashion, and, over the years, tanned complexions became more desirable—at least among Caucasians.

E. B. McCollum's 1922 discovery that an essential nutrient, which he named vitamin D, was synthesized by the human skin in the presence of ultraviolet light, further enhanced the image of the sun as a healthful influence. A method was devised to reproduce the sun's ultraviolet light in an electrical appliance, and thousands of American and European children spent days playing under sunlamps during winter months. In 1924 University of Wisconsin biochemist Harry Steenbock published his research on the synthesis of vitamin D through the irradiation of animal fats (Apple 1986). Rickets became a rarity; radiation acquired another hygienic function.

In this context, then, quite different from that of the 1980s, the director of the Atomic Energy Commission likened the atom to the sun. Like all effective analogies, it held a good measure of literal truth. The physical processes that produce atomic radiation are similar (not identical) to those that produce solar radiation. Both forms of radiation are invisible to the naked eye. Both have some beneficial uses, and in the case of vitamin D production, function analogously. However, like the analogy between germs and criminals—like any analogy—the analogy between the atom and the sun carries meanings that are not at first obvious.

In this case, the analogy dictated an almost casual attitude toward atomic radiation that resulted in appalling abuses of the technology and contrasted sharply with earlier attitudes.[13] Children growing up in the early 1950s had shoes fitted by x-ray. Women went to beauty parlors to have superfluous hair removed from their legs by x-ray. Children had their tonsils literally burned out by x-ray. Dentists and physicians urged frequent and high-dosage radiation as diagnostic and therapeutic panaceas. Technicians worked without protection day after day, year after year, in the presence of radioactive materials. No one can claim that this is the "fault" of a simple analogy, but the casual attitudes engendered by widespread acceptance of Lilienthal's formulation for the "peaceful atom" created a cultural climate in which these practices seemed not to be dangerous— except in retrospect.[14]

Ironically, it is not the analogy that has changed: we still liken atomic "radiation" to solar "radiation." What has changed, in part because of the analogy, is our notion of the sun. The reality of the physical dangers of atomic radiation led researchers to reassess the physical dangers of overexposure to sunlight. As in the case of atomic radiation, evidence had long existed of the harmful effects of sunlight on human skin, but only recently has a sustained change of scientific opinion affected public policy and popular attitudes.

The symbolic characterization of invisible phenomena may seem a vague and, at best, interesting philosophical exercise unrelated to the problems of hazards research or emergency management. But it has been my effort to demonstrate that this symbolism is absolutely integral to the most fundamental aspects of hazards research: the definition of the problem at hand. At the very least, these examples suggest that policy-makers should subject their own assumptions to rigorous and frankly philosophical scrutiny, that they seek historical precedent as instruction, and that they entertain as many alternatives to received analogies as they, philosophically and historically, can muster.

NOTES

This research was made possible in part by a grant from the Wisconsin Educational Research Foundation, and in part by a Smithsonian Institution Postdoctoral Fellowship.

1. For example, on the culturally defined dimensions of pain, see Pernick 1985, esp. pp. 148–70.

2. These ideas are not new; they have roots in seventeenth-century European political theory. On *policey* and police in European political theory, see Rosen 1974: 124–54.

3. The separation of these two enterprises, which also may seem self-evident, is itself a particular cultural arrangement, making the separation neither arbitrary nor irrelevant.

4. From an advertisement for Ivory Soap in *St. Nicholas* 1885, part of the Warshaw Collection, Smithsonian Institute.

5. One should also note an advertisement for Ricksecker Tooth Powder in *Munsey's Magazine* (June 1895), Warshaw Collection, Smithsonian Institute.

6. See *Ye Book of Spotless Town*, Warshaw Collection, Smithsonian Institute.

7. From *Ye Book of Spotless Town*.

8. On the particular threat of Jews and Italians, see McLaughlin 1904: 236–37 and Reed 1912: 391.

9. See also Haller 1963, and Charles Rosenberg's "The Bitter Fruit: Heredity, Disease, and Social Thought" in Rosenberg 1976.

10. For a more extensive discussion of metaphor and expertise, see Brown 1986a: 33–54 and Brown 1985. Both sources include an extensive bibliography on metaphor and language theory. Especially helpful are Lakoff and Johnson 1980, Austin 1975, and Hesse 1963.

11. For other aspects of this cultural transformation, see Brown 1986b.

12. See the *New York Times*, January 20, 1925, p. 1; April 28, 1928, p. 21; May 23, 1928, p. 11; June 5, 1928, p. 1; June 14, 1928, p. 9, cited in Hilgartner 1982.

13. See Smith 1965.

14. There is also a medical-legal problem presented by the health effects of radiation: at lower levels, it acts slowly, sufficiently out of synchrony with the cadence of medical diagnosis and legal procedure to diffuse its definition as medical or legal "damage." See, e.g., recent litigation between the estate of Rose Cippolone and the R. J. Reynolds Company.

REFERENCES

Apple, Rima D.
  1986   "Bottled Sunshine: The Commercialization of Science, 1920–1940."
          Paper presented at the History of Science Society annual meeting,
          October 23–36, Pittsburgh.
Arendt, Hannah
  1958   "Totalitarian Imperialism." *Journal of Politics* 20 (February):
          20–30.
Austin, J. L.
  1975   *How to Do Things with Words.* Oxford: Clarendon Press.
Belfield, William T.
  1884   *On the Relations of Micro-Organisms to Disease.* Chicago: W. T.
          Keen.
Brown, JoAnne
  1985   "The Semantics of Profession: Metaphor and Power in the His-
          tory of Psychological Testing, 1890–1929." Doctoral dissertation,
          University of Wisconsin.
  1986a   "Professional Language: Words that Succeed." *Radical History
          Review* 34: 33–54.
  1986b   " 'A' is for 'Atom'; 'B' is for 'Bomb': Atomic Energy and American
          Public Education, 1945–1965." *Journal of American History* (June).
Bulletin of the Atomic Scientists
  1947   November.
Haller, Mark
  1963   *Eugenics: Hereditarian Attitudes in American Thought.* New Bruns-
          wick: Rutgers University Press.
Hesse, Brenda
  1963   *Models and Analogies in Science.* London and New York: Sheed and
          Ward.
Hilgartner, Stephen, Bell, Richard C., and O'Connor, Rory
  1982   *Nukespeak: Nuclear Language, Visions, and Mindset.* San Fran-
          cisco: Sierra Club Books.
Hygeia
  1923   "Jimmy Germ." September, 397.
Kevles, Daniel
  1985   *In the Name of Eugenics: Genetics and the Uses of Human Heredity.*
          Berkeley: University of California Press.
Lakoff, George, and Johnson, Mark
  1980   *Metaphors We Live By.* Chicago: University of Chicago Press.

McLaughlin, Allan
    1904   "Immigration and the Public Health." *Popular Science Monthly* 64 (January): 232–38.

New York Times
    1945   August 7, p. 4.

Pernick, Martin
    1985   *A Calculus of Suffering: Pain, Professionalism, and Anesthesia in Nineteenth-Century America.* New York: Columbia University Press.

Reed, Alfred C.
    1912   "The Medical Side of Immigration." *Popular Science Monthly*, pp. 383–404.
    1913   "Immigration and the Public Health." *Popular Science Monthly*, pp. 313–38.

Rosen, George
    1974   *From Medical Police to Social Medicine: Essays on the History of Health Care.* New York: Science History Publications.

Rosenberg, Charles
    1962   *The Cholera Years: The United States in 1832, 1849, and 1866.* Chicago: University of Chicago Press.
    1976   *No Other Gods: On Science and American Social Thought.* Baltimore: Johns Hopkins University Press.

Scientific American
    1904   "Dr. Morton's Theory of the Therapeutic Value of Radium Solutions." 90 (January 30): 5.

Smith, Alice Kimball
    1965   *A Peril and a Hope: The Scientists Movement in America, 1945–1947.* Chicago: University of Chicago Press.

Soddy, Frederick
    1909   *The Interpretation of Radium and the Structure of the Atom.* London: John Murray.

Starr, Paul
    1982   *The Social Transformation of American Medicine.* New York: Basic Books.

Warner, John Harley
    1982   "Exploring the Inner Labyrinths of Creation: Popular Microscopy in Nineteenth-Century America." *Journal of the History of Medicine and Allied Sciences* 37: 7–33.

Williams, Robert C., and Cantelon, Philip L., eds.
    1984   *The American Atom, 1939–1984: A Documentary History of Nuclear Policies from the Discovery of Fission to the Present.* Philadelphia: University of Pennsylvania Press.

JoAnne Brown

Yew, Elizabeth
1980   "Medical Inspection of Immigrants at Ellis Island, 1891–1924." *Bulletin of the New York Academy of Medicine* 56 (6) (June): 488–510.

Young, James Harvey
1961   *The Toadstool Millionaires*. Princeton: Princeton University Press.

CHAPTER 3

Conservatism, Efficiency, and the Value of Life

Douglas MacLean and Claudia Mills

Critics of current health and safety regulations frequently charge that these reflect a phobic shunning of new technology, a dreamer's zeal for a "risk-free" world. Conservative health and safety policies, such critics charge, are costly and inefficient, set in response to newspaper scare stories, and interest group pressures, rather than in accordance with a systematic, across-the-board risk policy. In the absence of some rational method for computing and comparing the costs of saving lives to other costs, or the costs of saving lives under one government program to the costs of saving lives in other programs, we are spending too little to save lives and protect health and safety in some areas, and far too much in others.

Yet in spheres of personal concern, most feel it is only prudent to err on the side of safety. We do not go too near the edge of the cliff if the ground is unfamiliar; we take along an umbrella if we think it might rain; we throw out food that has been in the refrigerator a while (or at least we do not eat it); and so on. In the face of uncertainty about the possible outcomes of the risks we assume in our personal lives, "better safe than sorry" is the recommended motto. To err is human, but to err on the side of safety is good common sense.

Caution can become phobic, however, and we often recognize when it has, even though it may be impossible to draw a clear line. We do not avoid cliffs at *any* distance, *always* carry umbrellas, or throw out *all* left-over food. Most of us develop sensible personal policies, but policies that are still cautious in the face of uncertainty. But policy analysts and theorists often write as though conservative regulatory policies about health and safety go beyond a reasonable level of caution. It is part of our concern in this paper to examine whether or not this is so.

We also want to examine the argument that the inefficiencies attendant upon undue conservatism are best avoided by establishing some unified metric for comparing the values inherent in environmental decision-making. Environmental decisions require us to compare the value of saving lives to the value of improving health, and in turn to compare these to other kinds of benefits. We must compare the values we express in setting our environmental goals, which are often stated in vague and constricting legislation, against what we can realistically expect to accomplish in these areas, to determine what inefficiencies we should tolerate for the sake of pursuing social goals and fulfilling expectations.

We suggest that certain inefficiencies may and indeed should be tolerated in the area of health and safety regulation. In our view, living with certain controversies may be preferable to resolving them quickly through the use of even the best analytic methods. This is an issue of comparing some subtle values that may be served by living with unresolved controversies to the more obvious values served by resolving controversies and making decisions. The former, we argue, may well be worth some degree of inefficiency and delay.

We also argue, however, that health and safety policies could be made more rational and efficient than they are now, both by a better understanding of the nature of uncertainty and by more careful thought about the symbolic and cultural values embodied in our actions.

THREE LEVELS OF CONSERVATISM

Conservatism can be built into public health and safety policies at three levels.[1] First, it can be reflected in laws. The statutes that create and give mandates to regulatory agencies, for example, call for standards that protect the public health with "an adequate margin of safety" (the EPA mandate under the Clean Air Act); ban food additives that are carcinogenic (the Delaney Amendment to the Food and Drug Act); assure "to the extent feasible" that "no employee will suffer material impairment of health" (the OSHA mandate under the Occupational Safety and Health Act); and so on.

The standards called for by these laws are always vague, however, so it is left to the agencies entrusted with their implementation to establish policies that will guide their decisions and determine their priorities. This is a second level where conservatism can enter. Decision-makers can set standards to protect against worst-case scenarios, relying on the most pessimistic of a range of risk estimates—an approach common, for example, in hurricane evacuation and earthquake planning. Policy-makers can decide to set costly standards, if they believe social values call for greater protection in their particular area (e.g., the workplace, air and water standards, food additives) than in other areas where individuals act alone, together, or through government to reduce risks.

A third level of possible conservative bias occurs in risk assessment, in the scientific enterprise of identifying risks and estimating their magnitudes. (This level, of course, cannot be neatly separated from the level of risk management, anymore than facts can be neatly separated from values.) How should the scientists who provide the data for risk management cope with the uncertainties they confront? Which tests should they do? How should they report their results? And how should they extrapolate from laboratory experiments to the more realistic environments that regulations aim to control? All these questions involve uncertainties in response to which risk assessors may choose to be conservative.

THE ARGUMENT AGAINST CONSERVATISM

The argument against conservatism at the first two levels is similar: protecting health to the extent feasible or to ensure an adequate margin of safety is excessively costly and involves a misallocation of resources. If some agencies are willing, whether by law or by policy, to spend more per life saved than other agencies, then our risk budget is misallocated. We are spending more money to save fewer lives than we could if we were less selectively cautious. Worse still, if we tried generally to achieve absolute safety or zero risk, we would probably achieve net negative effects by diverting resources away from pursuing other goods (like education or material comfort) that inadvertently improve our health and safety. We can tax workers to fund research to reduce the risk of ulcers and heart attacks—but if we refunded that same money to workers, they might reduce their own risks of stress-related illness more directly by simply taking a vacation. Similarly, a slightly carcinogenic food additive may protect against other diseases or may keep the public from eating other less healthy substitutes.

The argument against conservatism at the level of risk assessment rests on the charge that if scientists make conservative assumptions, they are usurping the risk management function. They are making policy choices that should be made instead by legislators and administrators, who are open to public scrutiny and political accountability. Scientific data should not err on the side of caution but reflect without bias the full range of uncertainties involved. If this is not feasible, then the data should reflect best mean estimates, not conservative upper-bound estimates of the uncertainties in the hazards we risk.

The case for the critics of conservatism can also be buttressed with dramatic examples of inefficiency in risk management. Here are a few of the outstanding ones (see Morrall 1986).[2] The Food and Drug Administration recently proposed a ban of the cosmetic coloring Orange No. 17, which would have averted a calculated risk of one in ten billion, saving an estimated one life in two thousand years. Ten rules currently proposed and under consideration from several agencies for which data are available would save a total of ninety lives per year (nearly two million Americans die annually) at an estimated cost of more than one hundred million dollars per life saved. Some of these proposals will surely be rejected. They include from one agency, OSHA, a proposed safety rule for oil and gas well service with an estimated cost of one hundred thousand dollars per life saved, as well as a proposed health rule for formaldehyde exposure with an estimated cost of seventy-two *billion* dollars per life saved. OSHA is far more conservative in setting health standards, especially to protect workers from carcinogens, than in setting safety standards, an emphasis that, within reasonable bounds, many would defend. But if we assume that other similar health and safety opportunities abound, then OSHA would be grossly misallocating resources if these proposals, outgrowths of its special conservative concern to protect workers from cancer risks, were approved. Likewise, to take only one example from the domain of natural hazards, huge costs are invested in radar systems for early detection of tornadoes, but such systems save very few lives.

A DEFENSE OF CONSERVATISM AT
THE FIRST TWO LEVELS

The criticism of conservatism at the first two levels in many ways reflects a typical policy theorist's view of an ideal world. It suggests that the politics, management, and science of risk are discrete and can remain somewhat independent, even though what takes place at one level will obviously influence what happens at other levels. It suggests that managers can employ analytic techniques to combine what we want (as politically and otherwise expressed) and what we know (as read off from assessments) into reasonable decisions. It further suggests that what we want is the highly abstract general goal of "risk reduction," rather than the specific goals of cleaner air, a safer workplace, water we need not be afraid to drink, food without additives that cause cancer, mutual succor in time of disaster, and so on.

This idealized view is deeply flawed. Risk assessment and risk management are not easily isolated facets of the policy-making process; nor is the goal of health and safety regulation best understood as that of aiming at some kind of global or generalized risk reduction. Very few persons, we suggest, have a stated goal of "reducing risk" in their lives generally, as shown by what analysts take to be widely held inconsistent attitudes toward risk (e.g., the same individual who pickets a local nuclear reactor willingly goes rock-climbing). That we want not some abstract goal of risk reduction, but the particular goals of clean air, safe water, and so forth, is further suggested by the fact that the political process has served up a motley set of laws and agencies to regulate health and safety, each with its own mandate, rather than one omnibus risk-reduction bill authorizing one agency to make efficient trade-offs across all these different realms. We turn now to examine one revelatory case history: decision-making at OSHA.

FEASIBILITY AT OSHA: PRUDENT OR PHOBIC?

The history of the Occupational Safety and Health Act suggests that what its proponents cared about was not reducing risk generally but protecting worker health and safety. Its passage followed closely upon the major mine disaster in November 1968, which took seventy-eight lives in Farmington, West Virginia. The accident crystallized a supersaturated atmosphere of public opinion that supported occupational safety and health legislation. The most controversial part of the OSH Act, Section 6 (b)(5), which instructs the Secretary of Labor to set standards that "most adequately [assure], to the extent feasible on the best available evidence, that no employee will suffer material impairment of health or functional capacity even if such employee has regular exposure to the hazard dealt with by such standard for the period of his working life," was first introduced as an amendment by Senator Javitz to make the Senate bill *less* conservative. The original Senate bill called for standards to assure "that no employee will suffer any impairment of health or functional capacity, or diminished life expectancy" (Subcommittee on Labor 1971: 834). Senator Javitz explained his amendment as a compromise between this original bill, "which might be interpreted to require absolute health and safety in all cases, regardless of feasibility, and the Administration bill, which contains no criteria for standards at all" (Subcommittee on Labor 1971: 197). The feasibility clause was a compromise between those who thought the standard should be driven by health considerations, not cost balancing, and those who feared the standards called for the impossible goal of eliminating risks altogether from the workplace.

The idea that occupational health standards should be determined by their feasibility rather than by some cost-balancing method was evidently considered necessary to realize the kind of healthy workplace that had enormous political support. There are strong reasons to believe that existing industry standards at the time were already economically efficient, but they clearly were not thought to be adequate. George Meany, speaking for the AFL-CIO, had said in Congressional hearings:

> Every year thousands of workers die slow, often agonizing deaths from the effects of coal dust, asbestos, beryllium, lead, cotton dust, carbon monoxide, cancer-causing chemicals, dyes, radiation, pesticides, and exotic fuels. Others suffer long illnesses. Thousands suffer from employment in artificially created harmful environments. [*Occupational Safety and Health Act of 1968*: 704, quoted in Kelman 1980: 243]

There was obviously a strong feeling that this situation must be changed and that a federal agency should be established to set health and safety standards. The strong and relatively conservative feasibility standard for toxic materials was already a compromise. Was it worse than the alternatives: cost-balancing standards or no standards at all? If we look at the OSH Act in its historical setting, it is difficult to see the feasibility standard as a phobic reaction to improbable hazards.

At the second or policy-making level as well, however, OSHA attempted to interpret the law in a way that would put a conservative emphasis on health but would nevertheless take economic impacts into consideration, balancing its concern for workers' health with considerations for the burden on industry of compliance. Its first toxic substance standard for asbestos reflected a compromise between industry pressure to keep the existing standard and union arguments that the standard should be lowered drastically; it set a significantly lower exposure level but allowed it to be phased in over time.

In formulating its standard for coke oven emissions, OSHA refused the recommendation of President Ford's Council on Wage and Price Stability to adopt cost-benefit analysis as its method for determining feasibility (*Exposure to Coke Oven Emissions* 1976). Most importantly, perhaps, it criticized all the existing methods for quantifying the values of life and health. But it also argued that the inherent uncertainties made cost-benefit analysis impractical. Partly because of the technology-forcing effect of the OSHA rules, the compliance costs to industry are too difficult to determine with the precision needed for reliable cost-benefit analysis, and scientific uncertainties make precise estimates of benefits impossible. Slightly different and equally plausible assumptions yield very different estimates of health and mortality effects, and the difficulties are compounded because many of these benefits are expected to occur perhaps twenty years hence. Thus, OSHA concluded, "there are insuperable obstacles to any attempt to estimate accurately and to reduce to dollar terms the value of any health regulation" (*Exposure to Coke Oven Emissions* 1976: 46750).

As the initial OSHA standards survived judicial review, the agency's working criteria for setting standards evolved. Feasibility was interpreted along technological, scientific, and economic dimensions. OSHA standards could be technology-forcing if the agency could show that the technologies needed to meet its standards were on the horizon. Standards could be based on partial and sometimes uncertain scientific evidence, because, given the nature of epidemiological evidence and the time lag involved between exposure and the onset of disease, OSHA would not be able to prove its dose-response estimates until after the damage to workers had been done. Yet OSHA could not impose on industry a burden so heavy that an entire industrial sector would be driven out of business. Through its interpretation of feasibility, the OSHA response to uncertainty was to make scientific conservatism and technological optimism its guiding principles.

What it chose *not* to do, it seemed, was to quantify benefits and costs, and attempt to maximize some expected value. In 1980 the Supreme Court struck down the OSHA benzene standard, reading the OSH Act to require that OSHA make quantitative risk assessments and show quantitatively that the benefits of the lowered exposure level bore a "reasonable relationship" to the costs (*Industrial Union Department. AFL-CIO v. American Petroleum, Inc.*, 100 S.Ct 2844, 1980). But in 1981 the Court upheld the OSHA refusal to use cost-benefit analysis as its criterion for setting standards in its cotton dust rule. Writing for a 5 to 3 majority, Justice Brennan said:

> Congress itself defined the basic relationship between costs and benefits, by placing the "benefit" of worker health above all other considerations save those making attainment of the "benefit" unachievable. Any standard based on a balancing of costs and benefits by the Secretary that strikes a different balance than that struck by Congress would be inconsistent with the command set forth in sec. 6 (b) (5). Thus cost-benefit analysis by OSHA is not required by the statute because feasibility analysis is required. [*American Textile Manufacturers Institute v. Donovan* 452 U.S. (1981): 490]

Feasibility analysis, as developed by OSHA, can be construed as its conservative response to uncertainty. It relies heavily on quantified data—on scientific and economic information and on technological projections—but it does not require that these be brought into a single metric with the goal of maximizing some expected value or pursuing efficiency. It is precisely because of the uncertainties involved that such a cost-balancing approach is thought to be useless or even damaging. It would indicate a level of precision and detailed knowledge that we simply do not possess.

We can be generally sympathetic with the OSHA interpretation of feasibility, given the clouds of uncertainty under which it must operate, and still recognize that the standard is flawed. The proposed rule for formaldehyde (assuming the seventy-two billion dollar estimated cost per life saved is correct) provides a case in point. Presumably this rule meets the health, technology, and economic criteria of the standard, but it reflects an irrational reaction nevertheless. A relative emphasis on carcinogens seems a defensible form of conservatism, given the kinds of uncertainties and latencies involved between exposure to carcinogens and subsequent cancers, but like all such efforts, it needs to be tempered with common sense.

The element of common sense seems notoriously to be missing when we compare the cost-effectiveness of the proposed formaldehyde rule to the proposed oil and gas well service safety rule. Even taking account of the different uncertainties that may be involved, cost estimates ranging over more than five orders of magnitude are deeply disturbing. Yet even this is not a reason to abandon the feasibility standard. At most, the standard needs further interpretation, but perhaps all we need is more common sense among risk managers. We will discuss below some ways of thinking about uncertainty and about the symbolic and expressive function of regulatory action that will help set limits to these kinds of inefficiencies.

AN ARGUMENT AGAINST CONSERVATISM AT THE THIRD LEVEL: COMPOUNDING CONSERVATIVE ASSUMPTIONS

Despite the OSHA refusal to interpret feasibility in terms of a cost-balancing method, ever since the benzene case the agency is required to rely on quantitative risk assessments. This is the third level where conservatism can enter, and it raises the most difficult and general theoretical issues.

The argument against conservatism in risk management presupposes an unrealistic degree of discreteness in the various factors that go into making decisions. The problem with conservatism in risk assessment is the converse. The methodology for assessing carcinogens essentially involves a number of discrete steps, and our knowledge is likely to be incomplete at each step. The case for making conservative assumptions has prima facie plausibility at each stage, but when they are aggregated the effects of conservatism can be compounded with dramatic results.

Risk assessments for cancer typically involve three major stages: estimates of the emissions level of a pollutant; estimates of exposure to the substance; and estimates of the cancer risk resulting from the exposure. Emission estimates tend to be the most straightforward part of the process, but even here uncertainties may enter about the state of the technology (as technologies improve, emission levels tend to come down); whether or how often a plant operates at full capacity; and the lifespan of the substance.

Exposure estimates are more complicated. They typically begin with a computer model that predicts how a substance will be dispersed and then combines the results of this estimate with information about the size, distribution, and behavior of the population that will be exposed. This allows ample room for worst-case assumptions about meteorological conditions, groundwater contamination, and so on, and for conservative assumptions about who will be exposed to what concentrations.

By far the most troubling stage, however, is in translating exposure estimates into risk estimates, which is done by constructing a dose-response function. Typically, scientists observe the effects of exposure to high concentrations of the substance in question, sometimes through epidemiological studies of workers, but more often through laboratory experiments on animals. Then they must make a number of assumptions to extrapolate from animals or workers to other human populations and from artificially high doses to actual exposure estimates.

This summary of the cancer risk assessment process clearly demonstrates how many different assumptions must be made in the face of uncertainty. The effects of compounding a conservative bias in each of these assumptions are staggering. To see this, let us look in some detail at a case study prepared for the EPA of the carcinogenicity of perchloroethylene (PCE), a common substance in dry cleaning fluids. Its authors faced decisions regarding three areas of uncertainty (Campbell et al., no date).

The first was whether to use a linear or a nonlinear function to extrapolate from high doses to low doses. A linear function assumes that the risk of cancer decreases proportionately, so that a substance that poses some cancer risk at high doses will pose a proportional risk even when a person is exposed to only one molecule. A nonlinear function allows for thresholds of exposure, with no risk of cancer involved when the dose is below a given level. Linear functions are the more conservative, and at low doses the difference can range up to several orders of magnitude.

Animal studies of PCE were done on mice and rats. The mouse study, it turned out, showed a higher response rate. The second assumption, then, was whether to use the mouse or the rat study. The third assumption was whether to extrapolate from animals to humans as a function of surface area or of body weight. Scientists are divided as to which method is more accurate. Because surface area increases less, proportionally, than weight as one moves from smaller to larger animals, surface area conversion is the more conservative method and leads to higher risk estimates. The difference in the two methods is roughly a factor of six for rats and a factor of thirteen for mice.

These three uncertainties, involving just two alternatives each, allow for eight different estimates. Based on the data in the PCE case, the low risk estimate (a nonlinear, weight-based extrapolation from the rat study) differs from the most conservative risk estimate (a linear, surface area extrapolation from the mouse study) by a factor of 35,000!

Albert Nichols and Richard Zeckhauser have recently argued against conservative risk assessments and defended an alternative procedure.[3] They argue that regulatory agencies often base emissions estimates on the assumptions that "plants operate at full capacity, though few actually do" (Nichols and Zeckhauser 1986: 14); that they rely on "old estimates . . . that are not representative of current technologies and controls" (i.e., actions taken because of state or local regulations or out of economic self-interest) (Nichols and Zeckhauser 1985: 5); that they assume substances will be used for longer than their average economic life (Nichols and Zeckhauser 1986: 15); and that regulated emissions levels will be fully complied with (Nichols and Zeckhauser 1985: 5–6). Conservative biases enter into exposure estimates by assuming unrealistically pessimistic meteorological data[4] or by estimating a maximum individual exposure that assumes "that some individuals are born and die at the point of maximum pollution concentration, and never leave that spot . . . [or take any] averting behavior" (Nichols and Zeckhauser 1986: 15).

DEFENDING CONSERVATIVE RISK ASSESSMENT: A CLOSER LOOK AT UNCERTAINTY

Even if these charges correctly reflect general regulatory practices, however, they do not support an argument against conservative responses to uncertainty of the kind we want to defend. To see this, we need to distinguish between different sources of "unsureness." We can be unsure about the effects of our actions either because our best scientific efforts do not allow precise predictions or because we have not bothered to find out what those effects are likely to be. The former unsureness is due in part to the state of the world; the latter is due to our limited efforts alone. Of course, real instances of unsureness will often combine both sources, but we will reserve the words "uncertainty" for the former and "ignorance" for the latter.

A conservative response to ignorance is reasonable only if action taken to reduce our ignorance would be too costly. Many of Nichols and Zeckhauser's examples of bias, which constitute a large part of their argument against conservatism, are cases of unreasonable ignorance. Regulators in these cases could reduce their unsureness and make more accurate estimates if they tried. Given the costs involved, they ought to try.

Before we consider Nichols and Zeckhauser's further arguments, we need to be more specific about the nature of uncertainty. The technical literature in decision theory discusses and debates two models of probability. In the *objective* model, probabilities are relative frequencies within ideal reference classes, where nothing is known to determine a finer, more relevant, set of reference classes. In the *subjective* model, on the other hand, a probability is a representation of decision-makers' beliefs about the world that make their set of beliefs coherent, explain their actions, or feel good to them.

Both these models are well understood, and in many situations it does not matter which one we use. The objective model can be applied to "random" events that show regularities over many repetitions. Thus, in the kinds of situations that concern us here, objective probabilities can be used to report the results of toxicological studies that determine cancer risks to a given animal population at the dose levels used in the experiments; objective probabilities determine cancer risks to humans where we have good epidemiological studies on human populations. In these cases the frequencies are known, and nothing can make our knowledge more fine-grained.

In the subjective model, probabilities are an expression of a decision-maker's degree of belief in a given outcome. Uncertainties about the probabilities express degrees of confidence in that belief. A well-calibrated decision-maker will have degrees of belief and confidence in different possible outcomes that correspond closely to the frequencies or objective probabilities. But subjective probabilities can be determined even where established frequencies are unavailable. This is an attractive feature of the subjective model.

It is important to stress, however, that the subjective model was originally developed solely for situations of individual decision-making or to select actions that will have no significant effects on others. Most real-life decision problems do not fit either model very well: objective probabilities are often not available, yet few decisions have no consequences for others.

Ian Hacking has made this point convincingly, criticizing subjective decision theorists who "assume without argument that their reasoning applies in public domains" (Hacking 1986: 141). If we cannot determine probabilities using the objective model in public domains, then we must admit that we are dealing with uncertainties and apply some other kind of reasoning. Hacking writes:

> If a hermit will produce some new technology in isolation, perhaps he may make a purely subjective calculation that is entirely his business, if that is how he wants to conduct his life. He is thereby comfortably lulled into an imitation of reasoning. Such imitations are not permissible in the public realm. . . . When there are no probabilities for a certain kind of possibility, I am reluctant to pretend to calculate, and I look with suspicion on others who would calculate on my behalf. [Hacking 1986: 153]

Nichols and Zeckhauser abhor the effects of compounding conservative assumptions in risk assessments, especially in selecting the dose-response function, but their argument leaves unclear which model of probability they think applies to these problems and therefore contains some subtle confusions. For example, they seem to concede that frequencies cannot be determined, so the objective model cannot be applied to select the dose-response function for cancer risks. They write, "Unfortunately, this function cannot be observed directly; a firm theoretical foundation for constructing it does not exist; and estimating it through controlled animal experiments would be prohibitively expensive, if not impossible" (Nichols and Zeckhauser 1986: 15).[5]

For just this reason, scientists engaged in risk assessments for regulatory agencies typically make conservative assumptions of the sort we have indicated above. They pick numbers or functions that they feel confident will either be correct or err on the side of safety. One could argue for a different approach, but there seems to be no alternative here but to rely on their professional judgments regarding the estimation of uncertainties.

Nichols and Zeckhauser's criticism of conservative estimates, however, appeals to the likelihood that these scientists will be wrong. "If all the parameters were distributed lognormally with the same variances and were independent, the product of five 90th percentile estimates would have a 99.8 percent chance of being too high" (Nichols and Zeckhauser 1985: 18). This kind of statement, however, makes sense only if the probabilities and uncertainties involved have the kind of determinancy that exists when frequencies have been well established. Uncertainties registered as confidence levels mean something different, and in public contexts it is not clear that the numbers that represent them mean very much at all, especially when the uncertainties involved reflect disagreement among experts about the most accurate method for making extrapolations.

This confusion is even clearer when we consider Nichols and Zeckhauser's alternative proposal. They defend an "expected-value" approach, which they explain in the following way:

> [Suppose] one set of assumptions predicts that the risk of cancer from a chemical is 1 in 10,000, while another set puts the risk substantially lower at 1 in 100,000. Suppose that risk assessors . . . report both figures along with their estimate that each one is correct—90 percent for the lower estimate and 10 percent for the higher estimate. . . . The expected-value approach . . . is simply the weighted average of the risk estimates, with the weight for each alternative equal to the subjective probability that it is correct. In our example, the expected value of the risk is about 2 in 100,000, which is roughly one-fifth the conservative estimate but almost twice the "most likely" estimate. [Nichols and Zeckhauser 1986: 21]

Again, this way of thinking treats the numbers with more respect than they deserve. Suppose, as is not unlikely, that the different estimates have been produced by different risk assessors; the higher estimate by the National Institute for Occupational Safety and Health, and the lower one by the Chemical Manufacturers Association. No doubt the scientists' different values are driving their judgments of the best estimate, but each will obviously think his or her own estimate is more likely to be correct than the other.

In this situation we might propose going to another scientist or taking the matter to some science court to estimate the likelihood that each estimate is correct. But this procedure also fails to appreciate the nature of the uncertainties involved, for even if 90 percent of the scientists think the lower estimate is more likely to be correct than the higher one, that is not necessarily a good reason to conclude that it is more likely at all to be correct, let alone nine times as likely. Reasonable individuals, trying to decide for themselves between these two estimates, would have to know why most scientists prefer one to the other. If "no firm theoretical foundation" gives a reason for preferring one over the other, then we simply do not know what the chances are that the worst-case estimate is correct.

Nichols and Zeckhauser also recommend that risk assessors be bound to an expected value approach so that decisions about conservatism can be made by risk managers. In this way, "fewer value judgments would be concealed in the risk-assessment process" (Nichols and Zeckhauser 1986: 22). Such an approach, however, takes the fact-value distinction, or the risk assessment–risk management distinction, too seriously. In situations involving genuine uncertainties, scientists should be encouraged to make and explain their best judgments, without having the judgments of policy analysts and theorists, who may not fully understand the scientific questions involved, forced on them.

In regulating health and safety, risk assessors and risk managers both have good reasons to err on the side of safety. Human lives are at stake, after all, and our priority should be to save lives rather than money when we genuinely do not know on which side we might err. But there is ample room within a policy of conservatism to avoid the kinds of extremes that are cited by the critics of regulatory agencies. Risk managers must be sure they are relying on good science and not ideologically driven science. These may not be easy to distinguish, especially where the real uncertainties involved are substantial. More important, they must ensure that conservative assumptions are not further compounded as a result of inexcusable ignorance. When ignorance is controlled, the costs of erring on the side of safety will not be nearly as great.

Above all, risk managers must set priorities within an agency. The embarrassing proposals out of OSHA suggest that these priorities are not being set as well as they might be. We turn now to one central controversy in the setting of priorities in health and safety regulation: the question of establishing a "social value" for human life. We suggest that while determining a social value for human life is a rational way of setting certain regulatory priorities, it also compromises other, equally important, regulatory objectives.

THE SYMBOLIC FUNCTION OF REGULATION

When we look at the extraordinary differentials between what is spent to save a life under different regulations spawned by different government agencies—recall the extravagantly disproportionate costs of the OSHA proposed formaldehyde and oil well rules—we can understand the rationale for establishing a standard "social value" of human life, a measure by which the costs of health and safety proposals can be assessed and compared across the board. Regulatory agencies do not set the price of life; they merely try to uncover public preferences for risk reduction from data about consumer safety decisions, wage rate differentials for hazardous occupations, opinion surveys, and contingent valuation studies. This is partly misleading, because another possible way to determine the value of life would be to examine regulatory decisions themselves. We look for the norm in other areas, of course, precisely to guide these decisions and evaluate existing regulatory policies. That is the sole purpose in determining a social value of human life.

This issue is a source of enduring controversy. Pricing life seems both necessary for holding regulatory agencies economically accountable, and morally repugnant. The moral issue, of course, is treating a "sacred" good as an economic commodity. Kant wrote that human beings have intrinsic worth or dignity, and that whatever has dignity is "above all price, and therefore admits of no equivalent" (Kant 1911: 434–45). But Robert Solow describes the issue more clearly: "It may well be socially destructive to admit the routine exchangeability of certain things. We would prefer to maintain that they are beyond price (although this sometimes means only that we would prefer not to know what this price really is)" (Solow 1981: 40).

Decisions about acceptable risk inevitably involve comparing the value of saving lives and protecting health against the cost of doing so. To make these decisions in a fully rational way, many would argue that we must be explicit about these costs and the amount we are willing to spend to save lives. This is to embark on what Allan Gibbard calls "technocratic moral reform." He suggests:

> A rationally grounded morality will be reformist—perhaps shockingly so. It will not appeal primarily to our capacities to be aroused, as traditional moral reform movements have done, but to ways of regimenting the considerations involved to produce rational, coherent judgments. ... We need, it seems, to train people in rational methods of risk assessment and so organize society that those methods really do determine policy with regard to risk. [Gibbard 1986: 99]

Why do "many, perhaps most of us," as Gibbard says, find this a chilling prospect?

The answer is not, as some have claimed, that human life has an infinite price. That is not what Kant meant in saying that humanity is "above all price." The reason is rather, as Solow observes, that we find it morally repugnant to see life as routinely exchangeable for other goods. We thus feel uncomfortable with even rationally defensible procedures for making difficult decisions that make an exchange rate for life prominent.

How can we make sense of this reaction? We would argue that the value of life is complex.[6] Human life has intrinsic value, which makes it worth saving and prolonging. This component of life's value favors efficient efforts to save more lives rather than fewer. It stands behind our support for rational methods of risk assessment. But human life is also sacred, and this component of its value can work in a different and conflicting direction. We will briefly explain what we take this sacred component to mean.

Durkheim regarded sacred values as "elementary forms" of religious life, by which he meant that even as societies become secular, there remains a kind of need that traditional religions fulfill in older or more primitive cultures (Durkheim 1915). This is a need to find rituals that strengthen social integration. "There can be no society," Durkheim wrote, "which does not feel the need of upholding and reaffirming at regular intervals the collective sentiments and the collective ideas which make its unity and its personality" (Durkheim 1915: 417).

As a pluralistic culture, we do not have a single unity and personality, but there are clearly some basic moral values that we all share and that, as Durkheim would point out, are universal. Rituals carry symbolic meaning that calls attention to these values. They are marked by special, perhaps nonrational behavior and actions, which draw the attention of the community to objects or relationships that have a special place in the life of the group. Because rituals are symbolic, they rely on conventional forms of behavior, which can differ from group to group. But in all societies, especially in those areas where we find it necessary to "humanize" parts of our existence, we will find characteristic activities marked by rituals (Hampshire 1983). They surround birth, sex, and marriage, for example, and they also surround death and the taking of life.

Precisely because health and safety decisions have obvious economic consequences, we need to guard especially against treating human life as exchangeable in these contexts, and some policies and procedures that are inefficient but highly symbolic can be an effective guard. Startling examples of inefficient, ritualized behavior are common in our dealings with hazards and risks. We need only consider our willingness to engage in rescue missions when identified individuals are involved, to act as if—or certainly to give the appearance that—costs are not a consideration.

To argue that we must respect the sacred value of human life in these situations is not to deny in any way the value of efficiency in life-saving and the importance of saving more lives rather than fewer when we can. The point is a more subtle one. It is to suggest that there may be irreconcilable tensions between our rationalistic, revisionist sentiments, on the one hand, and our conservative, ritualistic sentiments, on the other. A rationalistic decision procedure may unavoidably threaten some of these sentiments, which may suggest not making that procedure too absolute, too open, or too openly identified with public agencies like EPA that were created to pursue moral as well as economic goals. We must perhaps be willing to live with some controversies rather than resolving them technocratically and to tolerate "pockets" or modest levels of inefficiency for this purpose.

Some examples here suggest the way in which honoring sacred values may involve behavior that is deliberately inefficient—but also show that such inefficiencies should indeed remain within bounds. Consider certain symbolic elements of weddings and funerals, which focus on the refusal to hold the costs incurred in their observance to usual standards of efficiency. All but the most unsentimental bride chooses a special dress to wear on her wedding day, traditionally a dress that costs far more than any other dress she owns and that will never be worn again, except perhaps at her own daughter's wedding. The ceremony would be as legally binding if the bride wore her ordinary work clothes, but the choice of a special dress makes an unmistakable statement that the wedding day is special, different from all others; it marks the magnitude of the change made in the lives of those committing themselves in marriage. Yet, even so, most brides are not willing to spend more than a fixed amount on their wedding finery, and those with the most lavish weddings are not viewed as having made the deepest commitment. The deliberate inefficiency of wedding arrangements has symbolic value, but this value is not laid out on a linear scale. It is signaled by a discontinuity with ordinary economic thinking, but the discontinuity is modest, not radical, in scope.

Likewise, we bury or even cremate our dead in a dignified coffin, although a cardboard box would dispose of "the remains" equally well. We are willing to spend good money on an object of beauty and craftsmanship that will be destroyed forever only days after its purchase. This is a way in which we signal our reverence for the deceased, in which we echo Kant's dictum that human life has not a price, but a dignity. Yet, despite many a funeral director's fond hopes, we rarely feel that there is no amount of money that would be too great to spend to honor our dead.

We have a sense of which inefficiencies are fitting and which inappropriate or even ludicrous.

Turning again to the symbolic and expressive function of health and safety regulation, we may also recognize the symbolic role of public figures like the administrator of EPA. When he or she appears at a press conference to announce a regulatory decision, often about some hazard that has generated widespread public anxiety, people may be less concerned to know that he or she has found the ideal cost-benefit ratio than to be reassured that things we value deeply—our health, the environment, posterity—are being guarded and protected by the agency we have created to be the trustee of these values. Like it or not, the actions of EPA have important symbolic and expressive significance. We might not approve of taboos like refusing even to look at cost-benefit analyses, but we ought at least to be sensitive to the kinds of symbolic importance they might have.[7]

These considerations support the general conclusion that we should look critically and perhaps even suspiciously at suggestions that we should apply some analytic method universally for making environmental decisions. The comparisons and trade-offs we must make are often context-dependent or involve symbolic elements. These comparisons make the justification of our decisions very situation-specific.

We hope to have suggested here why certain inefficiencies in regulatory decision-making are better tolerated than eliminated, but also some ways in which such efficiencies can be confined within limits. We have argued for conservatism in health and safety regulation, but for a bounded conservatism. This seems to us a decent and sensible way to proceed when human lives and sacred values are at stake.

NOTES

1. While we discuss a conservative bias in regulatory policy, which may lead to a systematic overassessment of risk, Clayton Gillette (in this volume) points to an opposing bias in the adjudicative system, which may instead systematically *underassess* social risk.

2. The bases for the estimates in this article are not described in detail. Morrall says that they are taken from agencies' estimates at the time of the decision, some of which he revised in order to make them all comparable. Thus, he sets fifty nonfatal hospitalizations, or two permanent disabilities, equivalent to a life saved,

and monetizes all these benefits, in order to include reductions of nonfatal injuries and property damage, which weigh in the decisions of many agencies.

More controversially, Morrall uses a 10 percent discount rate for both benefits and costs, which many risk analysts, including ourselves, would reject. He writes: "Discounting costs but not benefits leads to absurd results, such as that a rule saving 100 lives a decade from now is more desirable than a rule of equal cost saving 99 lives right away." Such a result seems to us not only to be not absurd but morally justifiable. Nevertheless, Morrall's comparisons are illuminating, and the range of differences in cost-effectiveness would likely remain nearly as great even using different assumptions.

3. Their argument appears in two versions. A longer and more technical presentation is Nichols and Zeckhauser 1985. A shorter, nontechnical version of this paper is Nichols and Zeckhauser 1986.

4. According to Nichols and Zeckhauser (1986: 15): in estimating exposure to benzene from the maleic anhydride plants, for example, EPA used data from Pittsburgh, where, in its own words, "meteorological conditions that minimize ground-level concentrations . . . are common." A later critique by the industry, using local meteorological data for each plant, suggested that the EPA estimates were more than 50 percent too high on average.

5. Nichols and Zeckhauser (1985) write: neither epidemiological data nor laboratory experiments with animals can detect low-level risks; the sample sizes needed to detect small increments in risk are simply too large. Thus, risks to the general population ordinarily are assessed by studying individuals with unusually high exposures (often workers) or giving animals doses far beyond those likely to be encountered by people. Various mathematical models have been developed to perform the necessary extrapolations. Unfortunately, current theory does not provide unambiguous support for any one of them, nor can empirical tests determine which is most accurate.

6. This point is argued more fully in MacLean 1983 and 1986a.

7. It might be objected to our defense of the symbolic importance of public policies that, as Murray Edelman has noted, the symbolic aspects of a policy may blind the mass public to the fact that the policy's material impacts in fact work against its interests and in favor of dominant groups. See Edelman 1964. It is interesting here, however, that the Reagan administration, strongly probusiness and proindustry, led the movement toward subjecting health and safety measures to cost-benefit analyses—that is, toward overriding the symbolic values at stake in favor of a concern with efficiency.

REFERENCES

Campbell, G. L., Cohan, D., and North, D. W.
  no date *The Application of Decision Analysis to Toxic Substances: Proposed Methodology and Two Case Studies.* U.S. Environmental Protection Agency, Contract 68–01–6054. Washington, D.C.: Office of Pesticides and Toxic Substances.

Durkheim, Emile
  1915 *The Elementary Forms of Religious Life.* Trans. J. W. Swain. London: Allen and Unwin.

Edelman, Murray
  1964 *The Symbolic Uses of Politics.* Urbana: University of Illinois Press.

Exposure to Coke Oven Emissions
  1976 41 Federal Register.

Gibbard, Allan
  1986 "Risk and Value," in *Values at Risk*, Douglas MacLean, ed.

Hacking, Ian
  1986 "Culpable Ignorance of Interference Effects," in *Values at Risk*, Douglas MacLean, ed.

Hampshire, Stuart
  1983 *Morality and Conflict.* Cambridge: Harvard University Press.

Kant, Immanuel
  1911 *Grundlegung zur Metaphysik der Sitten.* Berlin: Prussian Academy edition, vol. 3. Trans. J. W. Ellington, under the title *Grounding for the Metaphysics of Morals.* Indianapolis: Hackett, 1981.

Kelman, Steven
  1980 "Occupational Safety and Health Administration," in *The Politics of Regulation*, James Q. Wilson, ed. New York: Basic Books.

MacLean, Douglas
  1983 "Valuing Human Life," in *Uncertain Power*, D. Zinberg, ed. New York: Pergamon.
  1986a "Social Values and the Distribution of Risk," in *Values at Risk*, Douglas MacLean, ed.
  1986b Ed. *Values at Risk.* Totowa, N.J.: Rowman and Littlefield.

Morrall, John
  1986 "A Review of the Record." *Regulation* 10 (November/December): 25–34.

Nichols, Albert, and Zeckhauser, Richard
  1985 "The Dangers of Caution: Conservatism in Assessment and Mismanagement of Risk." Discussion paper 2–85–11. Cambridge: Har-

vard University, Energy and Environmental Policy Centers, John F. Kennedy School of Government, Energy and Environmental Policy Centers.

1986   "The Perils of Prudence: How Conservative Risk Assessments Distort Regulation." *Regulation* 10 (November/December): 13–24.

Solow, Robert

1981   "Defending Cost-Benefit Analysis: Replies to Steven Kelman." *Regulation* 5 (March/April): 4041.

Subcommittee on Labor of the Senate Committee on Labor and Public Welfare

1971   *Legislative History of the Occupational Safety and Health Act of 1970.* Washington, D.C.: U.S. Government Printing Office.

PART II

Historical Development

CHAPTER 4

Risks and Society

Some Historical Cases and Contemporary Comparisons

Joel A. Tarr

Given our present concern with risk and risk analysis, it is curious that the current literature largely lacks an extended consideration of how persons perceived and dealt with various risks in the past, under different social and cultural conditions. Covello and Mumpower observe that the history of risk analysis could serve the useful purpose of providing perspectives on contemporary risk issues, illuminate the intellectual antecedents of current thinking about risk, clarify the differences between risk analysis and management today and in the past, and provide a basis for anticipating future directions in risk analysis and management (Covello and Mumpower 1985).

The study of historical cases of risk could also serve to enhance our understanding of the present, through careful use of the historical tool of analogy and through the analysis of changing patterns of social responsiveness to various risks. As a discipline, history would be of particular utility in forming perspectives on risk because of its concern with larger social processes. For, as Douglas and Wildavsky observe, the "type of society generates the type of accountability and focuses concern on particular dangers" (Douglas and Wildavsky 1982, 6–7).

An approach to the study of risk that looked to the past would be especially valuable in regard to past phenomena that society experienced as hazardous, but where both public and experts came to believe that the risk had been eliminated or controlled—only to have concern reappear at a later time. The explanations as to why these risks disappeared from society's agenda relate to a number of factors, including effective regulation, scientific and technological advances, improved instrumentation for detection and analysis, a belief in the wisdom and infallibility of experts, as well as shifts in society's social and cultural values. This paper will present a discussion of three historical cases involving risks that society thought it had eliminated or controlled, only to have them reassert themselves. The cases to be explored are epidemic disease, electricity, and drought. They represent biological, technological, and natural hazards.

BIOLOGICAL HAZARD: CHOLERA

Epidemics, observes Charles E. Rosenberg, our leading historian of medicine, are historically associated with the components of fear and sudden and widespread death. They are highly visible social phenomena, with a clearly marked beginning and end. From the perspective of analyzing risk, they can serve as remarkably useful devices because they provide a focus "capable of illuminating fundamental patterns of social values and institutional practice" (Rosenberg 1989). Risk from epidemic disease is of particular interest because of the changing paradigms of explanation and causation followed during the nineteenth and twentieth centuries. Essentially, the shift is from competing hypotheses of disease causation based on religious and philosophical factors to theories of contagion and anti-contagionism (atmospheric and other environmental conditions in the locality), and then to the acceptance of bacterial science based on the germ theory (see chapter 2, above). As Rosenberg notes, explanatory frameworks served the purpose of managing and controlling the "arbitrariness" of disease within the framework of the cultural values of the society (Rosenberg 1976; 1989).

During the nineteenth century, when medicine was struggling to become a "science" and a profession, ideas of "popular" medicine competed with various hypotheses based on scholastic concepts and clinical observation to produce great uncertainty about the causation and treatment of life-threatening diseases. These concepts often had specific cultural links. While the rise of the public health paradigm and the development of bacterial science appeared to point the way toward greatly reducing risk from infectious disease through public health measures, sanitary reform, and preventive medicine, many exceptions and anomalies remained. This section will discuss the evolution of attitudes in regard to one severe epidemic disease—cholera—and make some observations concerning the historical epidemic and our current epidemic of AIDS.

While American society in the nineteenth century experienced epidemics of several different diseases, cholera was probably the century's most feared and characteristic epidemic disease. Malaria, tuberculosis, and typhoid fever claimed many more victims than cholera but their symptoms were less sudden and fearful. Before the nineteenth century, cholera was a disease confined to the Far East. After 1817, however, as trade and travel increased due to transportation and communications improvements, it spread throughout the world. In one sense, cholera in the United States can be viewed as a by-product of technological progress. As a disease, cholera moves along any pathway leading to the human digestive tract; its onset is usually sudden. It has extreme symptoms, including diarrhea, spasmodic vomiting, cramps, and dehydration. In the most severe epidemics, cholera was spread by sewage contamination of water supplies, but the etiology of the disease was not understood for much of the century.

Cholera visited the United States four times in the nineteenth century: 1832–34; 1848–54; 1866; and 1873, when it was confined to the Mississippi Valley. This discussion will limit itself to the first three epidemics. Because it occurred several times over the course of the century during a period of great advances in regard to preventive medicine and public health, it provides us with a window through which to examine shifting societal responses in regard to a feared disease.

When cholera appeared in American ports in 1832, the medical "profession" divided sharply about the causes and remedies for cholera. In addition, lay therapists of all kinds flourished, pushing remedies ranging from botanic medicine to immersion in icy water (Starr 1982: 30–59). More orthodox physicians generally divided into three groups: contagionists, contingent contagionists, and anti-contagionists, with the majority in the latter camp. Most physicians believed that the causes of cholera lay in the atmosphere and that it was due to local conditions such as stagnant water or decaying organic matter. They found little evidence that it was contagious. A few contagionists advocated quarantines and isolation as a way to deal with the disease, but most medical opinion was opposed (Coleman 1987). Some physicians believed in a theory of contingent contagionism that suggested that the disease became contagious under certain conditions of filth, but they were also in a minority. American physicians thought largely in scholastic terms, hoping by chains of reasoning to discover the "true philosophy" of a disease and few physicians believed that disease was a specific, well-defined biological entity (Rosenberg 1962).

Even though the "experts" divided over the contagious or noncontagious nature of cholera, with most arguing for non-contagion, the popular behavioral response was, wherever possible, to flee the cities when outbreaks occurred. Those who left were largely from the more affluent classes, while the poor, more limited in their mobility, were forced to remain (Cassedy 1984). The mass of the population clearly disagreed with the physicians (the "experts") concerning the noncontagious nature of cholera and believed it was spread by a specific entity. They refused to rent their buildings for use as cholera hospitals, to work as nurses with the sick and, in some towns, prevented travelers from entering, even murdering strangers (especially foreigners) suspected of carrying the disease (Rosenberg 1962). In addition, they often opposed various efforts of public authorities to cope with the epidemic. In New York City, they regarded the hospitals as little more than "charnel houses" and blocked attempts to transport the sick to them. They attacked and beat physicians and city officials attempting to enforce sanitary regulations, and formed mobs who opposed the order of the Special Medical Council calling for immediate burial of the dead. In some cases, the dead were buried secretly, making it impossible to collect accurate mortality statistics.

Many Americans believed that cholera was God's judgment on the sinful and that only those of irregular habits had to fear the disease. Concern over exposure to risk, therefore, could be selective and did not warrant any special precautions. For the religiously orthodox, it also had the function of promoting the "cause of righteousness" by removing God's enemies. Orthodox ministers reinforced these beliefs and saw those who were stricken as sinners receiving their deserved reward. More liberal clergymen viewed cholera as a result of the failure of the victims to observe the laws of nature and their insistence on living in intemperance, filth, and vice.

The poor (including a disproportionate number of immigrants and blacks) suffered the most from cholera because they lived under the most crowded conditions and because they could not afford to flee the city. Inasmuch as many affluent Americans believed that both poverty and cholera were a result of idleness and intemperance, it appeared logical that the poor would suffer the most, while the more virtuous "respectable" classes escaped its depredations. Some commentators saw the epidemics as a warning that immigration needed to be restricted, while a few political radicals took the position that the suffering of the poor was a result of human injustice.

When cholera appeared in Europe in 1831, the city councils in a number of Atlantic coastal cities, acting on the belief that cholera was contagious and would soon appear in the New World, approved quarantine regulations for goods and passengers from infected ports in Europe. Many inland cities followed their lead. In addition, many cities throughout the nation established quarantines, formed boards of health, publicized methods of dealing with cholera, established special cholera hospitals, attempted to clean the streets of accumulated filth, and made efforts to remove the poor from the slums. Because many physicians and ministers believed that personal habits such as the drinking of intoxicating beverages and the eating of "coarse and indigestible" foods were "predisposing" causes of the disease in a cholera atmosphere, their sale was often banned (Rosenberg 1962).

Whatever the vigor of the public policy response during the time of the epidemic, most remedial measures proved to be ad hoc and temporary. In some communities the boards of health ceased to exist, hospitals were closed, and the streets reverted to their normal filthy conditions. Little permanent institutional change took place as a result of the 1832–34 epidemic. While there was a great outpouring of literature, little of it was statistical in nature, making analysis and comparison difficult.

In 1849 the United States was exposed to another wave of the feared epidemic. The response of society to cholera in this year was not dramatically different from that in 1832–34, suggesting that not much learning about disease etiology and risk mitigation had occurred in the seventeen-year period. Some physicians did place an increased emphasis on the relationship between filth and disease, maintaining that cholera might be a "portable" disease due to a "ferment" evolving from filthy conditions. The growth of medical statistics and surveys of urban conditions helped form a belief in the specificity of the disease, as compared with interpretations based on vague moral factors (Cassedy 1984). Many physicians, however, continued to argue that moral lapses could induce cholera. While numerous cities considered instituting permanent sanitary mechanisms, little of a permanent nature was done and the streets remained squalid. This half-hearted response reflects the continued confusion over the best response to the risk from the disease. Reflecting the belief that cholera was God's punishment, President Zachary Taylor recommended a day of national prayer, fasting, and humiliation (Andrew Jackson had refused to recommend such a fast day in 1833). Moral failings still appeared to many Americans as the main element in disease causation, and proper moral behavior and prayer as the surest method of reducing risk.

The nation's experience with cholera in 1866, and especially that of New York City, differed considerably from that witnessed during the previous epidemics. Although the New York population was much larger than it had been in 1849, for instance, there were only one-tenth as many cholera deaths. Since the previous cholera period, considerable learning had occurred with regard to disease etiology, the role of sanitation in mitigating the effects of cholera, and the collection of statistics of morbidity and mortality (Duffy 1974). Analysis of bills of mortality, vital statistics registers, and census reports convinced physicians and others concerned with public health that many deaths from disease could be avoided through appropriate sanitary measures.

The key element in New York in the reduction of risk from cholera was the policies of the Metropolitan Board of Health, an organization formed early in 1866 by the State Legislature to sanitize the city. Underlying its actions was the belief by its physician leadership that cholera was contagious and related to polluted water supply (Duffy 1974). These two hypotheses derived primarily from the work of two European "experts," Dr. John Snow of London, who theorized that cholera was a contagious disease with a poison found in the feces and vomitus of cholera patients, and Max von Pettenkofer, a Bavarian sanitarian who maintained that there was a connection between water and cholera. In addition, the ideas of British sanitarians such as Edwin Chadwick (a convinced anticontagionist) and Southwood Smith concerning the necessity of sanitizing the city played an important role (Cassedy 1984). Although physicians still differed about contagionist and anti-contagionist origins of disease, most agreed that cholera was portable and transmissible.

The Metropolitan Board of Health's success in cleaning the city streets and slums reflected its powerful organization. The Board divided the streets into districts, and sanitary inspectors (all physicians) were appointed for each one. All cases of cholera were reported to the neighborhood police station (professional police were themselves a new organization), the information telegraphed to the Board's central office, and a wagonload of disinfectants sent immediately to the infected house. A so-called moveable corps made house-to-house visits and provided food and clothing to families stricken by cholera. Streets were cleaned of manure, cisterns were emptied, and thousands of privies disinfected.

Through its efforts, the Metropolitan Board of Health seemingly freed New York City from the savage effects of cholera experienced in previous epidemics. While many still held the belief that cholera afflicted the "dirty, the intemperate, and the degraded" most severely, the moral explanation had been tempered by a more statistically and scientifically based explanatory frame (Duffy 1974; Rosenberg 1962).

CHOLERA AND AIDS

Cholera and other fearful epidemic diseases such as yellow fever had receded far from the public memory during the last third of this century, as had concern over other infectious diseases such as typhoid and typhus. These had largely been brought under control by state policy, oriented toward improving sanitation and providing clean water and sewerage. Even sexually transmitted diseases such as syphilis and gonorrhea were downgraded as threats to health because of their amenability to drug therapy. Other infectious diseases succumbed to penicillin, streptomycin, antitoxins, sulfonamides, and antibiotics in the more recent decades (Dowling 1977).

The onset of the AIDS epidemic in the 1980s, as Allan M. Brandt has noted, "threatened our sense of medical security" and made explicit "the complex interaction of social, cultural, and biological forces" (Brandt 1987). In this sense, it repeated our society's experience with cholera, as the response to AIDS went through cycles of moral blaming of victims and attempts to segregate them, confusion over etiology and vectors, clashes between expert and popular responses to contagion, and important questions about the role of the state in limiting civil rights (Brandt 1987; Rosenberg 1986; 1989; Kirby, chapter 1, above).

Because of the similarities of AIDS to other epidemic diseases, some public health authorities have argued that it will eventually be controlled by the conventional techniques for responding to epidemics. That is, the "well-tested methods of surveillance, research, prevention, and treatment" for dealing with risk from epidemic disease would eventually result in its confinement and control (Fox 1986). Other students of the epidemic, particularly in its social and institutional dimensions, have been less sanguine.

Daniel Fox, for instance, argues that a "crisis of authority" in health care reduces society's ability to react effectively to this epidemic as it has in response to epidemics in the recent past. That is, just as was discovered in regard to cholera, it is not desirable to "substitute individual for collective responsibility for social welfare" (Fox 1986). Charles Rosenberg views AIDS as atypical in a number of ways, including its geographic spread, the rapidity of its identification as a unified clinical entity, and the special character of its victims (Rosenberg 1989). Whatever the ultimate judgment regarding the place of AIDS within the larger history of disease, the comparisons between it and other classic epidemics, as well as the strategies devised for control, provide a valuable intellectual bench mark for medical experts, makers of medical policy, and society at large.

RISK FROM NEW TECHNOLOGIES: THE CASE OF ELECTRICITY

I have no panacea for all the ills which may follow the use of high potential currents under conditions usually found in large cities. I can no more say how to make electricity safe in such cases than I can say how to make railroad travel safe, or how to make steamboat travel safe, or how to make the use of illuminating gas safe, nor the use of steam boilers safe. No improvement of our modern civilization has ever been introduced but that it involved considerable risk.

So wrote Elihu Thomson, electrical inventor and entrepreneur, in 1889.

How much risk is society prepared to accept from new technologies that involve aspects of the unknown and hence of uncertainty? Is society today more or less prepared to accept the unknown than in the nineteenth century? One indication of our preference for certainty is the extent to which contemporary society has formalized technological risk assessment. Increasing numbers of scientists and analysts are attempting to identify and measure risks, as risk assessment emerges as a profession, and government engages on both the legislative and bureaucratic levels in regulating and managing a variety of hazards.

One explanation for the expansion of risk assessment activities is the argument that the hazards facing society today differ in both character and magnitude from those of yesterday and have potential effects that are latent, long-term, involuntary, and irreversible. Supposedly, the complexity of technological development and the speed of scientific and technological change have also accelerated (Covello and Mumpower 1985). But many nineteenth-century technologies appeared complex and mysterious as well as hazardous to those who first experienced them. These elements of concern often produced fantasies about the effects of the technology as well as attempts at evaluation or analysis of the risks involved, and rejection, modification, or acceptance of the technology.

Of the major nineteenth-century technological innovations, few had as much mystery and uncertainty associated with them as electricity. Although knowledge of electricity went back to the eighteenth century, it was not until the late nineteenth century that the public began to encounter electricity at home and in the workplace. Because of its mystery, many in society viewed electrical technology as menacing, while others saw it as an opportunity. Popular images about the risks inherent in electricity ranged from the fanciful to the real. One popular image, for instance, held that excess electrical charge was accumulating in the world and presented a danger to humankind and to nature. Nature was supposedly being thrown out of balance and would at some point restore itself in a cataclysmic fashion. Adverse weather, health problems, and animal distemper were all blamed on electricity, and fairs and amusement parks abounded with electrically-related wonders (Marvin 1988).

Electricity was also used for medical purposes and supposedly had curative powers as a vital force. Both expert and quack uses of electricity for medical purposes abounded. Entrepreneurs peddled nostrums with miraculous electrical properties for problems ranging from snakebite to hair loss. Sears, Roebuck, and Company peddled a "Heidelberg Electric Belt" guaranteed to make a new man of its wearer in a month; electrical corsets were available for women to ward off unwanted attentions (Marvin 1988). Physicians used electrotherapy both to revitalize and as a sedative, and articles about its theory and practice were published in the most widely read medical journals (Rosner 1988).

The author of the standard text on "medical electricity," George M. Beard, was a pioneer in the study of neuroses and the discoverer of neurasthenia. Beard found that many of his patients complained of vague and unclassifiable symptoms, of anxiety, excessive fatigue, irrational fears, and erratic sexual behavior. He defined these symptoms as those of neurasthenia, and held that it was the result of a weakness of the nervous system. Beard maintained that the nervous system was a closed and continuous channel with a fixed quantity of electrical force coursing through it. This nervous force transmitted messages from one part of the body to another and served as the "raw material" of consciousness. Beard compared the human body to a dynamo that could produce only a limited amount of nervous force; the lamps might dim because of the stresses of modern life. Thus, mental illness was viewed as resulting from environmental stress rather than any psychological causes.

Interestingly, Beard found that the inventions of Thomas Edison—all relating to electricity—had done more than any other factor to increase the demands upon the nervous force of Americans. In order to cure the effects of neurasthenia, Beard prescribed a variety of methods including the use of electricity itself (Rosenberg 1976).

High voltage electricity obviously held other dangers besides its supposed relationship to human or natural imbalance of various kinds. These risks included a threat of physical injury and of fire: risks that were identified and assessed by the pioneer electrical inventors and entrepreneurs who constructed the first electrical power systems. How these risks were to be managed became a matter of public debate between major innovators in the field in the so-called battle of the systems, between small-scale direct current (DC) and large-scale, alternating current (AC). The major controversy was between Thomas Edison, originator and advocate of the DC system, and George Westinghouse, promoter of AC. Westinghouse had designed and produced an alternating current incandescent lighting system, believing that alternating current was more economical than DC and would capture a larger share of the market. Edison, on the other hand, believed that AC, which used overhead wires, was dangerous to both electrical workmen and to the public because of its high voltage and its poor reliability. He believed that the public would accept electricity in homes only if it could be shown to be a safe system and rejected AC on these grounds (Passer 1953).

Edison believed that any electrical accident would damage the public's image of electricity and reduce the chances of widespread adoption, regardless of the specific technology being used. Because AC had more potential for harmful accidents, Edison undertook a media campaign to show that it was unsafe. At his West Orange, New Jersey, laboratory, he conducted experiments in which high-voltage AC current was used to kill animals and he supported a campaign to convince the state of New York to use AC for the first human electrocution, conducted in 1890. The Edison interests also promoted legislation, such as the prohibition of overhead lines, limitations of voltage, and the requirement of safety devices to reduce risk from AC power systems. Although no States adopted restrictive legislation, several large cities outlawed overhead wires and limited voltages in residences (Passer 1953). According to W. Bernard Carlson and A. J. Millard, Edison's position was dictated by long-term considerations of the success of the electrical industry with the public rather than of immediate financial advantage (Carlson and Millard 1987).

The AC companies attempted to meet the Edison challenge by advertising the safety of their system and by developing safety devices. Their development and installation, however, did not necessarily guarantee that hazard in AC would be eliminated, for customers frequently ignored safety equipment and did not follow recommended installation procedures (Carlson and Millard 1987). Eventually, because of several critical innovations that gave it technical and efficiency advantages over its DC rival, AC conquered the electrical power and light market, generating over 95 percent of the electric energy annually produced in the United States. Direct current disappeared in a gradual fashion, through the synthesis of the two systems—by "a combination of coupling and merging" at the technical and institutional levels (Hughes 1983).

The values that appeared most determinate in driving the electrification of American cities, regardless of system, appeared to be those of efficiency and cost-effectiveness compared to earlier methods of providing power and light. Not all nations, however, were so ready to embrace electricity, especially in regard to streetcars. Cities in France, Great Britain, and Germany, for instance, required the burial of wiring as early as the 1870s (in this case for the telegraph) at a time when American cities were stringing thousands of miles of wire along their busy streets. The pattern differed among separate European cities, but such regulations were generally in effect before rather than after construction, contrasting with the United States where burial of wires generally took place after serious accidents. These restrictions, and the conservative attitude toward the hazard of aboveground wiring that they represented, contributed to substantial lags in the electrification of European streetcar lines compared to the United States (McKay 1976).

How do we account for the difference? Historian John P. McKay argues that late nineteenth-century European society had a more conservative attitude toward electrical innovation and risk than did American society. Part of the conservatism was based on concern over the danger of live wires to passengers and pedestrians, and fear that increased speed would accelerate accident rates. In addition, electrical transmission lines interfered with telegraph and telephone reception, and caused the electrolysis of gas and water mains. This technological conservatism, however, included not only concern over danger, but also over aesthetic effects. Here a value judgment as to the quality of the urban environment came into play. This attitude was most pronounced in large cities, where poles and wires along historical boulevards and squares were considered offensive. The municipal authorities in Berlin, Dresden, Brussels, Budapest, Paris, and Vienna would not permit overhead wires in the central parts of cities. In some cities, limitations also extended to the outlying areas (McKay 1976).

A combination of factors, therefore, including aesthetic objections, a tradition of public authority and regulation, and a limited term for franchises, resulted in a substantial lag between the pace of traction electrification in Europe compared to the United States. These factors combined to produce a search in Europe for a technological alternative to the electric streetcar powered by overhead wires. Among these innovations were the storage-battery car, the surface-conduit system, and the surface-contact system. More significant were the attempts to develop "mixed" systems that combined overhead conductors plus other alternatives on the same car and the same line. Even where the overhead system was fully adopted, it was considerably modified, especially in regard to visual effects. Lines were installed more carefully and poles were made of steel and handsomely decorated. In contrast with America, bulky overhead feeder cables were required to be underground and concealed rather than strung in the air (McKay 1976).

Objections to the stringing of electric and other wires along the streets were voiced in America. These objections involved the same set of factors as did those in Europe: concerns over safety and aesthetic factors. However, the American environment differed in several crucial ways, among them a weaker tradition of municipal regulation, a multiplicity of firms installing a variety of electrical systems, and a greater emphasis on the primacy of low costs. Aesthetic objections were raised over unsightly wires and poles, and the hazard they presented, but had little effect during the initial decades of electrification.

Many accidents also occurred involving wires but, although there were complaints, it was not until well into the twentieth century that some American cities moved to require the underground placement of wires, especially in the central business districts. However, in contrast to European cities, action came after wires were already in place and not before construction had begun (Zueblin 1916). Thus, in evaluating this experience, it is necessary to balance the various economic gains made by rapid technological implementation in this country but with higher accident and aesthetic costs, against the reverse in Europe.

As the nation became more electrified, the public accepted electricity as a commonplace, even though it continued to have a high level of uncertainty and risk involved. One of the major factors behind the founding of the National Bureau of Standards in 1901, for instance, was the need of the electrical industry for uniform measures. Eventually, although primarily catering to industrial needs during its first years, the Bureau of Standards moved into the safety field.

In 1914 the Bureau published a set of safety rules for the electrical industry, followed in 1915 by the first nationwide electrical safety code (Cochrane 1966). This code met strong opposition from the electrical power industry, which argued that the formulation of a safety code "gave undue publicity to the hazards of electricity" (Cochrane 1966). Lacking any authority to enforce its rules, the Bureau was driven to issue a special circular explaining its code. The circular included an account of one hundred typical electrical accidents occurring in 1913, most of them fatal. By 1920, however, less than half the States had adopted the electrical code although a number of cities had adopted extended regulations based on negotiations between electricians, builders, and city governments (Rose 1988).

During the 1920s, with the development of many electrical appliances, electricity became a magic fluid, supposedly reducing the household burdens of women and providing light and heat throughout residential and work environments. Working-class women especially benefited from the power of electricity, although upper-income women, for whom electrical appliances may have meant dispensing with servants, suffered "incipient proletarianization" (Cowan 1983).

Electrical utilities were especially aggressive in promoting the electrification of the home. In Chicago, for instance, Samuel Insull opened neighborhood and suburban Electric Shops that in actuality were small department stores selling consumer products. His utilities made available low-priced installment plans to pay for home wiring and appliance purchases. Electricity made a move to the suburbs especially attractive because all new construction there was fitted for the use of electrical power. Every major group within American urban society increased its consumption of electricity during the decade. Thus, according to one historian of the electrical industry, the period from 1919 to 1932 witnessed "the birth of an energy-intensive society" (Platt 1988).

Aspects of electrical power distribution were called into question during the depression years of the 1930s, but these issues revolved around questions such as rate structures and monopoly control rather than dangers from electricity itself. Convictions about the benevolence of electrical energy, as distinguished from the malevolence of the privately owned utility companies, were reaffirmed by government-sponsored rural electrification, especially in the Tennessee Valley, and these held sway throughout the immediate postwar decades. While examinations of hazards continued, the studies were conducted under industry sponsorship and by national standards groups, and did not become matters of public debate as in the late nineteenth century (Dalziel 1954; 1968; 1972).

In her contribution to this volume, JoAnne Brown has demonstrated the manner in which atomic power was analogized to what was called "the greatest and most beneficent of nature's forces . . . the sun," thus transforming the threat of the atomic bomb into a "benign domestic influence." Similarly, it can be argued that the images of "Reddi-Kilowatt" or "Little Bill," the benevolent genii of electrical power, encouraged householders to have confidence that the risks of electricity were under control. These assurances of safety, testified to by "experts," included the health effects of human exposure to power-frequency fields (Nair et al. 1989; Brodeur 1989).

Within the last decade, concern over health hazards from electromagnetic fields has greatly increased again. Attention focused first on the aesthetic impact of large transmission towers, which is analogous to what happened in Europe a century ago. Concern then developed over the health effects of alternating currents in extra high voltage transmission lines (60-hertz fields) and towers. Today this concern has been generalized to a wide range of electrical appliances in the home and workplace.

These perceptions of risk reflect conflicting evidence concerning the impacts of electric power, as well as the ability of new instruments to identify unsuspected risks (Tarr and Jacobson 1987). Thus, just as in the case of epidemic disease, social concern over a hazard supposedly eliminated in the past has arisen again.

"NATURAL" HAZARDS: THE CASE OF THE GREAT PLAINS AND THE DUST BOWL

A major concern of those who deal with natural hazards has to do with the amount of risk the government should allow the public to assume. Sorensen and Mileti have identified ten programs designed to encourage self-protective behavior by the public prior to natural disaster. These programs are usually based on the "optimistic assumption" that by supplying citizens with information about risk from natural hazards they will make good judgments about protecting themselves and their property. However, note Sorensen and Mileti, "this optimism has been met by growing doubts as the toll inflicted by disasters continues to rise" (Sorensen and Mileti 1987).

This section of my chapter will present a case of a "natural" hazard—the dust bowl of the 1930s and succeeding droughts. The cause of exposure to risk appears here to be explained by the larger cultural context and adherence to a certain set of values that have perpetuated certain myths rather than by an institutional failure or the lack of availability of pertinent information.

The Great Plains is a broad topographic plain with a semiarid climate, grassland ecology, and an agricultural economy. Its most important climatic characteristics are its dryness and the unpredictability of the weather. For over a century, agricultural settlement has caused massive transformations in the region, with the eventual establishment of a vast dryland farming system for the production of grain. Settlers, often following a mandate that was viewed as fulfilling the national destiny, have continually moved down from east to west, along a gradient of declining precipitation and more frequent drought: that is, into areas, as William A. Riebsame notes, of "increasingly risky environments [where] . . . farmers worked closer to the margin of survival and resource sustainability" (Riebsame, in press).

In the centuries before settlement, the Great Plains had become the home of several hundred different types of grasses that helped hold the dirt in place and furnished food for vast numbers of animals, such as the bison. Although Amerindians had inhabited and "used" the plains, they essentially did little to alter the ecological order. The greatest changes came in the post–Civil War period, first with the activities of the cattlemen and the rise of the cattle empire, and then after 1886 with the arrival of the farmers who came to take advantage of government policies intended to dispose of public lands as quickly as possible. Severe droughts in the 1890s set back settlement, but it increased again with favorable government land policies after 1909. By the 1920s the region had been divided into thousands of relatively small "family" farms that grew one crop, wheat, as farmers converted the Plains from a grassland to a cropland. Both population and cultivated area have gone through cycles, with the region reaching its population peak in 1930 and its high point for cultivated area in 1983 (Riebsame, in press).

As farmers expanded their acreage in the twentieth century, they increasingly utilized machines to till the ground. As Donald C. Worster observes, "The grassland was to be torn up to make a vast wheat factory: a landscape tailored to the industrial age" (Worster 1979). The new "sodbusters" were expansionists, plowing up the grassland with several different mechanical innovations such as the one-way disk plow and the combined harvester-thresher. The number of hours it took to bring an acre of wheat to the granaries was reduced from fifty-eight hours in 1830 to under three hours in some sections of the Great Plains in the 1920s. Especially important were dry-farming techniques that were developed early in the century and that supposedly preserved moisture in the soil. According to Riebsame, dry farming was a "pseudo-science that rekindled the belief that most of the Plains could be successfully farmed" (Riebsame, in press).

Beginning in 1930, and continuing through 1936, much of the United States underwent a severe drought, often accompanied by intense heat. During this time all American States except Maine and Vermont suffered a precipitation deficiency of at least 15 percent of the historical mean, while twenty states set or equaled record lows for their entire weather history. The southern Great Plains, where the drought continued to 1941, experienced the most severe conditions. As historian Donald Worster notes, droughts are a fact of life on the plains but no one was prepared for the severe dust storms that followed. These dust storms consisted of so-called black blizzards and more common sand blows. According to the Soil Conservation Service, the number of storms where visibility was cut to less than a mile ranged from fourteen in 1932 to seventy-two in 1937 and down to seventeen in 1941 (Worster 1979).

The farmers who settled and plowed the southern Great Plains were optimists in that they consistently underrated the possibility of drought; when drought did come, they believed that it would be short-lived. They seldom believed that these temporary situations required them to change their habits or farming practices. Worster claims that they were "prouder of their ability to tough it out than to analyze their situation rationally, because they expect[ed] nature to be good to them and make them prosper" (Worster 1979). The dust storms offered a strong challenge to the farmer's assumptions of the inevitability of progress and the benignness of nature, but in spite of their severity they had only a temporary effect on farmers' beliefs. They responded to criticisms of their values and practices by defending them with increased vigor. Worster describes the tendency of the farmers to:

> fail to anticipate drought, underestimate its duration when it comes, expect rain momentarily, deny that they are as hard hit as outsiders believe, defend the region against critics, admit that some help would be useful, demand that the government act and act quickly, insist that federal aid be given without strings . . . vote for those politicians who confirm the people's optimism and pooh-pooh the need for major reform, resent interference by the bureaucrats, eagerly await the return of "normalcy" when the plains will once more proceed along the road of steady progress. [Worster 1979]

Thus, the region received more federal dollars from the New Deal than any other, but whenever New Deal administrators asked for innovation in regard to preventive farming practices, farmers strongly resisted them.

Some innovations were successfully implemented under the New Deal in regard to land management. Ecologists argued that a new equilibrium had to be created and a program for farming by ecological principles be devised. New Deal ecologists and agronomists established a Soil Conservation Service that restored some land to grasses, planted shelterbelts of trees, built terraces to conserve water, and retired land. In addition, other New Deal programs provided commodity credit and subsidized crop insurance.

When Dust Bowl farmers embraced conservation, they did it because it would make the land produce at a higher rate. To a large extent, however, Great Plains farmers were reluctant to abandon ingrained values; traditional approaches to the land focused on exploitation and profit. Innovations such as land use planning were abandoned in a decade, and market competition and technological innovation again took over in driving Great Plains development (Riebsame, in press).

These basic patterns of exploitation and expansion continued in spite of the return of drought and dust storms to the plains in the 1950s and 1970s. For some these events confirmed what they believed to be a regional climate pattern of drought every twenty years and were viewed as a warning signal of future disaster. But farmers saw the setbacks as only temporary and chose to believe that droughts could be controlled and that the Dust Bowl would not be repeated. While they possessed experiential and historical information suggesting the contrary, they chose to reject it. By the late-1970s and early 1980s, more land was in production in the

Great Plains than at any other time in our history, driven by interaction between the personal exploitive values of the farmers and government programs and speculative investments that encouraged extensive cultivation. For some authors, like Donald Worster, this pattern confirms that the culture of man, particularly as evidenced by the behavior of the Plains' farmers, drives them to take actions that upset the ecological order in the hope of profit and to therefore put themselves and their region at risk. The greatest risk, according to these environmentalists, is that there will be a return to Dust Bowl-like conditions as a result of poor farming practices and disregard of a fragile environment.

In the case of the Great Plains, the use of the Dust Bowl symbol as an impending environmental catastrophe unless ecologically destructive practices are changed, suggests an approach to dealing with hazard and uncertainty that would require massive cultural change. The Dust Bowl therefore becomes what Riebsame calls a "new ecological taboo—carrying with it a set of guidelines for human use of the Plains" (Riebsame, 1986). For the most fervent ecologists business farming is not suitable to the Plains environment, and a major cultural and value change towards ecologically sound farming or perhaps even towards the end of Plains exploitation is necessary to avert disaster. History, in this case, is interpreted and put to use in order to heighten perceptions and forebodings of risk.

For Riebsame, the use of the Dust Bowl taboo has actually hindered the adoption of more incremental and continual methods of agricultural adjustment. He notes that the 1930s drought, rather than being part of a twenty-year drought cycle, was actually the most extreme event in over 350 years and that repetition of events of such magnitude is unlikely in the near future. His view of history, perhaps, is informed by a somewhat longer perspective than that of Worster, as well as the use of measurement in a less ideological manner. At the same time, however, while he maintains that drought is not nearly as severe a risk to the Great Plains environment as some think, he warns of other environmentally dangerous but more subtle effects of modern farming, such as hydrologic changes, runoff increases and groundwater depletion, soil transformations due to tillage and compaction, and soil erosion. These receive less attention than merited, as concern over drought, and technologies to conquer drought, dominate our attention. In light of this, he predicts that the Great Plains development in the future will probably follow a continuation of past trends, making it increasingly vulnerable to changes, be they environmental or market-led (Riebsame 1986; in press).

CONCLUSIONS

The three cases presented here have offered examples of how history and historical case studies can serve a useful function in the area of risk analysis and hazard management. The cases chosen were those in areas where hazards, once thought to be controlled, reasserted themselves, putting individuals and even society at risk. In all three areas considered—epidemics, electricity, and the Great Plains—society reacted with elements of mystery and uncertainty in its initial encounters, as prevailing culture and values shaped responses. Thus, cholera, in its first appearances in the early nineteenth century, was often blamed on the moral infirmity of its victims as well as being treated with a variety of heroic therapies. For electricity, the early decades of its development were marked by battles between rival systems and claims about which system was most hazardous as well as by various speculative and fanciful interpretations of its effects. Finally, the farmers who transformed the Great Plains from grassland to cropland believed in the essential benevolence of nature and the importance of technology in reaping its bounty.

In each case, advances in science and technology were critical in removing uncertainties and reassuring both professionals and nonprofessionals that hazards were under control. In the cholera example, advances in epidemiology and sanitary science brought control after a long period of uncertainty in understanding causation. In regard to electricity, the advocates of AC were able to quiet fears about their product by developing safety devices, but even more importantly by making improvements that gave it large cost and efficiency advantages over the rival DC current. Finally, in the case of the Great Plains, technological advances such as dry farming, improvements in plows and harrows, or superior irrigation systems suggested that nature was under control. Social belief that the "magic bullets" supplied by science and technology would solve its problems seemed confirmed.

In each of these cases, however, control and guarantee of almost no risk proved illusory. Cholera has been replaced by AIDS, concerns about the health effects of electric and magnetic fields are voiced by both scientists and nonscientists, and the Great Plains are undergoing severe stress involving changes in factors such as soil chemistry, water quality, and groundwater depletion, as well as vulnerability to wind erosion. Society is no longer sure that "magic bullets" exist for every problem and risk, and new values questioning the earlier assumptions have gained increasing

Joel A. Tarr

strength. Only the future will tell whether or not this is merely another stage in the cycle of hazard control and the reassertion of confidence.

NOTE

The author thanks William Riebsame for introducing him to the questions of the historiography of the Great Plains, and Indira Nair for her perceptive suggestions in regard to the section on the hazards of electricity.

REFERENCES

Brandt, Allan M.
  1987   *No Magic Bullet: A Social History of Venereal Disease in the United States since 1880.* New York: Oxford University Press.
Brodeur, Paul
  1989   *Currents of Death: Powerlines, Computer Terminals and the Attempt to Cover-up their Threat to your Health.* New York: Simon and Schuster.
Carlson, W. Bernard, and Millard, A. J.
  1987   "Defining Risk within a Business Context: Thomas A. Edison, Elihu Thomson, and the ac/dc Controversy, 1885–1900," in *The Social and Cultural Construction of Risk: Issues, Methods, and Case Studies,* Vincent T. Covello et al., eds., 275–93.
Cassedy, James H.
  1984   *American Medicine and Statistical Thinking, 1800–1860.* Cambridge: Harvard University Press.
Coates, Vary T.
  1980   "Nineteenth Century Technology—Twentieth Century Problems: A Retrospective Mini-Assessment." Washington, D.C.: Office of Strategic Assessments and Special Studies, EPA.
Cochrane, Rexmond C.
  1966   *Measures for Progress: A History of the National Bureau of Standards.* Washington, D.C.: U.S. Department of Commerce.
Coleman, William
  1987   *Yellow Fever in the North: The Methods of Early Epidemiology.* Madison: University of Wisconsin Press.
Covello, Vincent T., et al., eds.
  1983   *The Analysis of Actual Versus Perceived Risks.* New York: Plenum Press.

Covello, Vincent T., and Mumpower, Jeryl
  1985   "Risk Analysis and Risk Management: An Historical Perspective."
          Risk Analysis 5, 2: 103–20.
Cowan, Ruth S.
  1983   *More Work for Mother: The Ironies of Household Technology from
          the Open Hearth to the Microwave.* New York: Free Press.
Dalziel, C. F.
  1954   "The Threshold of Perception Currents." *AIEE Transactions Power
          Apparatus and Systems* 73: 990–96.
  1972   "Electric Shock Hazard." *AIEE Spectrum* 41–50.
Dalziel, C. F., and Lee, W. R.
  1968   "Reevaluation of Lethal Electric Currents." *IEEE Trans. Industry
          and General Applications* IGA-4: 467–76.
Douglas, Mary, and Wildavsky, Aaron
  1982   *Risk and Culture.* Berkeley: University of California Press.
Dowling, Harry F.
  1977   *Fighting Infection: Conquests of the Twentieth Century.* Cambridge:
          Harvard University Press.
Duffy, John
  1974   *A History of Public Health in New York City 1866–1966.* New
          York: Russell Sage Foundation.
Fox, Daniel M.
  1986   "AIDS and the American Health Polity: The History and Pros-
          pects of a Crisis of Authority." *Milbank Memorial Quarterly* 64:
          Sup. 1:7–30.
Fox, Daniel M., et al.
  1989   "The Power of Professionalism: Policies for AIDS in Britain, Swe-
          den, and the United States." *Deadalus* 93–111.
Hughes, Thomas P.
  1983   *Networks of Power: Electrification in Western Society 1880–1930.*
          Baltimore: Johns Hopkins University Press.
Kates, Robert W., et al., eds.
  1985   *Perilous Progress: Managing the Hazards of Technology.* Boulder:
          Westview Press.
McKay, John P.
  1976   *Tramways and Trolleys: The Rise of Urban Mass Transport in
          Europe.* Princeton: Princeton University Press.
Marvin, Carolyn.
  1988   *When Old Technologies Were New: Thinking about Electric Com-
          munication in the Late Nineteenth Century.* New York: Oxford
          University Press.
Nair, Indira, et al.

1989   *Biological Effects of Power Frequency Electric and Magnetic Fields,* Background paper, Office of Technology Assessment-BP-E-53. Washington, D.C.: U.S. Government Printing Office.

Pacey, Arnold

1983   *The Culture of Technology.* Cambridge: MIT Press.

Passer, Harold C.

1953   *The Electrical Manufacturers 1875–1900.* Cambridge: Harvard University Press.

Perrow, Charles

1984   *Normal Accidents: Living with High-Risk Technologies.* New York: Basic Books.

Platt, H. L.

1988   "City Lights: The Electrification of the Chicago Region, 1880–1930," in *Technology and the Rise of the Networked City in Europe and America,* Joel A. Tarr and Gabriel Dupuy, eds., 246–81. Philadelphia: Temple University Press.

Riebsame, William E.

1986   "The Dust Bowl: Historical Image, Psychological Anchor, and Ecological Taboo." *Great Plains Quarterly* 6(2): 127–36.

in press "The United States Great Plains," in *The Earth as Transformed by Human Action,* B.L. Turner II, ed. New York: Cambridge University Press.

Rose, Mark H.

1988   "Urban Gas and Electric Systems and Social Change, 1900–1940," in *Technology and the Rise of the Networked City in Europe and America,* Joel A. Tarr and Gabriel Dupuy, eds., 229–45. Philadelphia: Temple University Press.

Rosenberg, Charles E.

1962   *The Cholera Years: The United States in 1832, 1849, and 1866.* Chicago: University of Chicago Press.

1976   "George M. Beard and American Nervousness," in *No Other Gods: On Science and American Social Thought,* 98–108. Baltimore: Johns Hopkins University Press.

1989   "What Is an Epidemic? AIDS in Historical Perspective." *Deadalus* 1–17.

Rosenkrantz, Barbara Gutmann

1979   "Damaged Goods: Dilemmas of Responsibility for Risk." *Milbank Memorial Fund Quarterly/Health and Society* 57(1).

Rosner, Lisa

1988   "The Professional Contest of Electrotherapeutics." *The Journal of the History of Medicine* 43–67.

Short, James F., Jr.

1984   "The Social Fabric at Risk: Toward the Social Transformation of
        Risk Analysis." *American Sociological Review* 49: 711–25.

Sorensen, John H., and Mileti, Dennis

1987   "Programs to Encourage Precautionary Behavior in Natural Dis-
        asters: Review and Evaluation," in *Taking Care: Why People Take
        Precautions*, N. Weinstein, ed. New York: Cambridge University
        Press.

Starr, Paul

1982   *The Social Transformation of American Medicine.* New York: Basic
        Books.

White, Gilbert F., and Haas, J. Eugene

1975   *Assessment of Research on Natural Hazards.* Cambridge: MIT
        Press.

Worster, Donald

1979   *Dust Bowl: The Southern Plains in the 1930s.* New York: Oxford
        University Press.

Wright, James D., and Rossi, Peter H., eds.

1981   *Social Science and Natural Hazards.* Cambridge: Abt Books.

Zueblin, Charles

1916   *American Municipal Progress.* New York: Macmillan, rev. ed.

CHAPTER 5

The History and Politics of Disaster Management in the United States

Roy S. Popkin

Disasters were a part of the American scene even before there was a United States. In 1755 a major earthquake struck the Boston area, and at the end of the Revolutionary War a hurricane prevented the reinforcing and resupplying of General Cornwallis's British troops at Yorktown, thus hastening the surrender that gave final victory to the American colonists. The first disaster legislation of the new republic was enacted by Congress in 1803 (May 1985; Bourgin 1983).

Over the years, disasters such as the Chicago fire, the San Francisco earthquake, the Johnstown flood, the Galveston hurricane, the 1936 floods along the Mississippi and Ohio rivers, Hurricane Camille, Tropical Storm Agnes, Three Mile Island, and Love Canal have marked milestones in the nation's development. Paralleling the many catastrophic events in American history has been the evolution of hazard response and relief activities by government and private agencies—beginning with locally-based relief and recovery efforts and disaster-specific federal legislation, expanding with the founding of the congressionally chartered American Red Cross in the latter part of the nineteenth century, and eventually developing in the mid-twentieth century into the complex of insurance providers, governmental and voluntary agencies, and their various programs involving preparedness and recovery.

Roy S. Popkin

Hazard mitigation activities designed to *prevent*, or at least reduce, damage and loss resulting from extreme natural events have been slower to evolve. Only in the last twenty years or so have disaster mitigation programs, other than U.S. Army Corps of Engineers flood control operations, become an important part of the governmental response to hazards. Activities aimed at reducing or preventing human and environmental suffering and losses from human-caused disasters, such as nuclear power plant accidents and toxic waste spills, are even more recent developments.

This paper surveys in greater detail the historical evolution of hazard management in the United States; it discusses the programs and politics currently affecting hazard response and mitigation, and suggests what directions the field will take in the future.

DEFINING DISASTER

Because "disaster" has a variety of formal or implied meanings, it is helpful to examine the definitions used in federal legislation and by the American Red Cross in order to understand the historical analysis and comments put forth in the remainder of this paper.

The detailed federal definition is contained in Public Law 93–288 (Bourgin 1983)—the May 22, 1974, act of Congress, which is the basis for today's federal disaster programs (new legislation revising the act is at time of writing being discussed by Congress). The act states:

> Major disaster means any hurricane, tornado, storm, flood, high water, wind-driven water, tidal wave, tsunami, earthquake, volcanic eruption, landslide, mudslide, snowstorm, drought, fire, explosion, or other catastrophe in any part of the United States which, in the determination of the President, causes damage of sufficient severity and magnitude to warrant major disaster assistance under this Act, above and beyond emergency services by the Federal government, to supplement the efforts and available resources of States, local governments, and disaster relief organizations in alleviating the damage, loss, hardship, or suffering caused thereby. [Bourgin 1983]

The federal definition has been interpreted to include aid to refugees from Cuba and assistance to families affected by toxic wastes. The Red Cross definition has been extended to encompass victims of one-family fires, persons affected by "social disasters" such as civil disorders, and families that are homeless and hungry. In fact, the homeless have also been brought within the purview of the federal disaster program and programs of numerous smaller voluntary agencies.

POLICIES AND PROGRAMS: A BRIEF HISTORY

This chapter examines what might be called the "institutionalization of the second commandment—to love thy neighbor." In the United States this process began in a small way in 1803 (Bourgin 1983), when Congress passed its first disaster legislation on behalf of the citizens of Portsmouth, New Hampshire, who, because of a catastrophe, were unable to pay customs house bonds on goods they were importing.

The Red Cross

It was not until almost a century after that first 1803 relief act that Congress chartered the American Red Cross as the nation's first formally recognized disaster relief agency. And it was not until 1950 that legislation was passed that outlined a more generalized approach by the federal government to disaster relief. In fact, the Federal Disaster Act of 1950 specifically stated:

> In providing such assistance hereunder, Federal agencies shall cooperate to the fullest extent possible with each other and with States and local governments, relief agencies, and the American National Red Cross, but nothing contained in this Act shall be construed to limit or in any way affect the responsibilities of the American National Red Cross under the Act approved January 5, 1905 (33 State. 509) as amended. [Bourgin 1983]

This caveat has been included in all subsequent major disaster relief legislation. The Red Cross continues to play a significant role in disaster relief and to influence disaster relief practices in the United States.

In many ways, the first major departure from piecemeal disaster legislation *was* the incorporation of the American Red Cross (although this was probably not viewed as disaster legislation). Originally founded as the American unit in an international effort to provide service to civilian and battlefield victims of war, the American Red Cross became the first national Red Cross society to concern itself with disaster relief (Buckingham 1977). The agency came into being in 1881 after the United States Senate ratified the Geneva Conventions. But its founder, Clara Barton, saw that, in addition to aid to war victims, disaster relief could be an equally important activity for the organization. Paradoxically, she could not sell the idea to the international Red Cross movement at the time; her disaster proposals, known as the "American amendment," were soundly defeated at conferences in Geneva. The American Red Cross was only a few months old when she sent a representative to the scene of a major forest fire that had devastated vast areas around Port Huron and Bad Axe, Michigan. The very first Red Cross disaster supplies were sent to Port Huron for victims of that fire.

By the time of the first big Johnstown flood, 1889, the Red Cross had grown considerably. Barton led a major relief operation in that ravaged Pennsylvania steel town. After the Sea Island, Georgia, hurricanes in 1893, she and the Red Cross organized a self-help program for the black population on the island. By the time of the San Francisco earthquake and fire, the capability of the Red Cross had grown sufficiently such that President Theodore Roosevelt put the agency in charge of spending the millions of dollars donated to the government for earthquake relief. For that disaster, direct federal expenditures for medical supplies and military assistance with mass care and debris clearance amounted to about $2.5 million, and about half of that was entrusted to the Red Cross.

The Red Cross introduced many innovative approaches to disaster relief in the United States. After the Cherry Mine disaster of 1909, the Red Cross and community and government leaders developed a committee that was the forerunner of present-day workers' compensation systems. After the famous Triangle Shirtwaist fire in lower Manhattan in 1901, Red Cross relief included financial aid to parents of immigrant workers who died in the fire, so that those parents—who, prior to the disaster, had been supported by their working daughters—could open small businesses to support themselves in their native countries.

In all, the Red Cross created a program of disaster response and relief that established expectations on the part of community leaders and individual families of consistent aid in times of disasters. The Red Cross continued to be the major source of assistance for victims of major disasters until the early 1960s, yet despite this major role, the organization received (and still receives) little funding from the federal government. Indeed, in the 1930s, the Red Cross undertook to distribute government-provided cloth, seeds, flour, and other assistance to drought victims but would not manage federal funds for those victims, preferring to remain entirely apolitical. Even today, the Red Cross reimburses the armed forces for costs involved in using military equipment, such as helicopters and trucks, in emergency relief operations.

Today the Red Cross disaster assistance program begins with local chapter response, supplemented with funds, personnel, and equipment from the national organization when needed (American Red Cross 1986). The agency provides emergency mass care—food, clothing, medical care —to supplement local medical facilities, and shelter for the displaced (generally about one-third of disaster victims, initially, although during the floods of 1936 the Red Cross at one time sheltered over one million homeless). Subsequently, the agency provides individualized assistance to families. Such aid could include total rebuilding of a home and replacement of its contents if the family involved has no insurance and no other resources. More frequently, however, the Red Cross provides materials and the family provides much of the labor.

During the 1955 flood relief operation in New England, the federal government, for the first time, began providing some Small Business Administration loan assistance to disaster victims, particularly those who had lost stores or other businesses. Since then, as government programs have expanded, the Red Cross role in individual family assistance has diminished, particularly in larger disasters receiving a presidential declaration and federal funds. However, federal programs have limitations regarding dollar amount and eligibility, so the Red Cross still provides a considerable amount of supplemental assistance. For example, after the Paris, Texas, tornado the Red Cross provided an average of $11,000 to each of sixty low-income families who lacked adequate insurance and were eligible for only $5,000 from government grant programs. However, without federally-funded disaster assistance programs, the Red Cross could not have continued to meet the needs of disaster victims. A study performed for the Red Cross Board of Governors after the Tropical Storm Agnes floods of 1972 showed that the organization, which spent $23 million to provide emergency assistance after that disaster, would have had to spend ten times that amount to provide the same level of help that had been given flood victims in 1955.

The Government's Role in Disaster

There are a number of histories of disaster policy and programs in the United States. In addition to the books by Peter May and Frank Bourgin already cited, Clark Norton's *Emergency Preparedness and Disaster Assis-*

tance: Federal Organization and Programs (1978) is also useful. Thomas Drabek's monograph, *The Professional Emergency Manager* (1987), reviews program and legislative history in terms of the evolving role and responsibilities of emergency managers and civil defense directors.

Disaster relief has traditionally been considered a local responsibility. In fact, civil defense authorities liken their activities to those of frontier neighbors rallying to raise a barn or to help a burned-out settler or farmer rebuild a home destroyed by fire. Until very recently, this local responsibility was supplemented only occasionally by federal assistance appropriated or authorized by Congress after a particular event (this practice was followed as late as 1972 to provide relief to victims of Tropical Storm Agnes)—the action often involving assistance by the military. Between 1803 and 1947, Congress enacted 128 pieces of special disaster-specific legislation (May 1985; Bourgin 1983). When army (or, beginning in the 1880s, Red Cross representatives) arrived on the scene of a disaster, they generally found ad hoc local or regional relief committees collecting funds and relief supplies, and performing recovery efforts.

As noted, the first general legislation concerning disasters, Public Law 81–875, was passed in 1950. However, it contained few provisions for victims (Bourgin 1983). Subsequent legislation did provide various forms of individual assistance, but it was not until Public Law 93–288, the Disaster Relief Act of 1974, that the full spectrum of current federal disaster assistance programs was included in a comprehensive piece of legislation. The Act authorized individual family grants, disaster food coupons, temporary housing, and disaster unemployment assistance, and also referred to emergency loans, restoration of public facilities, mental health counseling, and other forms of individual public assistance.

Although Public Law 81–875 in 1950 introduced federal disaster relief as an institution, Federal Emergency Management Agency (FEMA) historian Bourgin notes:

> Its seminal importance upon future disaster legislation was hardly predictable. Congress' immediate concern was to relieve the financial burdens of repairing the farm-to-market roads and bridges in the rural counties and townships in flooded areas of Minnesota and North Dakota. The amount appropriated was only $5 million. There was little debate and it got little notice at the time. [Bourgin 1983]

Why, then, is so limited a bill considered so important to the history of disaster institutions? As Bourgin (1983) notes, it was the first piece of permanent and general disaster legislation enacted by Congress, and its concepts and authorities became the model of all succeeding federal disaster laws in effect today. Public Law 81–875 is in fact the "granddaddy" of them all.

Public Law 81–875 was designed to supplement State and local government resources, as had the previous disaster-specific laws, and it followed on a series of other congressional acts providing various forms of disaster assistance to be administered by various federal agencies (e.g., since 1936 Congress had allocated $15 million to the Corps of Engineers for flood control purposes, and since 1934, $39 million to the Bureau of Public Roads to fix flood damaged roads and bridges). The Reconstruction Finance Corporation (RFC) was established to offer loans at a reduced cost to businesses for disaster repair and construction; in addition, federal loans to farmers in "distressed emergency areas" were also implemented. The 1950 disaster relief legislation was also preceded by two other nondisaster-specific actions by the 80th Congress: Public Law 80–233 in 1947 authorized the distribution of government surplus property to State and local government for disaster relief, and Public Law 80–85 in 1948, part of a deficiency appropriation act, provided $500,000 to be available until June 30, 1950, for disaster relief. The 1948 Act was followed by a similar measure a year later, which appropriated a full $1 million to a presidential disaster relief emergency fund. These acts provided the language and pattern for all future disaster appropriations. The 1950 Act similarly set a pattern for the future: it supplemented State and local capabilities and resources, and called for the governor of a State involved in a disaster to certify a need for assistance to the President (Bourgin 1983).

Even though this particular law was limited in scope, the House Report on the bill established an important principle: "the bill provides a framework for the Federal Government under which prompt action can be taken in meeting the needs of stricken areas, and it will establish a general Government policy with respect to emergency relief in all future disasters instead of meeting the problem after it occurs" (Bourgin 1983). Some members of Congress questioned how severe a disaster had to be before the President would provide assistance. As Bourgin reports:

> An interesting colloquy took place when Senator Robertson (Va.) asked Chairman McClellan (Ark.), as floor manager of the bill, could a disaster affecting three or four counties constitute a major disaster? Suppose it affected only as few as 150 persons in a single county? Was it not a major disaster to the Senator if his home was washed away by a flood

and destroyed? To these questions, McClelland replied that he would not answer them since this would be the President's decision. To this, he added, "however, we can certainly rely upon whomever may be the President of the United States having some judgement and also some humanitarian feelings in making a decision as to what is a major disaster, where people have suffered or are about to suffer and where the Federal government should step in and assist." [Bourgin, 1983]

Congress also questioned how much it was "reasonable" to expect States or local governments to provide. No fixed percentage was determined, and the matter was left unsettled. Although later laws established fixed percentages as a State or locality's matching share, the federal government has included provisions to "lend" that money so restoration can proceed immediately.

Bourgin also recalls that under Public Law 81–875, costs paid by the federal government were only for "emergency repairs" and temporary replacement, which in many cases may not have meant much more than filling up the pot holes in the roads and throwing together temporary timbered bridges. Few States at the time had emergency funds of any kind for local government public facilities repair (Bourgin 1983).

Still, even this limited legislation set a precedent. It has evolved into a series of preparedness and response programs, which in 1980 obligated over $1 billion for disaster assistance (not including disaster loans); in comparison, less than $3 million was allocated under thirteen presidential major disaster declarations in 1953 (Bourgin 1983; FEMA 1987).

Space does not permit a detailed chronology of disaster legislation enacted since 1950 (see Tables 5.1–5.4). However, since the path from 1950 to 1974 was far from direct and, as May (1985) says, "without grand philosophical debate concerning the Federal rolls," some highlights can help explain the evolution of today's programs and institutions. If nothing else, these highlights underscore Burton, Kates, and White's point in *Environment as Hazard* (1978) that all major flood-related laws but one in the twentieth century were preceded by great floods somewhere in the United States.

In the years following passage of Public Law 81–875, Congress passed legislation providing temporary housing and emergency shelter for the disaster homeless, drought relief for farmers, and surplus federal equipment and supplies for use by States in disaster response. They extended the programs to include U.S. Pacific territories and to provide States as well

Table 5.1. Chronology of U.S. Disaster Relief Legislation

Year	Relief Provisions	Comments (key votes)
1947 (PL80–233)	Surplus federal property made available to state governments upon presidential approval	Formalized existing practice of donating surplus property
1950 (PL81–875)	Disaster Relief Act of 1950: authorized funding for repair of local public facilities upon presidential approval	Formalized existing practice (House: 232–25; Senate: voice vote)
1951 (PL82–107)	Authorized federal provision of emergency housing	Response to Kansas-Missouri flood of 1951; formalized existing practice
1953 (PL83–134)	Permitted donation of federal surplus property of individuals	Response to 1953 Worcester, Mass., tornado
1962 (PL87–502)	Added grants for repair of state facilities; added Guam, American Samoa, and Pacific Territories	Response to state and territorial needs
1964 (PL88–451)	Alaskan relief program—special loan and grant provisions	Disaster-specific relief
1965 (PL89–41)	Pacific Northwest floods relief program —special loan and grants	Disaster-specific relief
1965 (PL89–339)	Hurricane Betsy relief program for Florida, Louisiana, and Mississippi	Disaster-specific relief
1966 (PL89–769)	Disaster Relief Act of 1966: —Rural communities made eligible —Funding for damage to higher education facilities —Funding for repair of public facilities under construction	Amendments to the 1950 act extending disaster-specific provisions from above acts Indiana tornado in 1965 solidified the act's support
1969 (PL91–79)	Disaster Relief Act of 1969: —Funding for debris removal from private property —Distribution of food coupons —Unemployment compensation for disaster victims —SBA, FHA, VA loan revisions —Private timber purchase allowed	New general relief act, limited to 15 months' duration Followed California mudslide and Hurricane Camille
1970 (PL91–606)	Disaster Assistance Act of 1970: most provisions of the 1969 act, plus the following: —Grants to individuals for temporary housing/relocation —Funding for legal services —Community payments for tax loss —Revision of SBA loan provisions	Emphasis on expanding relief assistance for individuals Outgrowth of the 1969 act and Hurricane Camille response (Senate: 54–0; House: voice vote)
1971 (PL92–209)	Funding for repair, replacement, or reconstruction of nonprofit medical facilities	Amendment to 1970 act, arising from the 1971 San Fernando earthquake

Table 5.1. Continued

Year	Relief Provisions	Comments (key votes)
1972 (PL92–385)	Hurricane Agnes relief program, special loans and grants	Disaster-specific relief
1974 (PL93–288)	Disaster Relief Amendments of 1974: —Distinguished "major disasters" from "emergencies" —Authorized funding for mental health counseling, recovery planning councils, community loans, state disaster planning, parks and recreation repairs	Amendments to the 1970 act enacted instead of Nixon administration bill calling for new federalism approach (Senate: 91–0 orig. bill; 78–7 conference; House: 374–4 conference version)
1977 (PL95–51)	Reauthorization of the 1974 bill through fiscal year 1980	(Senate: voice vote; House: 393–5)
1980 (PL96–568)	Reauthorization for one year, review to take place prior to longer term reauthorization Funding for repair of nonprofit libraries hit by Hurricane Agnes	Concern over Carter's use of disaster funds for Cuban refugees and Love Canal

SOURCES: Executive Office of the President, Office of Emergency Preparedness, Disaster Preparedness (Washington, D.C.: U.S. Government Printing Office, January 1972), pp. 167–73; Congressional Quarterly, CQ Almanac, 1947–80 issues; U.S. Congressional Record, relevant sections for each law 1947–80; May 1985.

as local communities with aid for restoring damaged public facilities. Of special importance were two disaster-specific acts—Public Law 88–451, amendments to the Alaska Omnibus Act following the 1964 Good Friday earthquake that devastated parts of Anchorage and southwestern Alaska; and the Southeast Hurricane Disaster Relief Act, enacted *during* relief operations following Hurricane Betsy, which hit Florida, Louisiana, and Mississippi in 1965. The Alaska-related legislation provided forgiveness for certain federal loans to farmers and homeowners, and aided repayment of mortgages on damaged dwellings. The Hurricane Betsy law— enacted because of "a need for special measures designed to aid and accelerate . . . and to otherwise rehabilitate these devastated areas"—provided that mobile homes used for temporary housing could ultimately be sold to the hurricane victims for a "fair and equitable price," and, most importantly, that $1,800 of any SBA or FHA disaster loan could be canceled or "forgiven" after the first $500 was repaid (Bourgin 1983).

This latter provision became an important method of federal disaster assistance until passage of the 1974 Disaster Relief Act. The "forgiveness feature"—in effect, a federal grant—was increased to $2,500 for victims of Hurricane Camille in 1969, then to $5,000 (retroactively, for a year or

Table 5.2. The Development of Financial Relief Following Disaster

Year	Loan Provisions	Comments (key votes)
I. Small Business Administration Loan Provisions		
1934 (PL73–160)	Reconstruction Finance Corp. authorized to make loans to nonprofit corporations for repair of disaster damages to building or infrastructures	Temporary program covering damages for "earthquakes, conflagration, tornado, cyclone, floods"
1936 (PL74–525)	Reauthorization of RFC loan program	Covered 1935–36; total loan limit of $50 million
1937 (PL75–5)	Disaster Loan Corporation created with disaster loan program like the RFC program	Open-ended legislation
1953 (PL83–163)	Small Business Act of 1953: —Liquidated Disaster Loan Corporation	Provided agency-level disaster declaration
	—Authorized SBA to make loans "as the administration may determine to be necessary for floods or other catastrophes"	Applicants not required to apply elsewhere first; 3% interest rate, 20-year limit for homes, 10-year business
1955 (PL84–268)	Authorized SBA loans as a result of "production disasters" to businesses with "economic injury"	
1956 (PL84–402)	Extended business disaster loans to a 20-year limit	Amendment to 1953 act
1964 (PL88–451)	Alaskan relief program; special loan provisions including 30-year limit on home loans	Disaster-specific relief
1965 (PL89–41)	Pacific Northwest floods relief program; similar loan provisions to Alaskan relief program	Disaster-specific relief
1965 (PL89–59)	Extended 30-year limit to all loans and added deferment of payments for "hardship" cases	General legislation that arose from the above disaster-specific provisions
1965 (PL89–339)	Hurricane Betsy relief program; authorized cancellation of up to $1,800 on any loan	Disaster-specific relief
1965 (PL90–448)	Added "riots or civil disorders" as category for disaster loan	Response to urban riots
1969 (PL91–79)	Disaster Relief Act of 1969: —Extended $1,800 forgiveness to all declared "major disasters" —Raised ceiling on homeowner and business loan amounts plus other changes in interest rates	Provisions limited to 15 months' duration

Table 5.2. Continued

Year	Loan Provisions	Comments (key votes)
1970 (PL91–606)	Disaster Relief Act of 1970: —Increased forgiveness —Revised interest rate to range of 4⅞ to 5⅜%	Open-ended legislation
1972 (PL92–385)	Hurricane Agnes relief program: —Lowered interest rates and increased forgiveness for disasters in 1971 and 1972	Temporary relief program (Senate: 76–2; House: 359–1)
1973 (PL93–24)	Eliminated forgiveness clause and set a higher interest rate to equal Farmers Home Administration	Seeking uniformity in disaster loan programs
1975 (PL94–68)	Revised formula for interest rates on loans, attached to cost of governmental borrowing	Increased rate that year to 6⅞%
1976 (PL94–305)	Authorized SBA loans for farmers	SBA loans more desirable than FmHA loans
1977 (PL95–89)	Lowered interest rates on disaster loans	Temporary provisions in response to drought
1980 (PL96–302)	Reauthorization of SBA loan program through 1984 —Provided farmers must be rejected by FmHA before SBA disaster loan can be approved —Increased interest rates, 5% for emergency loan, 10% if private funding is available	Attempt to get SBA out of farmer loan business Outgrowth of bills vetoed or defeated, 1978 and 1979 (Senate: 91–2; House: 210–193)

II. Farmers Home Administration Loan Provisions

Year	Loan Provisions	Comments (key votes)
1949 (PL81–38)	Authorized agriculture secretary to make loans to farmers and stockmen for production disasters; terms to be established by the agriculture secretary	Provided agency-level disaster declaration Applicants must show cannot get loans elsewhere
1953 (PL83–115)	Added "economic disaster" loans to above provisions	
1961 (PL87–128)	Provided real estate and operating loans, not limited to disasters; continued emergency loans at 3%	Kennedy administration major farm legislation
1962 (PL87–832)	Made oyster planters eligible for FmHA loan programs	Response to the "mysterious 'virus x'"
1964–73 (PL88–451 89–339 91–79)	The legislation noted here applied to both SBA and FmHA (see above discussion)	During this period PL89–41 and PL89–59 did not apply to FmHA

Table 5.2. Continued

Year	Loan Provisions	Comments (key votes)
91–606 92–385 93–24)	Eliminated FmHA "test for credit elsewhere"	
1974 (PL93–237)	Extended retroactively the $5,000 forgiveness and 1% loan features of PL92–385	Temporary legislation covering December 1972 to April 1973
1975 (PL94–68)	—Added aquaculture farmers —Reinstated "test for credit elsewhere" —Interest rate 5% for amount of loss; additional amounts at market interest rate	Aquaculture to outgrowth of oyster farmer legislation (Senate: voice vote; House: 398–0)
1978 (PL95–334)	—Created new economic emergency program allowing borrowing up to $400,000 for up to 30 years —Revised limits upward on other loan programs	Response to "heavy lobbying" by the American Agriculture Movement farmer organization (Senate: voice vote; House: 362–28)
1980 (PL96–438)	—Placed limits on amount an individual farmer could borrow, to be lowered further in future —Required net worth of applicant be considered before emergency loan could be granted, with agency discretion over granting loans if private loans available	Response in part to a "60 Minutes" television exposé of disaster loans Passage delayed because of negotiations over SBA loan provisions for farmers

SOURCES: A Report to Congress: "A Review of Federal Disaster Loan Authority" (January 1977) in U.S. House of Representatives, Committee on Small Business, Subcommittee on SBA, Federal Natural Disaster Assistance Program (Hearings held April 6, June 9, 13, and 17, 1977) (Washington, D.C.: U.S. Government Printing Office, 1977), Congressional Quarterly CQ Almanac, 1976; May 1985.

so) for victims of Tropical Storm Agnes and other major disasters such as the Rapid City floods in 1972. At the same time, disaster loan interest rates fluctuated from year to year, based sometimes on a standard low percentage (they were as low as 1 percent after Agnes) and sometimes on the rate charged for government bonds. In any event, such loans were always less costly than commercial loans.

Insurance

Beyond immediate government and private agency assistance, insurance is, of course, a major resource for many families, with fire insurance or home-owners' comprehensive insurance providing basic assistance for many

Table 5.3. The Origins of U.S. Flood Legislation

Year	Action Taken	Comments (key votes)
	I. Study Phase prior to Permanent Legislation	
1949	Truman urged enactment of a flood insurance/indemnification program	House appropriations said such a program needs further study before consideration
1951	Truman message to Congress, proposing flood insurance	Part of funding request for midwest flood relief program
1952	Truman special message, urging enactment of his proposal	"Exploratory" meetings with insurance industry
1956 (PL84–1016)	Eisenhower called for flood damage indemnity program in his state of the union address; Federal Flood Insurance Act of 1956. Housing and Home Finance administrator to establish flood insurance, loan contracts, and reinsurance programs	The proposal was labeled "an experimental program" (Senate: 61–7; House: voice vote) Program never started, see 1957 action
1957	Flood insurance program was never started because the House failed to provide funding	(House vote on funding, rejected twice: 97–127 and 186–218)
1962–63	Senate passed bills calling for study of flood insurance	Response to flooding in mid-Atlantic states
1965 (PL89–339)	Hurricane Betsy relief mandated HUD study of flood insurance	Study issued in 1966 calling for flood insurance program
	II. Legislative Phase	
1967	National Flood Insurance Act 1967: provided for private insurers selling of federally subsidized flood insurance, with federal reinsurance provisions	Administration bill based on 1966 HUD report Remained in conference at end of year, not enacted
1968 (PL90–448)	National Flood Insurance Act of 1968: included as title VIII of the Housing and Development Act	Provisions of 1967 bill, but with Senate-proposed federal flood insurance fund
1973 (PL93–234)	Flood Disaster Protection Act of 1973: expanded flood damage coverage and provided sanctions for communities in flood zones failing to participate	Provisions enacted to induce more participation (Senate: voice vote; House: 359–21)

Sources: Congressional Quarterly, Congress and the Nation, vol. 1, p. 488; Congressional Quarterly, CQ Almanac, 1956–73; U.S. Congressional Record, relevant sections 1949–51; May 1985.

Table 5.4. Regulatory Provisions for Hazardous Areas

Year	Action Taken	Comments (key votes)

I. Floodplain Regulations

Year	Action Taken	Comments (key votes)
1934	Federal report suggesting restrictions for floodplains	National Resources Board Report
1950s	Two presidential commissions recommend nonstructural actions	1950 Water Policy Commission; 1955 Water Policy Committee
1960	Flood control act of 1960 mandated Corps of Engineers state/local technical assistance	Corps of Engineers started a floodplain information program
1966 (Executive Order 11296)	Johnson directed federal agencies to consider flood hazards in location decisions	Response to federal task force report calling for flood hazard mitigation
1968 (PL90–448)	National Flood Insurance Act of 1968: required local adoption of floodplain regulations as a condition for flood insurance	Established a quid pro quo between insurance availability and floodplain regulation; weak enforcement
1973 (PL93–234)	Flood Disaster Protection Act of 1973: made adoption of flood regulations a requirement for eligibility for loans from federally guaranteed banks	Considerably strengthened the 1968 act's floodplain regulation sanctions
1974 (PL93–288)	Disaster Relief Act of 1974: required efforts to "mitigate" future disaster losses as condition for federal aid	Section 406 of the act, sanctions apply to the act's relief provisions
1974 (PL93–251)	Water Resources Development Act of 1974: federal agencies must consider nonstructural alternatives to flood control	Mild attempt to shift emphasis from "structural" control methods like dams
1977 (Executive Order 11988)	Required agencies to issue regulations discouraging development in floodplains	Agency response was limited; follow-up memorandum issues in 1979
1977 (PL95–128)	1977 Housing and Community Development Act: relaxed flood insurance sanctions	Weakened 1973 provisions (Senate: 49–36; House: 220–169)
1982 (PL97–348)	Coastal Barriers Resources Act: prohibited federal flood insurance for new construction or improvements in undeveloped barrier islands	Part of more general legislation to protect barrier islands (Senate: voice vote; House: 399–4)

II. Earthquake Hazards Provisions

Year	Action Taken	Comments (key votes)
1970s	Several bills proposing changes in funding and organization of earthquake research activities	Several followed the 1971 San Fernando earthquake

Table 5.4. Continued

Year	Action Taken	Comments (key votes)
1977 (PL95–124)	Earthquake Hazards Reduction Act of 1977: increased spending and multiagency research effort to be centrally coordinated by FEMA	Similar to 1976 rejection (Senate: voice vote; House: 229–12)
1980 (PL96–472)	Reauthorization of the 1977 act clarifying the FEMA role and adding "multihazard" mitigation planning efforts	Response in part to perceived lack of FEMA leadership

SOURCES: U.S. Congress, Office of Technology Assessment, "Issues and Options in Flood Hazards Management, A Background Paper" (OTA-BP-X-3) (Washington, D.C.: Office of Technology Assessment, February 1980); Congressional Quarterly, CQ Almanac, 1976–82, May 1985.

(homeowners' policies now generally include extended windstorm coverage). Since the widespread issuance of such coverage began in the 1950s and 60s, the Red Cross has noted a sharp drop in the need to fund medical aid for tornado victims. However, traditional insurance policies do not cover flood damages, the insurance industry having abandoned such coverage many years ago after suffering major losses following a series of floods early in this century (Kunreuther and Dacy 1969). Additionally, earthquake insurance, while commercially available, is not purchased by many families: the deductibles are high and the policies expensive. There is currently no all-risk insurance available, although the possibility has been discussed by government and the insurance industry officials, and conceivably could be realized. The insurance industry is, at the time of writing, exploring with the Federal Insurance Administration within FEMA the possibility of issuing partially subsidized earthquake insurance through a program somewhat similar to the current flood insurance program.

The move toward a federal flood insurance program began in 1949 with President Truman, who subsequently cited the need for such a program in his 1951 State of the Union message (May 1985; Bourgin 1983). After major flooding in 1955, President Eisenhower also called for a flood damage indemnity program, and in 1956 a flood insurance program was established—but never funded, partly because no one could reasonably indicate what it might cost. After the Hurricane Betsy Relief Bill mandated a HUD study of flood insurance and the study recommended such a program, Congress passed the National Flood Insurance Act in 1967, which enabled private insurers to sell federally subsidized flood insurance with federal reinsurance (Bourgin 1983). Later amendments expanded flood damage coverage, mandated mapping of hazard areas, required insurance coverage of new buildings, and also made insurance available for certain existing structures. As the program evolved, the subsidized rates were restricted to structures outside designated high-hazard areas.

President Johnson's Executive Order 11296, in 1966, directed federal agencies to consider flood hazards in deciding where to locate federal facilities, and a subsequent order, no. 11988 by President Carter, required federal agencies to issue regulations discouraging development in flood plains. The 1973 amendments to the flood insurance law made adoption of local flood regulations a requirement for eligibility for the flood insurance program. In addition, victims receiving federally funded assistance were required to purchase flood insurance against future disasters. On the recommendation of the Red Cross, the possible financial burden this might cause low-income families was minimized by permitting them to use part of their IFG (Individual Family Grant) monies to purchase flood insurance. Built into the flood insurance program is a significant section—1362—that involves relocation of families from persistent flood hazard areas. This, and the various provisions calling for mapping and rezoning of hazardous areas, made the National Flood Insurance Program the nation's first land use control law.

Mitigation Programs

Beyond postdisaster aid and insurance, the nation's system of disaster programs now includes institutionalized methods for relieving (or preventing) suffering due to disasters. Mitigation at the federal level first began in 1936 when Congress appropriated funds to the U.S. Army Corps of Engineers to build dams, levees, and other flood control works (May 1985; Bourgin 1983). While Corps-built flood works have undoubtedly prevented billions of dollars in losses and much loss of life, this kind of flood mitigation has not been the panacea originally envisioned. In some instances, for example, up-river dams or channelization have actually intensified problems downstream, and serious devastation has resulted. As early as the 1950s, two Presidential Commissions recommended "nonstructural approaches"—land use controls, floodproofing, insurance, relocation—to flood hazard mitigation, and a subsequent 1960 law mandated that the Corps of Engineers provide technical assistance to State and local governments to encourage such action (Norton 1978; Bourgin 1983).

Clearly, hazard mitigation can mean many things. To some planners and social scientists it includes relief and rehabilitation, insurance, and other short-term actions to ameliorate losses, but to most others it means preventive actions that will forestall all future disasters and accompanying losses. The Flood Insurance Act and subsequent amendments contain a number of hazard mitigation provisions: notably, the previously mentioned section 1362, which, unfortunately, has never been adequately funded. As a result, relocations have been infrequent, although one report that examined various community flood mitigation plans found that relocation was included in over thirty cases. Indeed, the most noted relocation project, clearance of floodways after the 1972 Rapid City flood, was accomplished without any significant 1362 participation. Instead, a determined mayor found federal funds in a variety of other unrelated, but applicable, programs. The section has been used, however, in Jackson, Mississippi, parts of Texas, Oklahoma, and elsewhere.

The 1974 Disaster Relief Act and later amendments require efforts to mitigate future losses as a condition for federal aid. Under that law, interagency hazard mitigation teams must survey a disaster area and, within fifteen days, come up with a series of recommendations concerning the prevention of future losses. Although the recommendations are neither mandatory nor accompanied by offers of funding, a great many are adopted, some with limited federal funding.

Other major hazard mitigation laws now in force include the 1977 Earthquake Hazards Reduction Act (May 1985), which provides increased federal funds for research, planning, and education concerning earthquakes. The funds have been used to support such projects as the Southern California Earthquake Preparedness Project and the Central United States Earthquake Consortium. FEMA was designated to coordinate the research and planning funded by the Act, and in 1980 Congress strengthened this role by adding multihazard planning to the agency's responsibilities. In that context, the agency is promoting integrated emergency management (IEM) for all hazards (including enemy attack). Thus, FEMA attempts to cooperate with other agencies on various problems—for example, with the Army Corps of Engineers, the National Oceanographic and Atmospheric Administration, and State and regional agencies concerning evacuation planning along coasts vulnerable to hurricanes. Congress also passed, in 1982, the Coastal Barrier Resources Act (May 1985), which, among other things, prohibits federal flood insurance for projects on undeveloped coastal islands. Congress has also mandated emergency planning around nuclear power plants and the new Chemical Emergency Response Plan.

THE RESPONSIBILITY FOR DISASTER MANAGEMENT

Who is in charge of all this? Historically, the responsibility for federal disaster and hazard mitigation programs has been fragmented and often tied to whatever agency had responsibility for the nation's civil defense activities. The Housing and Home Finance Administration was originally responsible for those activities included in the 1950 act, but in 1953 the Federal Civil Defense Administration was created as an independent agency responsible for civil defense and disaster relief activities. In 1958 the Office of Civil Defense Mobilization within the White House took over responsibility for disaster relief, civil defense, and defense mobilization. Three years later the Office of Emergency Planning (which in 1968 was renamed the Office of Emergency Preparedness) in the White House assumed these tasks, although civil defense was later shifted to the Defense Department's Civil Preparedness Agency (DCPA). From 1973 to 1979 the Federal Disaster Assistance Administration within the Department of Housing and Urban Development was responsible for disaster relief and flood insurance; civil defense activities remained the responsibility of DCPA and continuity of government was in the hands of the little-known Federal Preparedness Agency within the General Services Administration (May 1985; Bourgin 1983).

In 1979 these various responsibilities came together with the establishment of FEMA, which now manages disaster relief, civil defense, and federal preparedness. Incorporated within FEMA are the Federal Disaster Assistance Administration, the Federal Preparedness Agency, the Defense Civic Preparedness Agency, the U.S. Fire Administration, and the Federal Insurance Administration. Only the latter two retained their names and identities within the FEMA structure. Some emergency planning functions of the National Weather Service and the Nuclear Regulatory Commission were also ultimately moved to FEMA.

Thus, the present power and responsibility for disaster management and mitigation are under FEMA, although increasing awareness of the potential for human-caused technological disasters results more and more in the involvement of other agencies such as the Department of Transportation, the Department of Energy, the Nuclear Regulatory Commission, and the Environmental Protection Agency. The U.S. Geological Survey, the Soil Conservation Service, the National Weather Service, the Corps of Engineers, and a number of other agencies all have ancillary roles.

Roy S. Popkin

May emphasizes that today's disaster policies have, more often than not, evolved from specific situations and are not the result of any grand design (May 1985). From this writer's perspective, as one who has been involved directly in both the use and evolution of disaster programs and policies, May seems to be right. A good deal of what is current law and practice did evolve from specific disasters, discussions among a few participants at a particular meeting or conference, limited testimony at congressional hearings and, sometimes, interpretations of regulations made by one or two persons on an emergency basis. Examples of these processes follow, but it is instructive to first examine a few issues concerning disaster victims and the extent of disaster as a national problem.

Central to the activities of all disaster programs are, of course, the victims. Victims have been studied, restudied, reduced to statistics, and generalized about in hundreds of different ways, and findings from such studies are often used as a measure of the effectiveness of disaster relief programs. An individual victim, however, is rarely part of an organized group, although there have been a number of cases of victims taking group action in an effort to speed up relief efforts or to demand resolution of underlying problems, as happened at Love Canal. Often, at least to the news media and some researchers, disaster casualties seem to be twice victimized—first by the disaster itself and subsequently by the relief processes themselves.

It is hard to tell how many Americans are disaster victims each year. Rossi estimated that perhaps 1.5 to 2.5 million persons were exposed to disaster events annually, although the researchers could not determine how many persons actually became victims in the sense that they suffered significant loss or injury (Rossi et al. 1983). The study did seem to indicate that the disaster victimization rate in the United States is at most 1 percent. Red Cross and FEMA annual reports tend to show that less than half of 1 percent of the nation's population needed financial or other substantive assistance beyond what insurance policies provided. Thus, the nation's disaster victim population is relatively small, particularly when compared to the number of persons affected by other great national problems. (However, one should note that a repeat of the 1811–12 central United States earthquakes or a high-tide hurricane hitting a major eastern seaport could change this proportion quickly and dramatically.) However, when the victim population needs help, that need can be acute and require extremely costly emergency and long-term assistance.

As discussed earlier, federal assistance is supposed to supplement State resources. In the real world, the only time a State makes a substantial financial contribution to disaster relief is when, as in the case of Individual Family Grants, it is required to put up 25 percent of the money. Occasionally, a State is able to provide special funding, but usually the States and local communities and, in particular, local disaster victims, look to external sources for needed help. As May writes:

> In practice, the State agencies tend to be fairly impotent allies. Disaster relief is often relegated to the backwaters of State government, thereby limiting the visibility or political clout of the agencies within State legislatures. Because States contribute little to disaster agency operating budgets, the agencies' activities are not given careful scrutiny in budget reviews. This in turn further limits the visibility of the agencies as well as the size of their legislative constituencies. Moreover, when major disasters occur, State agencies are overshadowed. Typically, members of the governor's staff and federal officials step in to negotiate and coordinate the federal relief effort. [May 1985]

Claire Rubin (1985) agrees. In only one of the fourteen communities she and her colleagues studied did State government play a major role, because, she says, State government had little to offer. Similarly, the national Red Cross must usually augment the resources of its local chapters with national funds and staff. This inaction on the part of States is probably due to both a lack of ongoing concern on the part of those in power and a lack of money and resources. Rossi and his associates found that the local groups most concerned with natural hazards were emergency managers, Red Cross leaders, and insurance people—hardly a strong, politically influential group (Rossi et al. 1982). The Rossi study found, in surveying more than two thousand local and State leaders, that anything related to natural hazards or disasters rated twelfth or lower on a list of eighteen potential problems. Moreover, a National Governors Association survey of State emergency management programs found that, by and large, FEMA funding determined what a given State's agency was going to emphasize programatically. While Congress has authorized "dual use" of funds and supplies—for civil defense *and* disaster response—FEMA insists that adequate time and effort be devoted to civil defense activities and, for example, has recently notified States that FEMA-funded personnel should not be used for chemical emergency response planning under the Superfund amendments that mandate such planning at the State level.

In one area where States currently have major operational responsibility—the IFG grants—their performance has been mixed. It can take more than a year for a victim to receive such a grant. Such delays were not unusual in California, for example, when Proposition 13 sharply reduced State budgets, and few State workers were available for disaster casework. FEMA, too, has operational problems that are budget-related: for example, agencies have complained that locally hired FEMA temporary employees do not really know the federal programs and consequently give out misinformation. In consequence, FEMA operations in West Virginia, Pennsylvania, and South Carolina have been investigated by a number of agencies, including the GAO and the House Science, Space, and Technology Committee.

Nonetheless, individuals and communities do get help. In fiscal years 1982 through 1986, there were 119 major disaster declarations by the President, covering 1,072 counties. During that period FEMA obligated over $724 million for public assistance (repair of public facilities) and $296 million for individual assistance. More than 75,000 families were assisted with temporary housing—122,000 with individual family grants (FEMA 1987). During the same period, the Red Cross, reacting to disasters of all sizes, averaged well over 40,000 responses a year, and the number of families assisted was somewhat higher than those aided by FEMA, although the amount spent was, of course, considerably lower. During the same period there were over $1 billion worth of SBA/FMHA disaster loans allocated, and flood insurance policy holders received over $755 million (FEMA 1987).

The major assistance available to disaster victims today for their relief and rehabilitation following a presidentially declared disaster includes:

- Red Cross emergency assistance to respond to immediate needs until federal programs are in place and to supplement such programs if needed.
- Red Cross mass care for those who need food and shelter.
- Individual Family Grants of up to $5,000 (legislation raising the ceiling is now pending) to disaster victims.
- Low-interest SBA disaster loans for those who qualify.
- Disaster unemployment insurance and food stamps.
- Temporary housing provided with federal funds.
- Federally funded, locally provided mental health counseling.

In a disaster, emergency response is handled initially by the Red Cross and State and local agencies; public agencies manage evacuations, rescue, searches, traffic control, and other public safety measures. Additionally, State health departments become involved in supporting local medical efforts. If there is a presidential declaration, the federal team moves in to set up one-stop Disaster Assistance Centers where victims can apply for federal, Red Cross, and other aid. At present, new consolidated application forms and computerization are reducing the bureaucratic processes involved. As already mentioned, the President can, of course, make an "emergency declaration" at the request of a Governor. This makes available assistance such as snow removal, forest fire fighting, emergency help with river diking, and could also probably be used in the event of an epidemic or other situation requiring a mass evacuation but not necessarily implying major destruction.

One might still ask whether this help adequately meets the needs of the victims involved. The Colorado State University Hazards Assessment Laboratory was funded by National Voluntary Organizations Active in Disaster to determine if there were unmet needs of disaster victims (Mileti, Popkin, Farhar 1985). After interviewing a number of experienced emergency managers and relief workers, the research team found that there were such needs, but that they were largely in the areas of information and counseling; other unmet needs were more related to restoring quality of life than to basic recovery. Persons suffering most from loss of quality of life seemed to be the elderly or the long-time residents of an area. Thus, when it came down to basics, needs were largely being met.

Interestingly, when relief agencies conduct such studies, they usually find that persons are much more satisfied with relief efforts than the agencies expected them to be. The agencies seem to be more critical of their own weaknesses than are disaster victims who, of course, usually do not know what to expect. Only rarely do victims object to or organize against agencies' efforts.

Still, the success record is mixed. For example, the number of flood insurance policies in force seems to stay at the same level year after year. The approximately two million policy holders at any given time represent perhaps a sixth to a tenth of the floodplain occupants or coastal residents who should have coverage. The flood insurance agenda of the Reagan administration was to make the program self-sustaining (rather than subsidized, as Congress originally intended) by raising rates and increasing exclusions. FIA representatives have been clear about this change despite the objections of those who have to deal with the families involved.

At a recent meeting of floodplain managers, a representative of rural Kentucky constituencies questioned the rate increases and suggested they would prevent unemployed or low-income coal country families from buying flood insurance. An FIA panelist at the 1982 meeting of the Association of State Floodplain Managers said, "perhaps we have to write off rural America" to reach the goal of operating in the black. Most FEMA staff working on flood insurance or flood hazard mitigation are paid from premium collection money; flood insurance is not a FEMA budget line item.

As mentioned earlier, Section 1362 has similarly remained underfunded. However, when a proposed fiscal year 1988 FEMA budget went to Congress with the 1362 funds—little as they were—halved, Congress restored the allocation. As this example indicates, Congress does critically examine disaster legislation and how it is implemented. For example, a Senate investigation of charges that low-income victims were discriminated against after Hurricane Camille, in 1969, resulted in clear changes in the way the government and the Red Cross did their casework. Similarly, there have been difficulties regarding enforcing repayment of SBA loans (an oversight often attributable to "benign neglect") but after congressional complaints and GAO investigations, the situation has improved. Other GAO studies have assessed the FEMA role as lead agency in earthquake hazard reduction (the agency received a poor rating), the process for implementing Corps of Engineers flood control projects (from the day a flood control project study is initiated to the letting of contracts averages over 27 years), and matters concerning loan followup and repayment. Clearly, Congress is watching over the institutions responsible for hazard management.

How politically influential are government disaster programs? Two former federal disaster chiefs—Thomas Dunne, a Republican and head of the FDAA under Nixon and Carter, and William Willcox, a Democrat and head of FDAA, and briefly FEMA, under Carter—say that political pressures were almost nil. The exceptions each cited related to ice storms and blizzards when Governors or members of Congress pressed for help that, coincidentally, was *not* provided in either instance. Both believe, and the evidence supports them, that political pressures exist most strongly at the State and local level, and usually involve recovery efforts or hazard mitigation recommendations that pit developers against mitigators, or involve some form of scapegoating. Willcox, then a Pennsylvania official, was on the Pennsylvania flood victim side and Dunne on the federal side during the 1972 Agnes recovery effort, when a major political row erupted concerning the effectiveness of federal assistance. At the time, HUD secretary George Romney was actually caught in a shouting confrontation with a flood victims' group on the steps of a Wilkes-Barre school. However, both Dunne and Willcox believe that local political frustration, not national politics, was the underlying problem.

The politics of disaster preparedness and recovery have been relatively low-key compared to those surrounding other major national issues, and, again, the politics of hazard mitigation is often much more politically intense and controversial at the local level, especially when it impinges on disaster recovery or commercial development. For example, after Hurricane Camille, most of the Mississippi County Commissioners who voted for stronger coastal property building codes were defeated in the following election because of those votes. The Commissioners had not even considered rezoning the gulf-front areas because those locations were the counties' best tax revenue sources.

If political action has been most volatile at the local and State level, congressional hearings on disaster response or disaster legislation have rarely commanded major media attention, except, perhaps, when they related to accusations of racial or economic bias in relief giving (as occurred during the Senate hearings concerning response to Hurricane Camille in 1969) or, as occurred more recently, when there was concern over the civil defense aspects of FEMA programs involving preparations for enemy attack or, more specifically, nuclear war. Oddly enough, however, the nation's first and only national land use control laws were enacted during a Republican administration as part of the National Flood Insurance Program. This legislation created little debate and received little attention by the media, and, hence, aroused little concern on the part of the public until the law's restrictions became the subject of local controversy. Although May (1985) characterizes disaster legislation of the past and much of the present as "log rolling" or "pork barreling," the legislation has not created the kind of nationwide controversy and uproar that surrounds such other legislation as omnibus water or highway project bills. Additional evidence of the apolitical nature of disaster programs—at least on the national level— is shown by May's finding of only a slight indication that the number of Presidential disaster declarations is greater in a Presidential election year (May 1985).

It is often said that our nation's concern about disaster and how to deal with it is most intense when stories and pictures of death, destruction, and human despair occupy front pages and the television news. Otherwise, the subject is a "low saliency issue" (Rossi et al. 1982). Indeed, the number of persons concerned with hazards when a disaster is not actually happening is small. If one includes emergency planners and managers, scientific and social researchers, earthquake and dam safety specialists, relief agency workers, weather forecasters, and dam and floodwall (levee) builders, the number of full-time, year-round job holders would probably total less than twenty-five thousand. The addition of fire fighters, rescue squad members, and insurance claims agents would, of course, make the figure somewhat larger. If one were to add a "victim" constituency of another 500,000 to 1 million persons who have suffered injury or serious loss in a given year, the population concerned about hazards may be one-half to 1 percent of the U.S population.

True, there is a theoretical constituency of many millions who are potentially at risk from various disasters, but experience shows that most of them do not become concerned until they are actually affected. While the politics of disaster is in many ways the politics of overcoming inertia, and all too often requires pain and suffering to initiate action, it is nonetheless politics worth pursuing. The need for hazard mitigation is no less compelling because those who recognize it are relatively few.

LOOKING AHEAD

There is hope for better response *and* better mitigation. Congress has considered amendments to the 1974 Act that would increase the amount of the IFG grant from $5,000 to $10,000 (FEMA recommended $7,500), extend the temporary housing period from a year to eighteen months (it once was unlimited), require that a percentage of State funds be used in restoring public facilities, and *require that perhaps 10 percent of all federal grants be applied toward hazard mitigation.* In contrast to these progressive measures, however, is the apparent agenda of the FEMA leadership. In short, its goal seems to be budget reduction. In 1976, Julius Becton, FEMA director, announced new approaches to Presidential declarations and other steps the agency was proposing that would save $75 million. However, the reductions would have required using a per capita formula that could have discriminated against smaller communities, and Congress stopped the proposals.

Not surprisingly in this era of Gramm-Rudman budget reduction, the current agenda still seems to be one of consolidating what exists and cutting costs at the same time. Consequently, disaster planning funding is down and research money is drying up, despite the repeatedly demonstrated positive benefits of planning and research. Moreover, there is a new emphasis and legislation—Title III of the 1986 Superfund Amendments and Reauthorization Act—putting more demands on emergency planners and managers, and raising questions concerning the whole future of emergency and disaster management. The new emphasis is on technological and environmental hazards, and the role of many individuals and agencies traditionally involved in hazard management is not clear; however, almost certainly they will be subject to a much greater work load.

Even before Title III, FEMA money was used to buy out families at Love Canal and Times Beach, and, in the past, local emergency management agencies have had to supply drinking water when underground sources were polluted. Now, questions are being raised about such things as who will help low-income families relocate or retrofit their homes if they have a severe radon gas problem. Recognizing the interdependence of technological and natural hazards, environmental laws already relate siting of waste treatment facilities to 100-year flood levels, and there is additional concern about the siting of nuclear power plants near earthquake faults. The Three Mile Island nuclear power plant sits on an island in the Susquehanna River—a river that rose thirty-six feet in 1972; the Trojan Nuclear Power Plant is close to Mount St. Helens. Clearly, we are becoming aware of a whole new set of disasters—technological disasters triggered by natural events—but no money is being appropriated to help understand and deal with these problems. In Title III, for example, Congress requires a great deal of planning but has allocated no money.

How effectively our nation's governments and emergency managers will deal with these problems remains to be seen. Experience and a few studies show emergency managers to be persistent creatures who are broadening their constituency to include floodplain managers, environmentalists, geologists, and others concerned with the nation's natural and human resources. While the current national political climate would seem to indicate a decrease in support for hazard management, the overall congressional legislative history indicates that politicians at the national level will probably continue and even increase their support in the long run, especially when and if major disasters occur and inspire future legislation.

Clearly, a great deal has happened in the forty years since the first major general disaster legislation was passed. However, the future is not determined; where we go from here depends on continuing efforts to create and maintain sufficient public awareness and concern to bring pressure on Congress and public officials at all levels to make disaster preparedness and hazard mitigation a significant issue.

At an earthquake preparedness meeting in Little Rock, Arkansas, in 1983, the emergency managers of the State of Kentucky and of Memphis agreed that any immediate attempt to get support for earthquake hazard zoning and retrofitting of seismic risk buildings would receive little political support; they worried that if such an effort were begun at that time, the whole cause of earthquake preparedness in the Mississippi Valley would be actually set back. But they agreed that they could start raising a new generation of voters who would be knowledgeable about earthquake risks and who would eventually pressure their representatives to do what needs to be done.

Their approach is probably correct. Only if we take the long view—to build a constituency for the future—will there exist the political support to institute broad hazard response and mitigation programs when the nation's economy is better able to support them.

REFERENCES

American Red Cross
1986   "Disaster Services Regulations and Procedures, the Red Cross Disaster Program." ARC 3002. Washington, D.C.: American Red Cross.
Association of State Floodplain Managers
1982   Annual Meeting Proceedings. Madison, Wis.: Association of State Floodplain Managers.
Bourgin, Frank R.
1983   A History of Federal Disaster Relief Legislation, 1950–1974. Washington, D.C.: Federal Emergency Management Agency.
Buckingham, Clyde
1977   Clara Barton. Alexandria, Va.: Mt. Vernon Publishing.
Burton, Ian, Kates, Robert, and White, Gilbert
1978   Environment as Hazard. New York: Oxford University Press.
Drabek, Thomas E.
1987   The Professional Emergency Manager: Structures and Strategies for Success. Boulder: University of Colorado, Institute of Behavioral Science.
Federal Emergency Management Agency (FEMA)
1985   Interagency Hazard Mitigation Report. FEMA–785–DR. Washington, D.C.: FEMA.

1987   Letter to author concerning disaster statistics.

Kunreuther, Howard, and Dacy, Douglas

1969   *The Economics of Natural Disaster*. New York: Free Press.

Kusler, Jon

1982   *Innovation in Local Flood Plain Management: A Summary of Community Experience*. NHRAIC special publication no. 4. Boulder: University of Colorado, Institute of Behavioral Science.

Lash, Douglas

1985   "Retrofitting Future Flood Losses." Paper presented at the International Symposium of Housing and Urban Development after Natural Disasters, October 23, 1985, Washington, D.C.

May, Peter J.

1985   *Recovering from Catastrophes: Federal Disaster Relief Policy and Politics*. Westport, Conn.: Greenwood Press.

Mileti, Dennis, Popkin, Roy, and Farhar, Barbara

1985   "Unmet Needs of Disaster Victims." Fort Collins: Colorado State University, Hazards Assessment Laboratory.

National Science Foundation

1980   *A Report on Flood Hazard Mitigation*. Washington, D.C.: National Science Foundation.

Norton, Clark F.

1978   *Emergency Preparedness and Disaster Assistance: Federal Organization and Programs*. Washington, D.C.: Congressional Research Service.

Office of Technology Assessment

1978   *Issues and Options in Flood Hazards Management*. Washington, D.C.: Office of Technology Assessment.

Popkin, Roy S.

1986   "Do Environmental Disasters Have a Good Side?" *EPA Journal* (March): 18–20.

Rossi, Peter H., Wright, James D., and Weber-Burdin, Eleanor

1982   *Natural Hazards and Public Choice: The State and Local Politics of Hazard Mitigation*. New York: Academic Press.

Rossi, Peter J., Wright, James D., and Weber-Burdin, Eleanor

1983   *Victims of the Environment: Loss from Natural Hazards in the United States 1970–1980*. New York: Plenum Press.

Rubin, Claire B.

1985   *Community Recovery from a Major Natural Disaster*. Boulder: University of Colorado, Institute of Behavioral Science.

Vinso, Joseph D.

1977   "Financial Implications of Natural Disasters: Some Preliminary Indications." *Mass Emergencies* 2(4): 205–17.

CHAPTER 6

Human Dimensions of Environmental Hazards

Complexity, Disparity, and the Search for Guidance

James K. Mitchell

In the last decade of the twentieth century, it is appropriate to take stock of research on the human dimensions of environmental hazards. There are three reasons for doing so. First, these hazards are no longer viewed as separately manageable threats external to society. They are now recognized as components of a major problematic—a complex web of interactions among peoples, environments, and technologies, characterized by multiple causes and consequences—that calls forth new types of intellectual and managerial responses. Second, the international scientific community is embarking on ambitious programs designed to provide the scientific basis for managing environmental hazards well into the next century. A review of what has already been learned about the human aspects of hazards can serve as a yardstick for assessing the prospects of proposed actions. Finally, nearly fifty years have elapsed since early studies of human response to environmental hazards were undertaken. Although subdivisions of the field have been reviewed periodically (White 1973; Mitchell 1974; 1984; Covello and Mumpower 1985; Whyte 1986; O'Riordan 1986; Drabek 1986a; Quarantelli 1986a), no comparative assessment of work in different subfields, or of broad developments in the entire subject, has yet been published.

What follows is not a full-blown review of research on people and environmental hazards. Rather it is an attempt to identify major trends and issues, to assess their implications, and to suggest some productive directions for future development of the field. Particular attention is paid to conceptual and theoretical developments, and to the role of human responses. I argue that the dominant characteristics of research on persons and hazards are complexity and disparity, accompanied by a search for guidance. Complexity stems from the nature of the hazards addressed. Disparity occurs in the variety of interpretations offered. The search for guidance is driven by an awareness of the need to devise rules for choosing among diverse contributions and the need for better organization of the intellectual domain if there is to be more effective use of hazards research knowledge to combat mounting hazard management problems.

ENVIRONMENTAL HAZARDS AS COMPLEX PHENOMENA

Environmental hazards are interactive phenomena that arise when instruments with the potential to cause loss come into contact with persons, property, or resources, thereby threatening life, emotional security, material welfare, and societal institutions. The degree of hazard can be expressed conceptually as a function of risk, exposure, vulnerability, and response:

Hazard = f (Risk × Exposure × Vulnerability × Response)

Risk is defined as the probability of a damaging event or circumstance. Exposure is a measure of the population at risk. Vulnerability is the potential for experiencing loss. Response is the degree to which society acts to reduce, avoid, or prevent loss. Hazards result from various combinations of these factors. Sometimes it is the rare physical event that produces catastrophe. But low probability risks may pose few threats if only small numbers of individuals are exposed, if those at risk have ample resources to rebound from loss, and if they are well protected. Likewise, in some societies, small departures from normal conditions may trigger disasters, whereas other societies may possess effective strategies for adjusting to much more extreme conditions. In short, hazards are *relative*, rather than *absolute*, phenomena. To paraphrase Zimmerman's famous description of natural resources, "hazards are not; they become" (Zimmerman 1933).

It is customary to divide environmental hazards into two groups: natural hazards and technological hazards. The former involve unusual or extreme geological, meteorological, hydrological, or biological processes (e.g., earthquakes, floods, drought, epidemic diseases). Technological hazards include potentially dangerous facilities, materials, processes, or systems created by human beings (e.g., nuclear power stations, toxic wastes). Although this is a convenient classification, it is an oversimplification. Inasmuch as hazards are interactive phenomena that involve persons and physical risk agents, it is misleading to adopt a classification based solely on criteria of physical risk. Natural and technological hazards both reflect interactions among populations, environments, and technologies, albeit in different mixtures and combinations.

Critics also argue that persons who must cope with the practical effects of hazard find that a causal distinction between natural and technological hazards is meaningless. Householders at risk, emergency managers, land use planners, and structural engineers are more likely to be concerned with developing the capacity to manage similar impacts, without being unduly concerned that they spring from different causes (Quarantelli 1986a; National Research Council 1983).

Finally, for many persons the most salient environmental hazards are complex "megaproblems" that blend natural, technological, and social risks (e.g., hunger, disease, and poverty). Bearing these objections in mind, I have retained the distinction between natural and technological hazards only because it has long been used by hazards researchers and has therefore affected the intellectual development of the field (Kasperson and Pijawka 1985).

Solzhenitsyn has observed that Americans have an almost obsessive interest in the subject of hazards and the desire to protect against them (Solzhenitsyn 1980). It is an interest that is increasingly shared by the residents of other countries. Formerly little-known places like Tangshan, Armero, Seveso, Bhopal, and Chernobyl are now widely recognized as the sites of acute disasters. Elsewhere, the impacts of chronic environmental hazards like drought, desertification, soil degradation, deforestation, and acid precipitation grow worse. Public health and pollution hazards that attend the production, use, and disposal of new chemicals and genetic materials are also increasingly evident. The AIDS pandemic constitutes yet another environmental hazard about which there is growing concern. Beyond these, just visible on the horizon, are hazards that threaten to alter life on earth, fundamentally and permanently, within a few generations. These include atmospheric warming, ozone depletion, and sea level rise.

Finally, the earth remains hostage to the potentially devastating environmental consequences of nuclear warfare.

In the last three decades scientific knowledge about the physical basis of environmental hazard has grown substantially. This is due to conceptual advances in the study of plate tectonics, atmospheric circulation, biogeochemical cycles, and ecology, together with the development of new instruments and techniques for gathering information (White 1985; 1987). As a result, it is now possible to identify the existence of systematic relationships among what were once thought of as separate agents of hazard. For example, apparently random variations in the intensity and location of coastal storms may be related to periodic El Nino occurrences and global changes in sea levels. These phenomena, in turn, may reflect long-term variations in sea surface temperatures and the buildup of greenhouse gases in the atmosphere. Thus, coastal erosion and flooding are elements in the first of several nested sets of hazard-related processes. Hazard agents are increasingly studied within macrolevel hazard systems rather than as individual phenomena. However, relatively little is known about physical, chemical, and biological linkages within such systems.

A further consequence of increased scientific knowledge is the discovery of subtle long-term hazards that affect the integrity of global life support systems rather than the immediate safety of persons and property. Termed "elusive" hazards (Kates 1985), the interaction of technologies and natural systems is a critically important process in their development. Among others these include: global atmospheric warming, acid precipitation, depletion of the stratospheric ozone layer, sea level rise, erosion of gene pools, soil degradation, deforestation, and desertification. They are cumulative, diffuse, and slow acting. The full extent of their impacts is mainly felt at regional and global scales rather than solely in local communities. Often these hazards can be detected only by sophisticated instruments. Other types of elusive hazards are also being uncovered at the opposite end of the geographic scale. For example, it has been found that poorly ventilated buildings are a major air pollution hazard, especially when they contain open fires used for cooking and heating. Women and children in developing nations are at particularly high risk (Smith 1988).

The basic concept of hazard as an interactive phenomenon is often not readily grasped, even by those who study hazards. Elusive hazards are particularly difficult to address. The trend toward conceptualizing physical risks in the form of hierarchical systems complicates understanding. But the complexities do not end there. Increasingly, researchers are becoming aware of the need to address hazards on an entirely different level of analysis. Like hunger, pollution, disease, and similar ills, environmental hazards are phenomena that involve the interaction of many aggregate stresses operating on many different temporal and spatial scales. Such complex bundles are referred to as problematics, syndromes, or concatenations (Currey and Hugo 1984; Clark 1986). Perhaps the most all-encompassing conception of this type is the Great Climacteric.

It has been suggested that we live in the culminating phase of an age of multiple crises—a Great Climacteric that began two hundred years ago with the coming of the Industrial Revolution (Burton and Kates 1986). Since then a massive transformation has been in progress, overturning traditional societies, fracturing established ways of organizing livelihoods and human tenure of the earth, and replacing them with new formations that are still evolving.

Although specific causes vary and other factors are at work, many of the global crises that now confront us can be viewed as offshoots of this process. Such crises include resource scarcity, ecological disruption, economic inequality, and political upheaval. Burgeoning environmental hazards also reflect the broader transformation. A "risk transition" is under way (Smith 1988). This is characterized by gradual reduction of some localized traditional hazards (e.g., waterborne infectious diseases), widespread increases in modern technology-based hazards, and the emergence of a new class of universal risks (e.g., global atmospheric changes: Mitchell 1988b).

Like the better-known "demographic transition" and its close counterpart, the "health transition," the risk transition may produce a new risk equilibrium in the future, characterized by a different mix and burden of risks than the present. Some observers contend that complex technological systems are inherently subject to failure (Perrow 1984). If the adoption of new technologies continues at its present rapid pace throughout the world, it will be very difficult to reduce the aggregate burden of environmental hazards.

Clearly, such hazards are exceedingly complex phenomena that have the potential to tax existing analytic capacities. To address them, it is necessary to take into consideration knowledge about natural systems, social systems, and about interactions between the two. As the preceding discussion suggests, knowledge about the natural components of environmental hazards has expanded rapidly in recent years. Have similar changes affected fields that address the human dimensions of hazard?

James K. Mitchell

THE HUMAN DIMENSIONS OF HAZARDS RESEARCH:
AN OVERVIEW

The roots of research on human aspects of hazards go back many centuries but most of the work has occurred during the past several decades (Covello and Mumpower 1985). A single comprehensive integrated body of studies pertaining to the human dimensions of hazard does not yet exist (Douglas 1985). Instead, the bulk of research has occurred in three distinct subfields: disaster research, natural hazards research, and risk analysis.

Disaster Research

The goal of disaster research is to provide knowledge about group behavior and social life under stress conditions (Quarantelli, Dynes, and Wenger 1986). This is usually accomplished by field interviews and by direct observation in postdisaster settings. Disaster research is widely regarded as a branch of sociology but important contributions have been made by psychologists, psychiatrists, and anthropologists (e.g., Wolfenstein 1957). The sociological perspective of symbolic interactionism has guided most studies, and organizational behavior during disasters has been a major theme (Quarantelli 1986b). Some researchers view disasters as subjects worthy of study in their own right, while others contend that they are valuable "social laboratories" for the analysis of stressful societal processes. However, the bulk of disaster research has a strong applied character and few theoretical models of social change have been formulated (Moore and Feldman 1962).

Disaster research did not emerge as an organized field until the 1950s, but several earlier contributions are worth noting. These include Prince's pathbreaking investigation of societal response to a munitions explosion in Halifax, Nova Scotia, during World War I (Prince 1920); Sorokin's broad analyses of wars, famines, and other societal catastrophes (Sorokin 1937; 1941), and studies of the effects of strategic bombing on civilian morale in Germany and Japan during World War II (U.S. Strategic Bombing Survey 1947a,b).

The U.S. Army has supported a number of American field teams that collected data on responses to natural and technological disasters during peacetime. Reflecting contemporary Cold War concerns, most of this research sought information likely to be useful in the control of wartime emergencies. These studies led to a Committee on Disaster Studies (1951–57) in the U.S. National Academy of Sciences (NAS) and a Disaster Research Group (1957–62). Both bodies continued the practice of gathering and publishing field information about postdisaster behavior in this and, occasionally, in other countries. When the Disaster Research Center was established at Ohio State University in 1963, the principal NAS disaster researchers transferred there, and it became the field's leading institution. The Center subsequently moved to the University of Delaware in 1984.

From 1948 to 1963, U.S. military and civil defense agencies provided most of the funding for disaster research. The military is no longer a major client, but the field retains a strong bias toward practical problems of interest to federal agencies, and much knowledge has been gathered concerning human behavior in the face of extreme stresses. A survey of publications during the past decade provides information on the distribution of research effort among different topics in disaster research (Drabek 1986b). The survey indicates percentages of studies, conclusions, and specific findings that apply to various disaster phases and social system levels. Individual, community, and organizational behavior continue to be the most favored and fruitful research topics. As in the past, most attention is directed to the response phase of disasters but Drabek believes that the growing body of work on recovery processes and disaster mitigation adjustments represents an extension of disaster research into new subject areas (Drabek 1986a: 413). Judged by the references he cites, it seems more likely that there is increasing collaboration and convergence between disaster researchers and others working in the related traditions of natural hazard research and risk analysis where such topics have long been studied.

Obvious gaps in disaster research remain to be filled. For example, few cross-societal and comparative studies of human response have been undertaken. Despite the fact that major strides have been made in documenting and interpreting postdisaster behavior, as well as in applying findings to modify disaster response programs, researchers are uneasy about the theoretical and conceptual bases of their field.

There has recently been an upsurge of interest in the definition of the central concept of disaster. According to one authority, finding an answer to the question "What is a disaster?" is "by far the most important task currently facing the field of disaster studies" (Quarantelli 1986a). After many decades of work there is no consensus; rather there is a great deal of confusion and contradiction about the nature of the phenomena under investigation. In addition to a redefinition of the concept of disaster, there is a need to place disasters in a larger framework. However, disaster researchers are cautioned not to substitute the term—or the concept—"hazards." The labels "risk situations" or "crises" are judged preferable to "hazards."

Natural Hazards Research

The genesis and status of natural hazards research has been well reported elsewhere (e.g., Mitchell 1984; Whyte 1986). Natural hazard researchers employ human ecological perspectives to investigate the interaction of human and nonhuman factors that generate, sustain, exacerbate, or mitigate hazards in geologic, meteorologic, hydrologic, and biologic systems (Whyte 1986). In other words, they examine the "goodness of fit" of the human use of the earth in the face of constraints imposed by its constituent physical processes. Variations in the severity of environmental hazards from place to place reflect the degree to which human activities are incompletely adjusted to such constraints. The degree of adjustment reflects the effects of inadvertent and deliberate human actions as well as the operation of extreme natural processes, and natural hazards researchers integrate information from both the natural and the social sciences.

The field is now in its fifth decade of existence. It grew out of attempts by geographers to explain the continuing failure of U.S. flood control policies to curb losses despite heavy investments in physical science research and engineering protection programs. During the 1940s and 50s most conventional analyses of flooding considered it a physical phenomenon that could best be dealt with by physical means. Flood probabilities and structural engineering responses were regarded as the principal factors that affect hazard; the attributes of human exposure and vulnerability were neglected. Oversimple characterizations of hazard still exist and are reflected in some of the arguments advanced to support proposals for heavy investment in physical science and engineering research during the forthcoming International Decade of Natural Disaster Reduction (Mitchell 1988a).

Under the direction of Gilbert F. White, the principles of natural hazards research were developed at the University of Chicago (Platt 1986). Researchers first focused attention on exposure, as reflected in the human occupance of floodplains. They pointed out that it is influenced by many nonphysical factors, including demands for the use of floodplain resources, the availability of alternatives, human assessments of flood risk, and judgments about the efficacy of flood protection works. Thus, human perceptions of risk and behavior in the face of risk play important roles in the creation of hazard. Subsequently, psychologists, economists, and other behavioral scientists have joined with geographers to develop the theoretical bases of the field around concepts of decision-making in the face of uncertainty (Fischhoff et al. 1981). Natural hazards research now encompasses a wide range of natural and technological hazards throughout the world (Burton, Kates, and White 1978; Kates 1978).

Many natural hazards researchers maintain close working relationships with hazard managers. Research findings are often directed toward the improvement of public policy. Because hazards are interpreted as joint products of human actions and natural processes, improvements in management can be achieved by changing the human or nonhuman components of hazard. In the case of persons at risk from flooding, managers may opt to permit victims to bear the losses or redistribute them by means of relief or insurance schemes. Conversely, they may reduce losses by keeping floods away from human populations (e.g., building levees, seeding hurricanes); by keeping populations away from floods (e.g., restricting the use of flood-prone areas, establishing warning systems); or by a combination of different types of measures (e.g., engineering works and insurance, warning and relief systems, comprehensive floodplain management).

Early research often generated recommendations for expanding the range of management alternatives available to persons at risk. Frequently this involved the manipulation of factors that affect exposure and the integration of previously separate adjustments into packages composed of mutually reinforcing alternatives (e.g., National Flood Insurance Program; comprehensive floodplain management). More recently, researchers have also turned attention to factors that influence collective vulnerability to loss and they have uncovered serious limitations to human freedom of action, especially in poor societies that lack the resources necessary to permit optimal management strategies (Hewitt 1983). Some explanations now seek to elucidate a variety of structural and contextual relations in which hazards are embedded. With the advent of contributions by sociologists, anthropologists, and political scientists, the field has also taken on a more varied philosophical coloring. It now includes various positivist, materialist, and pragmatist research "schools" (Wescoat 1987; Blaikie and Brookfield 1987; Hewitt 1983).

James K. Mitchell

Risk Analysis

Risk analysis is the youngest, and perhaps the largest, of the three main subdivisions of research on the human dimensions of hazards. It is primarily concerned with the identification, measurement, and evaluation of risks. Here the term "risk" refers both to the frequency and severity of threatening events (Lowrance 1976: 70). Although the principles of risk analysis apply to natural threats like earthquakes, most of the work to date has focused on engineering and health risks of nonnatural threats, such as toxic chemicals. As illustrated by recent events at Three Mile Island (1979), Mexico City (1984), Bhopal (1984), and Chernobyl (1986), the benefits of modern technology are accompanied by major hazards. Potentially hazardous technologies are rapidly being adopted throughout the world and there is an acute lack of information upon which to base risk management decisions.

Early work in risk analysis grew out of the need to establish the reliability of technologies and products before marketing and to meet regulatory standards for safety. For example, in the United States at the end of the nineteenth century, the Underwriters Laboratory was set up to undertake systematic testing of electrical equipment as a means for reducing losses caused by fires in buildings (Mehr and Cammack 1976). Later, governmental agencies were created to perform similar tests on food additives, drugs, and consumer appliances.

Testing programs can reveal some risks but they suffer from several limitations. For example, some observers challenge the validity of extrapolating the results of tests on laboratory animals to determine whether drugs or other materials are safe for use by humans. Similarly, it is often impossible to test particularly risky technologies to the point of failure because society is unwilling to bear the negative consequences. Therefore, initial assessments must rest on various surrogate measures of risk and on probabilistic risk data derived from modeling experiments.

Probability theory has strongly influenced the philosophy and methodology of risk analysis (Covello and Mumpower 1985). This is clearly reflected in the influential Reactor Safety Study (WASH 1400), authored by Norman Rasmussen (U.S. Atomic Energy Commission 1974). The type of "fault tree analysis" used by Rasmussen was pioneered by engineers who worked on military and space research, and was later adapted for civilian use in the U.S. nuclear power industry. WASH-1400 is a benchmark study because it developed a probabilistic risk assessment methodology that could be used to quantify risks of failure of a complex innovative technology before it is placed in operation.

Unfortunately, probabilistic risk assessments are themselves beset by limitations (Lowrance 1986). For example, it has proven difficult to identify all potential types of failure and to allow for the effects of synergistic failures among different subcomponents of large systems. Behavioral factors also complicate risk analysis. Despite the fact that very low probability events are—by definition—unlikely, individuals tend to exhibit greatly heightened concern about those that also have potentially catastrophic consequences (e.g., nuclear accidents).

Interest in the human dimensions of risk has been spurred by the question: "How safe is safe enough?" An engineer with experience of the electricity generating industry, Chauncy Starr, sought quantitative measures of the acceptability of risk by examining relationships between the number of deaths incurred in different jobs or activities and the associated economic benefits (Starr 1969). This has been dubbed the "revealed preference" approach to risk assessment. Later analysts introduced an alternative approach based on legal requirements and other social indicators (i.e., "implied preferences"). Starr's article emerged at a time when many worried about health and safety risks of nuclear pollution. Public interest in environmental quality began to wane during the late 1970s, but concern about technological hazards has remained strong, partly due to the reinforcing action of major industrial accidents.

During the last two decades, social science perspectives have begun to influence the field of risk analysis. It has been shown that there are wide variations in mental models of risk, including judgments of risk and criteria of risk acceptability (Fischhoff et al. 1981; Bogen and Spear 1987; McDaniels 1988). As a result, some risks are subject to considerable "social amplification" whereas others are underestimated (Kasperson et al. 1988). It has also been argued that risk perception and risk communication are deeply embedded in the structure of cultures and that these influences are reflected in the wide variety of institutional arrangements for coping with risk in different groups (Douglas 1966; Douglas and Wildavsky 1982; Kunreuther and Ley 1982). An increasing number of papers in the journal *Risk Analysis* have begun to treat considerations of social justice and other issues of ethics (Keeney 1984; Keller and Sarin 1988). These contributions call into question some of the assumptions of existing hazard management systems.

For example, the NAS has suggested that risk assessment and risk management are overlapping but separate tasks—one predominantly scientific and the other primarily legal, political, and administrative (National Research Council 1983). This interpretation has drawn strong opposition from those who argue that it is impossible to disentangle societal values from the process of identifying, estimating, and evaluating risks (Douglas 1985; Raynor and Cantor 1987).

Unlike disaster research and natural hazard research—both of which inform the work of public bodies, but are mainly carried on by academics —risk analysis practices are being systematically adopted by bureaucratic organizations. Several factors have combined to encourage its use as a procedure in public decision-making. Inquiries into spectacular disasters have turned up evidence of inadequate consideration of risks in existing technological systems: a recent report on the space shuttle Challenger concluded that the U.S. space program places too much reliance on subjective judgments and too little on formal risk assessment methods (Marshall 1988). Legislation frequently creates opportunities for expanding the field by calling for explicit consideration of risks in technology management practices (Poje 1988). Industries and government agencies involved with hazards provide ready-made constituencies for risk analysis expertise. Information about risks is often used by governments to evaluate proposals for the development of oil refineries and chemical plants (Snowball and Macgill 1984; Health and Safety Executive 1978; 1981) and the insurance industry requires systematic assessment of risks for the purposes of setting premiums and coverage limits (Friedman 1984). The "scientific" nature of risk analysis, complete with specialized terminology, mathematical equations, computer simulation models, laboratory experiments, and the like, lends itself to professionalization.

A Society for Risk Analysis has been formed to encourage communication and a sense of mutual identification among the several disciplines that are involved. At least in North America and Western Europe, risk analysis is becoming an aid to decision-making comparable to environmental impact assessment and technology assessment (Chrostowski, Pearsall, and Shaw 1985). Much less is known about risks in developing countries and centralized economies (Inhaber 1985; Karen, Bladen, and Wilson 1986).

COMPLEXITIES OF RESEARCH ON THE
HUMAN ASPECTS OF HAZARDS

Scientific knowledge of the physical bases and the human dimensions of environmental hazards reflects the complexity of the phenomena under investigation, but stems also from the different research agendas, perspectives, and methods of natural science and social science.

Contrasting Global Perspectives on Hazard

The natural sciences and the social sciences have adopted different conceptions of the global environment. These are reflected in Gabriel Garcia Marquez's apt phrase: "One Earth, Many Worlds" (Marquez 1986). Natural scientists increasingly view the Earth as a single system, and great progress has been made toward determining the system's characteristics (Malone 1986). Global models in the social sciences tend to break down into separate regional components: core/periphery; East-West; North/South; First, Second, Third, and Fourth Worlds (i.e., Many Worlds).

Most global models of society do not take explicit account of environmental factors, or tend to generalize from spatially limited samples. This has been well documented by Kates with reference to the first general theory of resource scarcity (Kates 1987a). Malthus based his formulation of the relationship between population and resources on his experience in one English parish. A century later, other scholars were making generalizations about scarcity using evidence drawn from an entire country. By the middle of the twentieth century, scarcity problems could be analyzed with data from subglobal regions, and within the past decade, the first models of scarcity based on global data have been formulated. As better information has become available from more areas, interpretations have become more complicated, to the point where it is now extremely difficult to make useful generalizations about scarcity at the global scale.

This finding also applies to studies of environmental hazards. Global information about risks and hazards is still incomplete, although geographic information systems with risk monitoring capabilities have been established (e.g., the U.N. Environment Program's Global Environmental Monitoring System—GEMS, and the related Global Resources Information Directory—GRID). There is already a great variety of subglobal models, each one based on a different set of premises and applied to a distinctive environment with a unique history of human use. For example, there are striking differences between conceptions of environmental constraints on society in Amazonia and Southeast Asia (Hutterer, Rambo, and Lovelace 1985).

In short, human ecological models of global environmental problems are likely to be constructed from the "bottom up," whereas natural science models are often formulated from the "top down." Finding ways to bridge the conceptual gap between the two is increasingly recognized as a major task (Los' 1986; Santos 1984), as is the need for greater knowledge. Information about natural hazards in developing nations is improving, but very little is known about technological hazards in the Third World (Inhaber 1985; Minor, Kawamura, and Lynes, 1986).

Lags in the Acquisition of Knowledge about Human Aspects of New Hazards.

Research on the human aspects of newly developing "elusive" hazards like global atmospheric warming has tended to lag behind work on their physical aspects. Apart from an extensive literature on human aspects of climatic change (Kates, Ausubel, and Berberian 1985), a few studies of soil degradation and erosion (Karan 1987; Blaikie 1985), and one volume that briefly considers human responses to the environmental consequences of nuclear war (Harwell and Hutchinson 1985), very little attention has been paid to human aspects of the vast suite of cumulative, long-term hazards that operate at regional and global scales. Not only are these hazards fundamentally different from the more familiar sudden onset/short duration hazards, they have the potential to undermine global habitability within a few generations.

To make matters worse, there is increasing evidence that it may take many years before changes in emphasis at the research frontier filter down to students. Most of the dissertations and theses now being written on hazards topics still reflect the concerns of an earlier phase. For example, between 1980 and 1986, 37 dissertations and 120 theses on environmental hazard topics were completed by American geography students. Fifty (32%) of these dealt with flood or drought; another 50 with other geological or meteorological hazards; 17 (11%) with hazardous industrial facilities and wastes (mainly nuclear); and the remainder with miscellaneous other biological and technological hazards (e.g., pesticides, oil spills, disease). Apart from the aforementioned drought studies and four theses on soil erosion and hunger, elusive hazards were almost totally ignored.

Much of the natural science research on elusive hazards has focused on problems of forecasting. Predicting human behavior is inherently difficult and this may help to account for the slow development of such studies in hazards research (Land and Schneider 1987). Elusive hazards also lack the urgency of more dramatic natural and technological disasters, because their consequences are not immediate or readily evident. Whatever the reason, research on nonhuman aspects of new environmental hazards has proceeded significantly faster and further than research on the human dimensions. This increases the likelihood that public policies for managing new types of hazards will be better informed about scientific and technological fixes than about behavioral fixes. Given the historically poor record of technological approaches to hazard management (ones not well grounded in knowledge about human behavior), this bodes ill for the future.

Neglect of the Human Dimensions of Hazards by Global Science and Technology Programs

There is evidence that important opportunities for cooperation between natural scientists and engineers on the one hand, and social scientists and hazards professionals on the other, are being overlooked or neglected—particularly at the global level. Two ambitious international programs, that together address most of the important global environmental hazards of the present and the foreseeable future, are now in the process of development. The International Geosphere Biosphere Program (IGBP) and the International Decade for Natural Disaster Reduction (IDNDR) are conceived on a grand scale, surpassing anything attempted in the field of international scientific collaboration, and are intended to provide the scientific underpinnings of global hazard management policies in the twenty-first century. As presently structured, neither devotes adequate attention or resources to the human dimensions of hazards.

The IGBP is a massive research initiative to be undertaken by earth scientists and biological scientists throughout the world under the sponsorship of the International Council of Scientific Unions (ICSU). It is intended "to describe and understand the interactive physical, chemical, and biological processes that regulate the total Earth system, the unique environment that it provides for life, the changes that are occurring in that system, and the manner by which these changes are influenced by human actions" (Malone 1986). The IGBP will involve five main program elements: (1) studies of key interactive processes such as biogeochemical cycles; (2) gathering of remotely sensed observations and data; (3) formulation of quantitative models of earth systems; (4) recovery of past environmental histories; and (5) development of a global data and communication system.

Although acknowledged in IGBP documents, the human dimensions of global environmental change are not addressed in proposed research projects. Under the names "Global Change," "Global Geosciences," and "Earth System Sciences," the IGBP has already drawn extensive funding commitments from U.S. agencies such as NASA and the National Science Foundation. There is no explicit reference to environmental hazards in the program's statement of objectives—nor elsewhere in most program documents—but concern about hazards is a basic motivating factor. This is made clear in recent congressional testimony where the IGBP is described as a "deliberate long-term, cost-effective program of international collaborative research that would generate the knowledge base required to deal intelligently with potential hazards" such as "'greenhouse' climatic warming, ozone depletion, acid deposition, deforestation, loss of biological diversity, desertification, and other anthropological impacts on the global environment" (Malone, congressional testimony 1987: 3).

The IGBP is potentially important to hazard researchers and hazards managers, yet in its present form the program lacks a risk assessment component and there is no indication that plans exist for translating the scientific research results into a form that is usable by policy makers, public agencies, and others who most need the information. As a result, much of its value for hazard management purposes will be delayed or lost (Mitchell 1988b). Plans for a Human Response to Global Change (HRGC) program are being developed by a group of organizations that includes the International Federation of Institutes of Advanced Study and the United Nations University, but this may be an entirely separate initiative from the IGBP.

The International Decade for Natural Disaster Reduction (IDNDR) is too likely to be a program of major proportions. It is designed "to provide knowledge and practices [to] reduce catastrophic loss of life, property damage, and social and economic disruption from natural hazards" including "earthquakes, wind storms, floods, tsunamis, landslides, volcanic eruptions, and wildfires" (National Research Council 1987: 2–4). Unfortunately, the IDNDR holds a narrow view of hazard and hazard reduction. The concept of hazard as interaction among physical risks and human responses is largely bypassed in favor of a focus solely on physical risks. Although failing to use *existing* scientific knowledge accounting for many inadequate societal responses to hazard, the program recommends a wide suite of *new* scientific initiatives. The IDNDR proposers have essentially cast aside hard-won experience from hazard research that demonstrates the necessity of mutual collaboration among scientists and users of scientific information.

In perhaps the program's most glaring flaw, no attempt is made to take hazards and hazards reduction into account in the context of economic development (Mitchell 1988b). Yet development of land and resources provides the chief stimulus to rising losses associated with natural hazards, and any hazard reduction program that hopes to make a significant dent in losses cannot afford to ignore them.

In short, both the IGBP and the IDNDR represent blueprints for a generation of global scientific research. They rest on expansive and optimistic assumptions about the role of natural science and engineering knowledge in the hazards policy arena. Unfortunately, both endeavors are poorly informed or influenced by the knowledge accumulated on the human dimensions of hazards since the end of World War II.

DISPARATE INTERPRETATIONS OF
HUMAN RESPONSES TO HAZARD

Theoretical and conceptual diversity is the hallmark of modern scholarship (Laudan 1984). To some it is a sign of intellectual health (Walker 1987); to others a cause for criticism. A few equate the existence of many different kinds of explanations with failure of the capacity to distinguish between sound and weak scholarship. In a critique of American higher education, Bloom considers that the bewildering diversity of contributions to knowledge stems from penetration of intellectual discourse by social mores that emphasize tolerance at the expense of making discriminating judgments (Bloom 1987). Some of those who accept this line of reasoning argue that failure to choose among alternative theorems leads to an overemphasis on uncertainty and to prescriptions for minimal change. It is not necessary to agree with Bloom's argument to realize that the existence of different modes of analysis poses difficulties for those who use scientific knowledge. Analysts, and more importantly, managers, may be unable to choose among competing interpretations.

For example, a team that recently investigated declining environmental quality in the Himalayas reported that experts cannot agree about what is wrong. Certainly, the problem includes deforestation, landslides, floods, heavy population pressure, and a host of other factors, many of which can be described as hazards. More to the point, "the problem . . . is that there is not a problem but a multiplicity of contending and contradictory problem definitions each of which takes its shape from the particular social and cultural context that it helps to sustain" (Thompson, Warburton, and Hatley 1986).

The complexities that attend the analysis of environmental hazards as physical phenomena and the difficulties of conducting cooperative research that involves both the social and natural sciences, mean that it is not surprising that there are many interpretations of the interactions between human beings and hazards. The next section reviews some of these differences, first in terms of general issues and then in a more detailed case study of recent debates about the human ecology of hazards.

Lay Wisdom

Students of natural hazards have long possessed a high regard for the general public's understanding of the risks it faces and the alternatives it chooses. Indeed, it is something of an article of faith among researchers that "average citizens" are much more capable of assessing and responding to natural hazards than they are given credit for by hazards managers. This is reflected in the popularity of proposals for instituting measures to buttress indigenous responses to hazard in developing nations, or to provide citizens in developed countries with better information about risks and potential adjustments (Klee 1980).

Unfortunately, recent studies have shown that there may be serious limitations to lay knowledge of technological hazards. In a world where new and potentially hazardous technologies are emerging daily, lay persons cannot rely on direct experience to guide decisions about risk, and may employ flawed "heuristics" to assess the likely threats (Fischhoff et al. 1981).

If confirmed by further research, this finding has serious consequences. It appears to strengthen the case for developing a cadre of experts and a range of specialized institutions for managing hazards, and implies that information about lay perceptions of hazard has fewer management applications than was once thought. This conclusion could encourage a reduction in the amount of effort directed toward understanding lay decision-making in the face of hazard.

The Context of Hazard

Should hazards be studied alone as an independent problem set, or are they best regarded as a dependent subset of larger problems? This issue has been present in research on natural hazards from the outset but it is now assuming increased importance. One of the major intellectual contributions of natural hazard research has been to shift the focus of attention from physical risks that threaten persons to the relationship between such risks and human responses. Now it is being argued that it is necessary to extend the concept of hazard to include contexts within which specific hazards are "embedded" (i.e., higher order hazards).

Evidence of the contextual character of hazard is common. Historians, in particular, have pointed to hierarchies of hazard. Among nineteenth-century residents of India, cholera was regarded as just one facet of "a broader catastrophe or cosmic upheaval that from time to time recurred" (Arnold 1986). It was judged to be an aspect of famine or political unrest, both of which were in turn seen as outcomes of colonial conquest. Similarly, natural disasters in southern Italy have often been interpreted— by residents and external observers—as expressions of the conditions of unemployment, isolation, poverty, emigration, and public corruption that constitute "the Southern Question" (Bosworth 1981; Alexander 1985).

In these examples it is relatively easy to recognize several orders of hazard, but hazardous characteristics of other contexts are not so obvious. In many cases, it is not clear how far the definitions of risk should be extended. A broad contextual definition (i.e., one that is grounded in socio-political variables rather than physical risks and human responses) raises especially thorny methodological and ethical problems. For example, should hazards include unpalatable ideologies and threats to human values such as "the risks of coercion, of deprivations of basic human rights, freedom, and dignity; of deprivation of equitable access to resources; of opportunities for self-fulfillment"? (Wenk 1986).

What empirical criteria would be used to distinguish hazardousness of the world's different economic, political, or governmental systems? How would judgments about ethics enter into consideration? Would threats to liberty be considered as serious, or more serious than, threats to life? (Kates 1987b). How shall contexts be analyzed from a hazards viewpoint if they cannot be unambiguously labeled "hazards"? For example, drought-induced food shortages are one specific expression of famine that is itself part of the general problem of hunger. But famine is rarely caused by drought alone; hunger need not involve famine. Changes in agricultural technology, rural development policy, food entitlements, and many other factors—including the political expediency of declaring a disaster—are often visible in developing countries (Brass 1986; Cant 1986; Steitz and Davis 1984). Such factors are not themselves hazards. They are flawed responses to the varied hazards that are commonly lumped together under the heading "underdevelopment."

Inasmuch as hazards are interactive phenomena that involve responses as well as risks, hunger stands revealed as a megahazard. It is a product of interaction among different types of risks (e.g., drought, failures of food conversion and storage technologies, disadvantaged access to resources) that affect human groups that experience varied degrees of exposure, have distinct levels of vulnerability, and practice diverse types of responses. By taking an expansive view of risks and hazards in this manner, it is possible to apply hazards research insights much further afield than originally conceived.

Many questions about the contextual nature of hazards remain to be answered, and it is probable that new investigative strategies will have to be developed. Three alternative ways of proceeding seem possible. Research might move in the direction of multilevel analyses of hazard with each level characterized by its own distinctive methods and concepts (e.g., drought, famine, hunger, scarcity, etc.). This merely continues present research trends and postpones the task of synthesis.

A second strategy might replace the analysis of hazards per se with the analysis of larger contextual problems. A similar suggestion has recently been made about research on international crises, undertaken by students of foreign policy. Haas argues that there is no longer a place for a separate field of international crisis studies but that the work could easily be accommodated under the umbrella of decision-making research (Haas 1986). Unfortunately, when applied to the subject of hazards, this alternative runs the risk of throwing the baby out with the bath water.

A third alternative seems more promising. Researchers might gradually push their investigations out from conventional conceptions of hazards as damaging events along "linkages" that connect with larger or different contexts. Wisner has shown how this might be done by taking account of progressively more spatially and more temporally remote factors that affect soil erosion in Africa (Wisner 1986). In a different but related example, White has characterized a gradually widening circle of hazard processes in Egyptian villages that begins with domestic water shortage, includes considerations of public health, and ends with the issue of empowering women to make decisions about their safety and the welfare of their children (White 1987). A further version of this approach is to view hazards as occurring at temporal or spatial "intersections" of different physical and human processes that may or may not proceed independently at other times and places.

The several variants of the third strategy all point toward more precise analysis of expanded hazard systems.

Hazard Ethics

Criteria of social justice used by hazards policy makers have an important bearing on the management of hazards. During the early years of research on human responses to hazard, issues of social justice went largely unexplored. The field focused on the decision-making processes of individual property owners threatened by natural hazards, and most analysts assumed a broadly humanitarian and utilitarian stance. As evidenced by the widespread use of cost-benefit analysis and related tools, the primary objective was to reduce losses, irrespective of distributional considerations.

Interest in issues of equity, fairness, and justice emerged as hazards research focused on new topics: institutional decision-making, sociopolitical and economic consequences of hazard, and, especially, technological threats. When industrial accidents or environmental contaminants produce hazards, humans can be held responsible both for creating the risks and for failing to provide protection for those on whom the risks are imposed. The concept of responsibility took on importance as increasing evidence of human contributions to natural hazards was uncovered. Floods are a hazard not simply because human populations occupy natural floodplains; flood regimes and floodplain geometry can be changed by both deliberate or inadvertent human agency. Precipitation and geological structure may predispose a hillside to failure but vegetation clearance, fires, and construction practices often trigger subsequent landslides. Recognition of substantial human capacity to alter natural risks is one reflection of a broader reassessment of human roles in the transformation of the globe (O'Riordan 1988).

This realization has produced far-reaching consequences, including a substantial weakening of legal arguments that natural hazards are "acts of God." However, there is disagreement about the scale of human intervention, which has led to continuing debates on the proper interpretation of data about the changing hazardousness of the earth (Shah 1983; Wijkman and Timberlake 1984; Thompson 1982; O'Riordan 1986). Depending on which of several interpretations of hazard are used, the most serious hazards are located either in the poorest and least developed societies that lack resources to reduce the vulnerability of exposed populations, or in nations of modest wealth that are undergoing rapid development capable of destabilizing existing hazard management systems (Little, Horowitz, and Nyerges 1987).

Growing acceptance of the concept that humans are responsible for at least some natural hazards, as well as all technological hazards, has strengthened interest in the establishment of criteria for responsible decision-making (*Law and Contemporary Problems* 1986). A risk-free society is unobtainable and hazard is implicit in all human endeavors, but it is still necessary to resolve the questions "Who shall bear what level of hazard?" and "How shall the costs and benefits of hazards management be distributed?" The search for answers has directed attention to philosophies of distributive justice, which is implicit in comparative international studies of legal mechanisms for managing hazard.

Despite the fact that elitists, utilitarians, egalitarians, and libertarians set out somewhat different criteria for just responses to hazard, it is clear that all the basic philosophies of justice assume society has an obligation to protect citizens. Although libertarians grant the state a right to intervene only to protect populations at risk from human acts that adversely change the degree of hazard, all philosophies of justice are converging on the use of a "social minimum" criterion for defining unacceptable hazard (Sterba 1986).

The topic of social justice is one aspect of the broader subject of ethics now beginning to receive serious scrutiny, and the number of publications is expanding rapidly (Sauer 1982; Wildavsky 1982; Elster 1985; *Ethics* 1985; Ives 1985; McKerlie 1986; Von Magnus 1984; Thompson 1984; Robinson 1986; Lemons 1983). Society pays most attention to ethical problems during hard times (Caplan and Callahan 1981), and these are partly defined by the number and depth of the "moral crises" that occur. To a significant extent, the upsurge of interest in hazard ethics is a function of "hard times" in hazards research. Researchers are burdened by a large number of complex issues they are not readily able to resolve. Hazards management is correspondingly impaired. However, those who look to ethics for help in resolving these problems are likely to be frustrated. Many different codes of environmental ethics exist (Tobin 1985) and there are strong differences among nations about the primacy of particular public and private values (Kates and Burton 1986).

In any event, ethical guidelines are difficult to formulate for abstract or hypothetical situations. Ethical considerations are likely to be different for private individuals and public officials (Kluge 1986). It is also unlikely that ethical assessments can be applied to risk assessment techniques or hazard analysis methods; each specific application will have to be judged by itself (Keeney 1984). Indeed, ethics scholars appear to agree that it is unwise to assess values divorced from the contexts in which they are applied (Weston 1985). Finally, Stone (1987) has suggested that the intellectual frameworks used to study ethical issues are in crisis and are inadequate to the task. Just as hazards are part of larger problematics, ethical issues are embedded in multiple conflicts whose resolution requires the development of new paradigms.

A CASE STUDY OF CONCEPTUAL DISPARITY: HUMAN ECOLOGICAL PERSPECTIVES ON HAZARDS

In light of the preceding discussion about risk perception, ethics, and contexts, it is no wonder that contemporary writings on hazards are marked by disparate explanations of human responses. It is not possible to examine all such explanations in detail but a case study of recent debates among scholars in the human ecology tradition of geography is instructive. Here, two distinct sets of theoretical and ideological perspectives are apparent. One highlights decision-making processes; the other, issues of political economy. These perspectives have played different roles in the interpretation of natural hazards on the one hand and technological hazards on the other.

James K. Mitchell

Natural Hazards

Natural hazards research has been strongly influenced by a decision-making perspective rooted in behavioral science. It attempts to explain how persons act in the face of hazard and focuses on boundedly rational choices among alternative adjustments to hazard under conditions of uncertainty. Some researchers have explored choices made by individuals at risk, paying particular attention to perceptual and behavioral factors that mediate the decision process (Mitchell 1984). Others have viewed hazard from the standpoint of professional managers who are either responsible for protecting potential victims or whose decisions can affect the safety of populations at risk. In the latter studies, institutional constraints on choice are paramount (Palm et al. 1983; 1985). Several models of hazard adjustment have also been formulated during the course of this work (Kates 1970; Mileti 1980).

A political economy perspective is also evident in natural hazards research. It emphasizes the elaboration of processes that create and maintain hazardous conditions. Here the view is that hazard is largely a reflection of structural inequalities within society. It is argued that victims of hazard are disproportionately found among groups in peripheral Third World nations that are becoming increasingly dependent due to the penetration of political and economic systems based in core regions.

There are a number of variants of this basic thesis: some emphasize the importance of maintaining indigenous systems for anticipating and responding to hazard as alternatives to government sponsored disaster relief and hazard mitigation schemes (Cuny 1983; Klee 1980; Richards 1986). Others address broad regional variations of vulnerability to hazard in terms of uneven access to resources (Hills 1982). A few have outlined long-term changes in patterns of hazard (Richards 1985). However, the chief differences among the various political economy studies derive from the fact that different conditions obtain in different parts of the world. Thus, there are subtle but significant differences among theories of hazard based on political economy applied to Latin America, sub-Saharan Africa, Southeast Asia, East Asia, and Oceania.

Perhaps because it emphasizes the evaluation of alternatives that confront persons at risk, the decision-making perspective finds ready application as an aid to natural hazards policy-making and management. Insofar as advocates of the political economy perspective sometimes effect radical critiques of socio-political and economic arrangements, that approach is less commonly adopted by agencies and institutions with hazard management responsibilities. Decision-making models have been successfully used to explain responses to hazard in many of the more developed nations and in segments of the Third World where problems of day-to-day survival have been overcome. They have been less successful when applied to the poorest nations where the acquisition of food and water, shelter, employment, and other necessities is a preeminent daily task.

A few critics have charged that the decision-making perspective is intrinsically flawed because it fails to address the larger socio-political context in which hazard occurs (Marston 1983). This type of criticism misses the point that such research does not ignore contexts; it usually assumes that a person or an institution at risk to hazard is capable of taking into account a multiplicity of contexts that would overwhelm the interpretive power of any more general theory of societal dynamics or institutional behavior. Moreover, much of the critique is misleading because it fails to take account of contrasts in the salience of different types of hazards in more developed and less developed countries. Scholars of decision-making have focused a great deal of attention on the occasional storms and industrial accidents that loom large on the roster of hazards in developed countries but—until recently—they devoted less effort to the salient hazards of less developed countries, where primary hazards include hunger, lack of potable water, and disease. As demonstrated by recent path-breaking work on domestic water supply decisions of individual householders and farmers in East Africa and Egypt, the decision-making perspective can, when correctly targeted, provide valuable knowledge about adjustments to primary hazards (White, Bradley, and White 1972; White 1987).

In reality, there is ample evidence in support of *both* interpretations of hazard. Although there are philosophical and ideological differences between proponent groups, the two viewpoints are not inherently incompatible. Disagreements arise because each tends to define hazard differently, to address different kinds of hazard, and to emphasize different explanatory variables. From the standpoint of theory development, a combination of both perspectives is both possible and desirable (Gold 1980; Werker 1985). For example, two geographers, prominently identified with the decision-making perspective, recently published companion reviews of hazards research that took note of the need to ground hazards in larger societal settings, including political contexts (Whyte 1986; O'Riordan 1986). Others are working toward this goal. Palm is exploring the potential of structuration theory for bridging the conceptual gap that separates students of decision-making from those who hold structural interpretations of hazard (Palm 1986; 1990).

One of the central tenets of structuration theory is the observation that human agency is both bounded by societal structures and enabled by them (Giddens 1976). The general popularity of structuration as a concept reflects a growing interest among social scientists to search for common ground between structuralist interpretations of society and approaches based on the primacy of human action. Wisner is seeking to close the gap in a different way, by extending systems models of hazard to take account of factors that are spatially and temporally remote from the contemporary interface between persons and hazardous environments. As illustrated in a study of soil erosion in Lesotho, the researcher begins with the current socio-political system and perceptions of hazard, gradually widening the investigative focus to bring the larger context into view (Wisner 1986).

I sense that both the integrative avenues currently being explored will prove to be productive, but are also likely to raise difficult conceptual issues for future researchers. One of these is the nature of the interactive unifying relationship between society and environment that is the basis of all human ecological thinking. Many in the hazards research community have conceived of this relationship in systems terms (Kates 1970; Mileti 1980; Geipel 1982). That is to say, hazard is seen as a discrete outcome of definable sets of processes that link separable components of physical and social systems. Once the system's elements have been identified and measured, the resulting hazard can be determined and modified.

However, it is also possible to posit the human ecological relationship in dialectical terms. This involves rejecting the dualism implied by the words "society" and "environment." These are no longer regarded as separable units but are in the process of becoming a different entity or entities, complete with new operational rules. The dialectic process might produce a new synthesis very like one of the original components; publications suggesting that natural hazards are almost entirely human creations may display this type of reductionism (Wijkman and Timberlake 1984). It is also possible that the new synthesis may be quite unlike either of its progenitors, and that a process of differentiation may be at work, leading to multiple products of synthesis (Bookchin 1987). Each of these interpretations has the potential to shape hazards research differently.

Technological Hazards

The development of research on technological hazards shows broad structural similarities to natural hazards research. Two theoretical approaches are taking shape that roughly correspond to the decision-making and political economy perspectives of natural hazards research. However, the order of emergence is different and one perspective is clearly dominant. It is only a decade since the first systematic studies of technological hazard were undertaken by geographers (Kates 1977; Whyte and Burton 1980). Several of the early workers were familiar with natural hazard research and carried over some of the same conceptual approaches; there is a general similarity between the Kates model of human adjustment to natural hazards (1970) and the Kasperson model of technological hazard management (Kates 1977).

Nonetheless, it became necessary to modify borrowed concepts to fit the context of technological hazard. At first this consisted of substituting or adding categories to natural hazard models; scientific discovery and "surprises" were added to the list of important hazard agents, and selected institutions were highlighted as creators, monitors, and regulators of hazard. More recently, a new type of model has evolved, in which technological hazard is now seen as the joint outcome of a linear causal sequence comprising human needs, technologies that are used to satisfy needs, adverse effects of technologies, and societal consequences. Specific causal chains for different hazards, and potential points of intervention for hazards management initiatives, are sought.

The search for causes and associated management opportunities is driven by keen public concern about the hazard potential of the continuing spate of new technologies and by the mounting toll of losses from existing technologies (e.g., automobile accidents). High priority is placed on identifying possible responses to new types of hazards, and on expanding the range of alternatives for coping with existing technological hazards.

By asking the question "What is hazard and how is it caused?" at the outset, students of technological hazard have come to recognize that it exists within a hierarchy of contexts (e.g., goals, instrumentalities, damage processes and consequences). Spatial and socio-political contexts of technological hazards have been addressed by some workers (Kirby 1986; Liverman 1986; Johnson and Zeigler 1986; Murauskas and Shelley 1986), but these investigations are of a fairly preliminary nature. Recent critiques call for a more thoroughgoing contextual "cultural approach" to the field (Rayner and Cantor 1987), and relatively little attention has been devoted to exploring individual behavior and individual decisions in the face of technological hazard. This is the opposite of early developments in natural hazards research. Indeed there is a certain asymmetry about the emergence of theory in these two fields.

Although students of technological hazard borrowed some decision-making theory from natural hazards research, this was not followed up by much empirical work. Instead the determination of hazard causes and management alternatives has been a primary goal of research. There is now renewed interest in decision-making in the face of technological hazard, including both normative and behavioral approaches (Buckley 1986; Machina 1987). In recent years a proposed behavioral theory of risk homeostasis has attracted favorable comment in the journal *Risk Analysis* (Wilde 1982; Slovic and Fischoff 1982; Graham 1982; Orr 1982; Cole and Withey 1982; Evans 1986; Wilde 1986). It centers on a decision-making model of driver behavior that highlights perceived alternatives for avoiding or preventing accidents, although it remains to be seen whether this will lead to further developments of a similar nature.

THE SEARCH FOR GUIDANCE

Many insights into the human dimensions of environmental hazards have already been acquired but further progress is hampered by the complexity of hazards themselves and by the range of different interpretations of the field. In view of these problems and the urgency of burgeoning hazards, how might future research best proceed? Two possible answers to this question are outlined below and a third is discussed in greater detail.

First, it is likely that a great variety of interpretive frameworks will continue to exist for the foreseeable future. Global models and top-down perspectives will sit uncomfortably alongside local field studies and bottom-up perspectives; structuralist contributions will vie with pragmatic managerial contributions. If this occurs, it may be productive to devise guidelines for applying alternative explanations of hazard, and alternative prescriptions for managing hazards. Under some circumstances it might be appropriate to apply one interpretive framework to a given hazard, whereas another set of circumstances might require use of a different framework to explain the same hazard. The task of developing guidelines would involve application of procedures for assessing the validity of different contributions to knowledge. This task would also require a canvas of existing sources of guidance for the making of complex choices (e.g., science, public policy, and ethics). The principles of weighing, balancing, and choosing among apparently incommensurable criteria and alternatives have already been developed in the field of environmental impact assessment and they might be adapted for this purpose (Clark et al. 1981; Biswas and Geping 1986).

A second approach to the problem of resolving disparate interpretations is to develop a more discriminating analysis of complex problems—one that rests on principles that are different from those of existing hazards research subfields. For example, recent work on discontinuous change processes in the natural sciences suggests that surprise and chaos might be among such principles (Wilson 1981; Peters 1987). This course of action seems likely to lead to the creation of a new "science of complexity" (Prigogine and Stengers 1984). Some of the path-breaking work conducted at the International Institute for Applied Systems Analysis (IIASA) falls under this heading (Clark and Munn 1986).

A third approach lies somewhere between the other two. It can be considered as a step beyond existing separate interpretations of hazard but not yet a full-blown unified science of complexity. This approach would seek to define and extend the common intellectual ground that is shared by the subfields of disaster research, natural hazards research, and risk analysis. It would be labeled "integrated hazards research."

TOWARD INTEGRATED HAZARDS RESEARCH

It will be recalled that three observations about the contemporary status of hazards research were made at the beginning of this chapter: the concept that hazards are a "problematic" rather than a series of separate problems; initiation of important new science and technology programs aimed at improving the management of global risks and hazards; and lack of a unified field of research on the human dimensions of hazard. In various ways, these observations underline the importance of integration as a theme in hazards research. They show that significant intellectual advances have been made by broadening conventional views of hazard and they suggest the direction in which further progress is to be found.

Integration has been an important theme in U.S. natural resources management. History is replete with examples of the gradual replacement of a host of specialized narrow measures for managing resources by a few broadly conceived strategies that integrate these measures in mutually supporting ways. White's explanation of the evolution of U.S. water resources management policy is typical (White 1969). At the outset it was common for single purposes (e.g., flood protection, water supply) to be met by single means (e.g., levees, reservoirs). Later the management system shifted to an intermediate stage dominated by either multiple purpose/single means adjustments or single purpose/multiple means adjustments. During this era, multipurpose dams were constructed for water supply, recreation, hydroelectric power, flood control, and other goals. Today, a third stage has been reached: multiple purposes are satisfied by multiple means. Integrated floodplain management seeks to combine a wide range of adjustments to satisfy many different types of demand for water.

Just as the concept of integration has helped to shape the search for innovative water management alternatives, adoption of the view that hazards constitute a problematic rather than a series of individual problems has helped to create a broader canvas for seeking solutions to hazards. But a hazards research paradigm, whether structured around hazards as separate phenomena or hazards as a problematic, also has limitations. Human interaction with the physical environment involves more than hazard. Humankind also exploits environmental opportunities for reward; as the Epicurean philosophers first recognized, the pursuit of pleasure can be as important as the avoidance of pain. Eventually, it will be necessary to integrate the analysis of hazard and the analysis of reward within a common research paradigm. Such a task will prove to be challenging, not least because the risks of losing potential rewards consume a great deal of space in contemporary literature. Of more than thirteen hundred nonfiction, hazard-related titles listed in the 1986 edition of *Books in Print*, the single largest group (29%) deals with risks in banking, investment, and insurance.

It is important to remember that studies of economic risk-taking have helped to shape thinking about environmental hazards. For example, they have provided much of the basis for developing normative decision theory, game theory, and behavioral decision theory—all of which have influenced our conceptions of human response to environmental hazard (Roumasset, Boussard, and Singh 1979). But it is also important to realize that rising concern about economic risks and business hazards has, in the past, often tended to draw public attention away from environmental hazards.

Policy-makers and hazard analysts increasingly recognize that both sets of hazards should be considered together. This realization is reflected in a series of international reports on environment and development (United Nations Conference on the Human Environment 1972; Independent Commission on International Development Issues 1980; Brandt Commission 1983; World Commission on Environment and Development 1987), in recent policy decisions taken by the World Bank, and in programs for the "sustainable development of the biosphere" (Clark and Munn 1986; Thibodeau and Field, 1984). Unfortunately, there is considerable resistance in the scientific community to taking an integrated view of hazards and development, and there is still a long way to go before the preceding initiatives are translated into changes in hazards management practices (Mitchell 1988a).

With these cautions in mind, I turn to the second observation at the beginning of this paper. Two global science and technology programs seek to integrate knowledge from the natural and biological sciences on the one hand (IGBP), and the natural and engineering sciences (IDNDR) on the other. However, both programs are little informed by knowledge about human behavior in the face of hazard. In the same way that the model of hazards as problematic should eventually be extended to encompass trade-offs between risks and rewards, the planned hazards research and management initiatives would benefit by inclusion of knowledge about the human dimensions of hazard. These dimensions include the decision calculus of hazards managers and others who apply the findings of hazards research directly to the reduction of threats and losses. It is not enough to advance the study of hazards by integrating various fields of intellectual inquiry; inquiry should be firmly linked to and informed by practice. To a significant degree, researchers in all three subfields of hazards research have shown that they are cognizant of the experience and needs of users in hazard management organizations.

The Siren song of a priori theory development has thus far been successfully resisted. Given the increasing interdependence of management and inquiry in a rapidly changing world, and the escalating scale of penalties for wrong judgments, it is to be hoped that this situation will continue.

Gradual convergence of the three subfields that address the human dimensions of hazards constitutes the third element in a program to achieve an integrated field of hazards research. This might proceed in two ways. First, it is important that investigators in different subfields of hazards research should make active efforts to learn from each other. For example, it is clear that students of technological hazard have succeeded in developing more specific and detailed models of technological failure than anything that has so far been produced for natural hazards. Conversely, individual models of decision-making in the face of risk are probably less well developed for technological hazards.

Mainstream students of risk analysis have recently come under criticism because they have neglected the cultural contexts of risk. Similar criticisms were leveled at natural hazards research in the mid 1970s. Risk analysts might examine how those in the natural hazards research community have adapted their field methods and are attempting to develop new investigative approaches to take account of these criticisms. Likewise, at least two, and perhaps all three, of the subfields are independently engaged in introspection about definitions of the field and basic principles. Collaborative attention to these matters, rather than separate endeavors, is likely to yield more insights and progress. Given the small numbers of interdisciplinary hazards researchers, relative to those who study hazards from narrow disciplinary perspectives, or from paradigms that lie wholly within either the natural or the social sciences, there are also pragmatic reasons for collaborating to gain access to as large an audience as possible.

Second, it will be necessary to develop additional concepts and methods suitable for addressing human aspects of hazard. These are necessary because society faces a problematic that includes new types of risks and rapidly changing scientific information about them. Others are needed to close the gap between global models of hazard, formulated in the natural sciences and the social sciences; to take account of the varying contexts in which hazards are embedded; and to bring different compatible interpretations of hazard together in a common framework. Inasmuch as the task of integrating disaster research, natural hazards research, and risk analysis involves common problems, a concerted approach is desirable, although the task of stimulating improved collaboration among the subfields will not be easy. There are few venues or media where such cooperation occurs at present. Although there is some overlap, the members of each group tend to have received their training in different fields, to belong to different professional organizations, to attend different meetings, and to subscribe to different journals. Those in one subfield may even profess little interest in the type of hazards research characteristic of another subfield. None of these barriers is insuperable and initial steps toward opening dialogue among researchers have been taken at the annual Hazards Workshops in Boulder, Colorado, periodic international emergency management meetings, and elsewhere.

EPILOGUE

It is—in my view—neither possible nor desirable for hazards research to become a monistic field of study. Given the diversity of hazards that exist and the wide range of human responses that are possible, there will continue to be many different approaches to the analysis of hazards and many different interpretations of findings. However, this does not mean that it is impossible to find common ground among the diverse components of hazards research or that the field would not benefit from a higher degree of intellectual integration. If hazards researchers are to provide policy-makers, hazards management professionals, and lay populations with sound guidance about hazards problems, it is essential to encourage conceptual simplicity and clarity, and to harness the field's disparate contributions in mutual reinforcement.

NOTE

Parts of this paper were prepared while the author was a visiting fellow at the East-West Center, Honolulu. Discussions with the following members of the center's Environment and Policy Institute helped to shape the ideas presented here: Norton Ginsburg, Kirk Smith, Satyesh Chakraborty, Joe Morgan. Many persons contributed insights and information, but the flaws are my own.

REFERENCES

Alexander, David
    1985   "Culture and the Environment in Italy." *Environmental Management* 9 (2): 121–34.
Arnold, David
    1986   "Cholera and Colonialism in British India." *Past and Present* (November): 118–51.
Berz, G.
    1984   "Research and Statistics on Natural Disasters in Insurance and Reinsurance Companies." *The Geneva Papers on Risk and Insurance* (April): 135–57.
Biswas, Asit K., and Geping, Qu, eds.
    1986   *Environmental Impact Assessment for Developing Countries.* London: Tycooly Publishing.

James K. Mitchell

Blaikie, Piers

1985   *The Political Economy of Soil Erosion in Developing Countries.*
London: Longman.

Blaikie, Piers, and Brookfield, Harold

1987   *Land Degradation and Society.* London: Methuen.

Bloom, Allan

1987   *The Closing of the American Mind.* New York: Simon and Schuster.

Bogen, Kenneth T., and Spear, Robert C.

1987   "Integrating Uncertainty and Interindividual Variability in Environmental Risk Assessment." *Risk Assessment* 7 (4): 427–36.

Bookchin, Murray

1987   "Thinking Ecologically: A Dialectical Approach." *Our Generation*
18 (2): 3–40.

Bosworth, R. J. B.

1981   "The Messina Earthquake of 28 December, 1908." *European Studies
Review* 11: 189–206.

Brandt Commission

1983   *Common Crisis: North-South Cooperation for World Recovery.*
Cambridge: MIT Press.

Brass, Paul R.

1986   "The Political Uses of Crisis: The Bihar Famine of 1966–67." *Journal of Asian Studies* 45 (2): 245–68.

Brasseur, Guy

1987   "The Endangered Ozone Layer: New Theories on Ozone Depletion." *Environment* 29 (1): 6–11, 39–45.

Buckley, James J.

1986   "Stochastic Dominance: An Approach to Decision Making under
Risk." *Risk Analysis* 6 (1): 35–42.

Burton, Ian, and Kates, Robert W.

1986   "The Great Climacteric, 1798–2048: The Transition to a Just and
Sustainable Human Environment," in *Themes from the Work of
Gilbert F. White*, Robert W. Kates and Ian Burton, eds., 339–60.

Burton, Ian, Kates, Robert W., and White, Gilbert F.

1978   *The Environment as Hazard.* New York: Oxford University Press.

Cant, Garth

1986   "Famine in the Sahel: Natural Disaster or Structural Violence?"
New Zealand Journal of Geography (April): 2–5.

Caplan, Arthur L., and Callahan, David

1981   *Ethics in Hard Times.* New York: Plenum Press.

Chen, R. S., Boulding, E., and Schneider, S. H., eds.

1983   *Social Science, Research and Climate Change: An Interdisciplinary
Appraisal.* Dordrecht: Reidel.

Chrostowski, Paul C., Pearsall, Lorraine J., and Shaw, Charles
  1985   "Risk Assessment as a Management Tool for Inactive Hazardous
          Materials Disposal Sites." *Environmental Management* 9 (5): 433–
          42.
Clark, D. B., et al.
  1981   *A Manual for the Assessment of Major Development Proposals.*
          London: Her Majesty's Stationery Office.
Clark, William C.
  1982   *Carbon Dioxide Review.* New York: Oxford University Press.
  1985   *On the Practical Implications of the Carbon Dioxide Question.*
          Geneva: World Meteorological Organization.
  1986   "Sustainable Development of the Biosphere: Themes for a Research
          Program," in *Sustainable Development of the Biosphere,* W. C.
          Clark and R. E. Munn, eds., 5–48. Cambridge: Cambridge Univer-
          sity Press.
Clark, William C., and Munn, R. E., eds.
  1986   *Sustainable Development of the Biosphere.* Cambridge: Cambridge
          University Press.
Cole, Gerald A., and Withey, Stephen B.
  1982   "The Risk of Aggregation." *Risk Analysis* 2 (4): 243–48.
Covello, Vincent T., and Mumpower, Jeryl
  1985   "Risk Analysis and Risk Management: An Historical Perspective."
          Risk Analysis 5 (2): 103–20.
Cuny, Frederick C.
  1983   *Disasters and Development.* New York: Oxford University Press.
Currey, Bruce, and Hugo, Graeme
  1984   *Famine as a Geographical Phenomenon.* Dordrecht: Reidel.
Dobell, A. R.
  1986   "The Public Servant as God: Taking Risks with the Public." *Cana-
          dian Public Administrator* 29 (4): 601–16.
Douglas, Mary
  1966   *Purity and Danger: An Analysis of Concepts of Pollution and
          Taboo.* London: Routledge and Kegan Paul.
  1985   *Risk Acceptability According to the Social Sciences.* New York:
          Russell Sage Foundation.
Douglas, Mary, and Wildavsky, Aaron
  1982   *Risk and Culture.* Berkeley: University of California Press.
Drabek, Thomas E.
  1986a   *Human Systems Responses to Disaster: An Inventory of Sociological
          Findings.* New York: Springer-Verlag.
  1986b   "The Problem of Taxonomy in Disaster Research." Unpublished
          paper, University of Denver.

Elster, Jon
    1985   "Rationality, Morality, and Collective Action." *Ethics* 96 (October): 136–55.
Ethics
    1985   Special issue on "Ethics and Nuclear Deterrence." 95 (3).
Evans, Gary W., ed.
    1982   *Environmental Stress.* Cambridge: Cambridge University Press.
Evans, Leonard
    1986   "Risk Homeostasis Theory and Traffic Accident Data." *Risk Analysis* 6 (1): 81–94.
Fischhoff, Baruch, Lichtenstein, Sarah, Slovic, Paul, Derby, Stephen L., and Keeney, Ralph L.
    1981   *Acceptable Risk.* Cambridge: Cambridge University Press.
Friedman, Don G.
    1984   "Natural Hazard Risk Assessment for an Insurance Program." *The Geneva Papers on Risk and Insurance* 9 (30): 57–128.
Friedman, D., and Mangano, J.
    1982   "Computer Simulation of the Earthquake Hazard in Montenegro." Paper presented at the fourth session of the International Consulting Board UNDP Project YUG/79/003, Titograd, Montenegro. October 26.
Geipel, Robert
    1982   *Disaster and Reconstruction.* London: Allen and Unwin.
Giddens, Anthony
    1976   *New Rules of Sociological Method.* London: Hutchinson.
Gold, John R.
    1980   *An Introduction to Behavioral Geography.* Oxford: Oxford University Press.
Graham, John D.
    1982   "On Wilde's 'Theory of Risk Homeostasis.'" *Risk Analysis* 2 (4): 235–38.
Haas, Michael
    1986   "Research on International Crisis: Obsolescence of an Approach?" *International Interactions* 13 (1): 23–58.
Hare, F. Kenneth
    1986   "The Challenge of Climatic Change." *Queen's Quarterly* 93 (2): 251–64.
Harwell, M. A., and Hutchinson, T. C., eds.
    1985   *Environmental Consequences of Nuclear War* (vol. 2). Chichester: John Wiley.
Health and Safety Executive
    1978   *Canvey: An Investigation of Potential Hazards from Operations in*

the Canvey Island/Thurrock Area. London: HMSO.

1981   *Canvey: A Second Report.* London: HMSO.

Hewitt, Kenneth, ed.

1983   *Interpretations of Calamity.* Boston: Allen and Unwin.

Hills, Theo L.

1982   "The Ecology of Hazardousness: the Experience of South America."
        GeoJournal 6 (2): 151–56.

Hutterer, Karl L., Rambo, A. Terry, and Lovelace, George

1985   *Cultural Values and Human Ecology in Southeast Asia.* Michigan
        papers on South and Southeast Asia, University of Michigan, no. 27.
        Ann Arbor: Center for South and Southeast Asian Studies.

Independent Commission on International Development Issues

1980   *North-South: A Program for Survival.* Cambridge: MIT Press.

Inhaber, Herbert

1985   "Risk in Developing Countries." *Risk Analysis* 5(2): 87.

Inhaber, H., and Norman, S.

1982   "The Increase in Risk Interest." *Risk Analysis* 2 (3): 119–20.

International Council of Scientific Unions

1986   *The International Geosphere Biosphere Programme: A Study of
        Global Change.* Paris. August.

Ives, J. H., ed.

1985   *The Export of Hazard: Transnational Corporations and Environ-
        mental Control Issues.* Boston: Routledge and Kegan Paul.

Johnson, James H., and Zeigler, Donald J.

1986   "Evacuation Planning for Technological Hazards: An Emerging
        Imperative." *Cities* (May): 148–56.

Karan, P. P.

1987   "Environment and Development in Bhutan." *Geografiska Annaler,*
        Series B—Human Geography, 69B (1): 15–26.

Karan, P. P., Bladen, Wilford A., and Wilson, James R.

1986   "Technological Hazards in the Third World." *Geographical Review*
        76 (2): 195–208.

Karl, Thomas R., and Riebsame, William E.

1984   "The Identification of 10– to 20–Year Temperature and Precipi-
        tation Fluctuations in the Contiguous United States." *Journal of
        Climate and Applied Meteorology* 23 (6): 950–66.

Kasperson, Roger E., et al.

1988   "The Social Amplification of Risk: A Conceptual Framework." *Risk
        Analysis* 8 (2): 177–88.

Kasperson, Roger E., and Kasperson, Jeanne X., eds.

1988   *Nuclear Risk Analysis in Comparative Perspective.* London: Allen
        and Unwin.

Kasperson, Roger E., and Pijawka, K. David

1985   "Societal Response to Hazards and Major Hazard Events." *Public Administration Review* 45: 7–18.

Kates, Robert W.

1970   *Natural Hazard in Human Ecological Perspective: Hypotheses and Models.* Natural Hazard Research Working Paper no. 14. Worcester: Clark University, Department of Geography. Reprinted in *Economic Geography*, 1971.

1977   *Managing Technological Hazard: Research Needs and Opportunities.* Monograph #25. Boulder: University of Colorado, Institute of Behavioral Science.

1978   *Risk Assessment of Environmental Hazard. SCOPE report #8.* New York: John Wiley.

1985   "Success, Strain, and Surprise." *Issues in Science and Technology* 2 (1): 46–58.

1987a   "The Human Environment: The Road Not Taken, the Road Still Beckoning." *Annals of the Association of American Geographers* 77 (4): 525–34.

1987b   "Life and Liberty are Human Rights." A Commentary for the Human Rights Symposium, Annual Meeting of the National Academy of Sciences, Washington, D.C. April 29.

Kates, Robert W., Ausubel, J.H., and Berberian, M., eds.

1985   *Climate Impact Assessment.* London: John Wiley.

Kates, Robert W., and Burton, Ian, eds.

1986   *Geography, Resources, and Environment:* vol. 2, *Themes from the Work of Gilbert F. White.* Chicago: University of Chicago Press.

Kates, Robert W., Hohenemser, C., and Kasperson, J. X., eds.

1985   *Perilous Progress: Managing the Hazards of Technology.* Boulder: Westview Press.

Kates, Robert W., and Kasperson, Jeanne X.

1983   "Comparative Risk Analysis of Technological Hazards (A Review)." *Proceedings of the National Academy of Sciences USA* 80 (November): 7027–38.

Keeney, Ralph L.

1984   "Ethics, Decision Analysis, and Public Risk." *Risk Analysis* 4 (2), 117–30.

Keller, L. Robin, and Sarin, Rakesh K.

1988   "Equity in Social Risk: Some Empirical Observations." *Risk Analysis* 8 (1): 135–46.

Kirby, Andrew

1986   "Technological Risks in Urban Areas: Introduction." *Cities* (May): 137–41.

Klee, Gary A.
    1980   *World Systems of Traditional Resource Management*. New York: John Wiley.

Kluge, Eike-Henner W.
    1986   "What is a Human Life Worth?" *Canadian Public Administration* 29 (4): 617–23.

Kotlyakov, V. M., Mather, J. R., Sdasyuk, G. V., White, G. F., et al.
    forth-   *Global Change: A Geographical Approach*. Moscow: Progress
    coming   Press.

Kunreuther, Howard C., and Ley, Eryl V., eds.
    1982   *The Risk Analysis Controversy: An Institutional Perspective*. New York: Springer-Verlag.

Land, Kenneth C., and Schneider, Stephen H., eds.
    1987   Special issue on "Forecasting in the Social and Natural Sciences." *Climatic Change* 11 (1/2).

Laudan, Larry
    1984   *Science and Values: The Aims of Science and Their Role in Scientific Debate*. Berkeley: University of California Press.

Law and Contemporary Problems
    1986   Special issue on "Responsibility." 49 (3).

Lemons, John
    1983   "Atmospheric Carbon Dioxide: Environmental Ethics and Environmental Facts." *Environmental Ethics* 5 (Spring): 21–32.

Little, Peter D., Horowitz, Michael M., and Nyerges, A. Endre
    1987   *Lands at Risk in the Third World: Local Level Perspectives*. Boulder: Westview Press.

Liverman, Diana M.
    1986   "The Vulnerability of Urban Areas to Technological Risks." *Cities* (May): 142–47.

Los', V. A.
    1986   "Global Problems as the Subject of Multidisciplinary Scientific Research." *Soviet Studies in Philosophy* (Fall): 5–30.

Lowrance, William W.
    1976   *Of Acceptable Risk: Science and the Determination of Public Safety*. Los Altos: William Kaufmann.
    1986   *Modern Science and Human Values*. New York: Oxford University Press.

McDaniels, Timothy
    1988   "Perceived Fairness in Risk Management." *Risk Analysis* 8 (1): 7–8.

Machina, Mark J.
    1987   "Decision-Making in the Presence of Risk." *Science* 236: 537–43.

McKerlie, Dennis
    1986   "Rights and Risk." *Canadian Journal of Philosophy* 16 (2): 239–52.
Malone, Thomas F.
    1986   "Integrating Studies of Global Change." *Environment* 28 (8): 6–11, 39–42.
Malone, Thomas F., and Roederer, J. G., eds.
    1985   *Global Change.* Cambridge: Cambridge University Press.
Marquez, Gabriel Garcia
    1986   *One Earth, Many Worlds.*
Marshall, Eliot
    1988   "Academy Panel Faults NASA's Safety Analysis." *Science* 239: 1233.
Marston, Sallie A.
    1983   "Natural Hazards Research: Towards a Political Economy Perspective." *Political Geography Quarterly* 2(4): 339–48.
Mehr, Robert I., and Cammack, Emerson
    1976   *Principles of Insurance.* Homewood, Ill.: R. D. Irwin.
Mileti, Dennis S.
    1980   "Human Adjustment to the Risk of Environmental Extremes." *Sociology and Social Research* 65: 327–47.
Minor, Michael, Kawamura, Kazahiko, and Lynes, Paul Finger
    1986   "Comment on 'Risk in Developing Countries.'" *Risk Analysis* 6 (1): 1–2.
Mitchell, James K.
    1974   "Natural Hazards Research," in *Perspectives on Environment,* Ian R. Manners and Marvin W. Mikesell, eds., 311–41. Washington, D.C.: Association of American Geographers.
    1984   "Hazard Perception Studies: Convergent Concerns and Divergent Approaches During the Past Decade," in *Environmental Perception and Behavior: An Inventory and Prospect,* Thomas F. Saarinen, David R. Seamon, and James L. Sell, eds., 33–59. Department of Geography Research Paper no. 209, University of Chicago.
    1988a   "Confronting Natural Disasters." *Environment* 30 (2): 25–29.
    1988b   "Risk Analysis," in *Global Change: A Geographical Approach,* R. Mather et al., eds. Moscow: Progress Press.
    1989   "Geographical Contributions to Research on Environmental Hazards," in *Geography in America,* Gary L. Gaile and Cort J. Willmott, eds., 410–24. Boston: Merrill.
Moore, Wilbert E., and Feldman, Arnold S.
    1962   "Society as a Tension-Management System," in *Behavioral Science and Civil Defense Disaster Research Group,* George Baker and Leonard S. Cottrell, Jr., eds., 93–105. Washington, D.C.: National Academy of Science.

Murauskas, G. Tomas, and Shelley, Fred M.

    1986   "Local Political Responses to Nuclear Waste Disposal." *Cities* (May): 157–62.

National Research Council

    1983   *Risk Assessment in the Federal Government: Managing the Process.* Washington, D.C.: National Academy Press.

    1987   *Confronting Natural Disasters: An International Decade for Natural Hazard Reduction.* Washington, D.C.: National Academy Press.

O'Riordan, Timothy

    1986   "Coping with Environmental Hazards," in *Themes from the Work of Gilbert F. White*, Kates and Burton, eds., 272–309.

    1988   "The Earth as Transformed by Human Action: An International Symposium." *Environment* 30 (1): 25–28.

Orr, Lloyd

    1982   "Goals, Risks, and Choices." *Risk Analysis* 2 (4): 239–42.

Palm, Risa

    1985   "Geography and Consumer Protection: Housing Market Response to Earthquake Hazards Disclosure." *Southeastern Geographer* 25 (1): 63–73.

    1986   "Coming Home." *Annals of the Association of American Geographers* 76 (4): 469–79.

    1990   *Natural Hazards: An Integrative Theory for Research and Planning.* Baltimore: Johns Hopkins University Press.

Palm, Risa, with Sallie A. Marston, Patricia Kellner, and David Smith

    1983   *Home Mortgage Lenders, Real Property Appraisers and Earthquake Hazards.* Monograph #38. Boulder: University of Colorado, Institute of Behavioral Science.

Pattison, William D.

    1964   "The Four Traditions of Geography." *Journal of Geography* 63 (5): 211–16.

Perrow, Charles

    1984   *Normal Accidents: Living with High-Risk Technologies.* New York: Basic Books.

Peters, Tom

    1987   *Thriving on Chaos: Handbook for a Management Revolution.* New York: Alfred A. Knopf.

Platt, Rutherford H.

    1986   "Floods and Man: A Geographer's Agenda," in *Themes from the Work of Gilbert F. White*, Kates and Burton, eds., 26–68.

Poje, Gerald V.

    1988   "Resources Needed for New Risk Analysis Opportunities." *Risk Analysis* 8 (1): 1–3.

Polanyi, K.
 1957   *The Great Transformation: The Political and Economic Origins of our Time.* Boston: Beacon.
Prigogine, Ilya, and Stengers, Isabelle
 1984   *Order Out of Chaos.* New York: Bantam.
Prince, S. H.
 1920   *Catastrophe and Social Change.* New York: Columbia University Press.
Quarantelli, E. L.
 1986a "What Should We Study? Questions and Suggestions for Researchers about the Concept of Disasters." Presidential Address to International Sociological Association Research Committee on Disasters, World Congress of Sociology, New Delhi. August.
 1986b *Disaster Studies.* Disaster Research Center Preliminary paper #111. Newark: University of Delaware.
Quarantelli, E. L., Dynes, R. R., and Wenger, D. E.
 1986   *The Disaster Research Center: Its History and Activities.* Disaster Research Center Miscellaneous Report #35. Newark: University of Delaware.
Raynor, Steve, and Cantor, Robin
 1987   "How Fair is Safe Enough? The Cultural Approach to Societal Technology Choice." *Risk Analysis* 7(1): 3–9.
Richards, Paul
 1985   *Indigenous Agricultural Revolution: Ecology and Food Production in West Africa.* Boulder: Westview Press.
 1986   *Coping with Hunger: Hazard and Experiment in an African Rice-Farming System.* London: Allen and Unwin.
Robinson, James C.
 1986   "Philosophical Origins of the Economic Valuation of Life." *The Milbank Quarterly* 64 (1): 133–55.
Roumasset, J. A., Boussard, Jean-Marc, and Singh, Inderjit, eds.
 1979   *Risk, Uncertainty, and Agricultural Development.* New York: Agricultural Development Council.
Santos, Milton
 1984   "Geography in the Late Twentieth Century: New Roles for a Threatened Discipline." *International Social Science Journal* 36 (4): 657–72.
Sauer, Gerald L.
 1982   "Imposed Risk Controversies: A Critical Analysis." *The Cato Journal* 2 (1): 231–50.
Shah, Bindi V.
 1983   "Is the Environment Becoming More Hazardous?: A Global Summary 1947–1980." *Disasters* 7 (3): 202–9.

Slovic, Paul, and Fischoff, Baruch
   1982   "Targeting Risks." *Risk Analysis* 2 (4): 227–34.
Smith, Kirk R.
   1988   *The Risk Transition*. Environment and Policy Institute Working
           Paper. Honolulu: East-West Center.
Snowball, D. J., and Macgill, S. M.
   1984   "Coping with Risk: The Case of Gas Facilities in Scotland." *Envi-
           ronment and Planning C: Government and Policy* 2 (3): 343–60.
Solzhenitsyn, Aleksandr I.
   1980   *East and West*. New York: Harper and Row.
Sorokin, Pitirim A.
   1937   *Social and Cultural Dynamics*. New York: American Books.
   1941   *The Crisis of our Age*. New York: E. P. Dutton.
Starr, Chauncey
   1969   "Social Benefit Versus Technological Risk: What is our Society
           Willing to Pay for Safety?" *Science* 165: 1232–38.
Steitz, Steven Thomas, and Davis, Morris
   1984   "The Political Matrix of Natural Disasters: Africa and Latin
           America." *International Journal of Mass Emergencies and Disasters*
           2 (2): 231–50.
Sterba, James P.
   1984   "Recent Work on Alternative Conceptions of Justice." *American
           Philosophical Quarterly* 23 (1): 1–22.
Stone, Christopher D.
   1987   *Earth and Other Ethics: The Case for Moral Pluralism*. New York:
           Harper and Row.
Susman, Paul, O'Keefe, Phil, and Wisner, Ben
   1983   "Global Disasters, a Radical Interpretation," in *Interpretations of
           Calamity*, Kenneth Hewitt, ed., 263–83.
Thibodeau, Francis R., and Field, Hermann H., eds.
   1984   *Sustaining Tomorrow: A Strategy for World Conservation and
           Development*. Hanover: University Press of New England.
Thompson, M., Warburton, M., and Hatley, T.
   1986   *Uncertainty on a Himalayan Scale*. London: Ethnographia.
Thompson, Paul B.
   1984   "Need and Safety: The Nuclear Power Debate." *Environmental
           Ethics* 6 (Spring): 57–69.
Thompson, Stephen A.
   1982   *Trends and Developments in Global Natural Disasters, 1947–1981*.
           Natural Hazard Research Working Paper #45. Boulder: University
           of Colorado, Institute of Behavioral Science.

James K. Mitchell

Tobin, Graham A.
   1985   "Environmental Ethics and Geography: Some Thoughts." *Geographical Perspectives* 55 (Spring): 6–14.
Tuan, Yi-Fu
   1979   *Landscapes of Fear*. New York: Pantheon Books.
United Nations Conference on the Human Environment
   1972   *Development and Environment*. Paris: Mouton.
U.S. Atomic Energy Commission
   1974   *Reactor Safety Study*. WASH 1400. Washington, D.C.
U.S. Strategic Bombing Survey
   1947a   *The Effects of Strategic Bombing on German Morale*. Washington, D.C.: U.S. Government Printing Office.
   1947b   *The Effects of Strategic Bombing on Japanese Morale*. Washington, D.C.: U.S. Government Printing Office.
Von Magnus, Eric
   1984   "Preference, Rationality, and Risk Taking." *Ethics* 94: 637–48.
Walker, R. B. J.
   1987   "Realism, Change, and International Political Theory." *International Studies Quarterly* 31: 65–86.
Watts, Michael D.
   1983   "On the Poverty of Theory: Natural Hazards Research in Context," in *Interpretations of Calamity*, Kenneth Hewitt, ed., 231–62.
Webster, Frank, and Robins, Kevin
   1986   *Information Technology: A Luddite Analysis*. Norwood, N.J.: Ablen Publishing Company.
Wenk, Edward, Jr.
   1986   *Tradeoffs: Imperatives of Choice in a High-Tech World*. Baltimore: Johns Hopkins University Press.
Werker, Scott
   1985   "Beyond the Dependency Paradigm." *Journal of Contemporary Asia* 15 (1): 79–95.
Wescoat, James L., Jr.
   1987   "The 'Practical Range of Choice' in Water Resources Geography." *Progress in Human Geography* 11: 41–59.
Weston, Anthony
   1985   "Beyond Intrinsic Value: Pragmatism in Environmental Ethics." *Environmental Ethics* 7 (4): 321–40.
White, Gilbert F.
   1969   *Strategies of American Water Management*. Ann Arbor: University of Michigan Press.
   1973   "Natural Hazards Research," in *Directions in Geography*, Richard J. Chorley, ed. London: Methuen.

1985   "Geographers in a Perilously Changing World." *Annals of the Association of American Geographers* 75 (1): 10–16.

1987   "Greenhouse Gases, Nile Snails, and Human Choice." Unpublished lecture, Distinguished Lecture Series on Behavioral Science 1985–86, University of Colorado, Institute of Behavioral Science.

White, Gilbert F., Bradley, David J., and White, Anne U.

1972   *Drawers of Water: Domestic Water Use in East Africa*. Chicago: University of Chicago Press.

Whyte, Anne V. T.

1986   "From Hazard Perception to Human Ecology," in *Themes from the Work of Gilbert F. White*, Kates and Burton, eds., 240–71.

Whyte, Anne V., and Burton, Ian, eds.

1980   *Environmental Risk Assessment. SCOPE report no. 15*. New York: John Wiley.

Wijkman, Anders, and Timberlake, Lloyd

1984   *Natural Disasters: Acts of God or Acts of Man?* Washington, D.C.: Earthscan.

Wildavsky, Aaron

1982   "Pollution as Moral Coercion: Culture, Risk Perception and Libertarian Values." *The Cato Journal* 2: 305–26.

Wilde, Gerald J. S.

1982   "The Theory of Risk Homeostasis: Implications for Safety and Health." *Risk Analysis* 2(4): 209–25.

1986   "Notes on the Interpretation of Traffic Accident Data and of Risk Homeostasis Theory: A Reply to L. Evans." *Risk Analysis* 6 (1): 95–102.

Wilson, Alan

1981   *Catastrophe Theory and Bifurcation*. London: Croom Helm.

Wisner, Ben

1986   "Land Management in Lesotho," in *Human Ecology and Geography*, Dieter Steiner and Ben Wisner, eds., 87–105. Zürcher Geographische Schriften #28, Technische Hochschule Zürich.

Wolfenstein, Martha

1957   *Disaster: A Psychological Essay*. Glencoe, Ill.: Free Press.

World Commission on Environment and Development

1987   *Our Common Future*. Oxford: Oxford University Press.

Ziegler, Donald J., Johnson, James H., Jr., and Brunn, Stanley D.

1983   *Technological Hazards*. Washington, D.C.: Association of American Geographers.

Zimmerman, Erich W.

1933   *World Resources and Industries*. New York: Harper and Brothers.

PART III

The Language and Practice of Control

CHAPTER 7

Institutional Biases in the Legal System's Risk Assessments

Clayton P. Gillette

We tend to envision the legal system, particularly its adjudicative component, as a mechanism for redressing a variety of injuries to which persons are susceptible.[1] Persons who engage in negligent conduct, manufacturers who produce defective goods, even those whose behavior is socially desirable and thus escape the opprobrium of "fault," may be held accountable when their activity causes harm to others.[2] Nevertheless, we do not rely on legal accountability to remedy all the slings and arrows of life. Those who suffer the hazards of growing old, of natural disaster, of genetic defects, find little relief in the law. In short, the legal system—at least at first glance—seemingly has little to say about "natural" as opposed to human-caused or technological hazards that pervade society. This appears quite appropriate, given the pragmatic limitation that the legal system functions only when there is an entity subject to its adjudicative or regulatory mandate. Natural forces simply fall outside the realm of those who can be held accountable.

On reflection, however, this dichotomy between the natural and the technological seems too simplistic. For when technology intervenes to reduce the probability or consequences of natural disaster, we subject those using the technology to high standards of care, notwithstanding that we might be worse off had they never intervened at all. Thus, those who enhance the quality of life by constructing dams to restrain flood waters, manufacturing vaccines that stave off lethal disease, or generating power without which we would be at the mercy of the elements, may find themselves subject to legal sanctions should their risk-reducing measures occasionally go awry.

That those who reduce the consequences of natural hazards are held responsible for their injury-producing activity suggests more than a social desire to compensate the injured. That objective would be accomplished by a social welfare scheme, void of the time and expense of a tort or regulatory system. The pervasiveness of the legal system suggests that society has additional concerns for the ways in which we minimize the total quantum of risk. Intervention by the legal system indicates a belief that legal rules can serve as incentives for socially desirable behavior. Thus, we can employ legal rules that induce private risk creators to serve as surrogates for the rest of us in determining the optimal level of natural and technological risk.

Ideally, the adjudicative component of the legal system—imposition of liability on risk creators—accomplishes this objective by imposing on injurers the costs of harm they cause. This process forces risk creators to internalize all the consequences of their conduct and thus induces them to compare social costs with the personal benefits of any activity. Presumably, only when the latter exceed the former will a prospective injurer engage in a risky activity. Thus, even the most self-interested actor is persuaded to consider the interests of others in deciding whether to generate a given level of risk. Similarly, the regulatory component of the legal system signals regulated groups that certain risks will not be tolerated or must be taken only under tightly controlled circumstances, enforced through the threat of fine or revocation of license necessary to continue in the risky business.

This is not to say that we seek some utopian "riskless" world.[3] To the contrary, legal doctrines, such as torts and nuisance, that permit redress of noncontractual harm largely permit exceptions to liability where the injurer has acted "reasonably"—a term often understood as action that, while risky, confers sufficient benefit to justify the risk.[4] Even under modern concepts of "strict" liability for defective products, evolving principles of law require that the product be "unreasonably" dangerous before injurers are required to compensate victims.[5] Thus, products that impose harm on occasional victims but confer benefits on a substantially larger population may not bear the costs of the injuries they cause, at least if the victim is deemed to have been adequately warned of the risk.[6]

The theory that assigns the enforcement of this internalization process to the legal system is best explained by basic economics. If society seeks an optimal level of risk, we must have both a forum for assessment and a class of parties interested in using that forum. If potential victims of technological risk are given "rights" (e.g., a right not to have their property polluted or a right not to be subjected to contraceptive devices that induce infection) and a mechanism for redress of infringement of those rights (e.g., the courts), then those injured have incentives to make viable claims that the technologies that injured them were not worth the risk. In short, the adjudicative component of the legal system provides the necessary incentives for victims to act as private attorneys-general for the rest of us in the debate about acceptable risk.

Modern risks, however, are often too complex to be mastered within the adjudicative system. Information concerning the source or avoidance costs of particular injuries may be so esoteric or expensive to uncover that even injured parties will not seek redress. Additionally, some potential harm may be so catastrophic that potential injurers would be incapable of paying for injuries should the risk materialize.

To address these concerns, society has created an adjunct to the adjudicative system. Rather than simply creating a forum for the claims of injured parties, modern risk assessment involves a new governmental body, the regulatory agency. With such agencies, as with adjudication, the ideal is to internalize the adverse effects of risky activities so that decisions about risks can be rendered, taking into account their net effects. The internalization process this time, however, emerges from expert bureaucrats who, according to classic theory, are sufficiently imbued with a sense of public interest that they consider all social costs and benefits before rendering a decision. From this combination of plaintiffs vindicating the public weal through the invisible hand of self-interested litigation, and technocrats accomplishing the same goal through regulation in the public interest, arises an optimal level of social risk.

That, in any event, is the story those of us heavily invested in the legal system like to tell ourselves. We debate the conditions under which one form of risk assessment is superior to the alternative and dicker about the relative merits of negligence and strict liability (Shavell 1984; Cooter 1984; Huber 1985; Krier and Gillette 1985). Yet for the most part we act as though proper management of either or both of these risk assessment mechanisms will avoid both those short-term hazards that are worth avoiding and long-term catastrophe.

Unfortunately, the world is more complicated than these mechanisms would allow. There can be little doubt that the incentives for optimal risk assessment the theory implies are substantial, but those incentives do not operate in a vacuum. The actors in these legal theaters, both adjudicative and regulatory, are subject to additional, and conflicting, incentives. These competing incentives often produce behavior inconsistent with what would be necessary to produce an optimal level of risk. Some of these incentives generate overassessment of risk; others lead to underassessment. The result, however, deviates substantially from any ideal system, and thereby belies reliance on the legal system as a panacea to risk.

These unfortunate incentives emerge from a variety of sources. Ignorance (or imperfect information), cognitive distortions, and bounded rationality all contribute to decision-making that deviates from what would be expected of the rational, self-interested, profit-maximizing individual hypothesized by economic models. I want, however, to focus on incentives that are particularly perverse because, like the model of fully rational, economic individuals, they flow from self-interest. Whatever their origin, these incentives drive behavior that prevents the legal system from realizing the ideal of internalization. The biases generated by these incentives, therefore, are inherent in the legal institutions that we use to produce social welfare, at least insofar as those institutions seek to use self-interest as a tool for achieving an optimum level of risk.

BIASES FOR OVERASSESSMENT OF RISK IN THE ADJUDICATIVE SYSTEM

Critics of adjudicative risk assessment generally maintain that the process overassesses risk. In this view, the villains are venal attorneys and compassionate but shortsighted juries. Attorneys are assumed to capture large contingent fees by appealing to emotions raised by an individual victim's plight while ignoring the social implications of imposing liability on those whose activities produce a net reduction in risk (Huber 1985). Juries identify too readily with victims and compensate for risks that, while real, were offset by the social benefits of the underlying activity. Viewing the courtroom contest as one between defenseless victims and wealthy risk producers, juries render verdicts that have the ironic effect of increasing

Table 7.1. Hypothetical Example of the Determinants of Optimal Cost Strategies

Accident Avoidance Costs	990	995	1,000	1,005	1,010
Expected Accident Costs	10,100	10,050	10,000	9,998	9,997
Net Social Benefit from Marginal Investment (decrease in accidents costs −5)	50	45	45	−3	−4

See text for discussion of alternative strategies.

total social risk. Fear of excessive liability induces manufacturers to vacate socially useful (if risky) businesses such as the production of vaccines or sale of insurance for medical malpractice.[7]

My current concern is less with these actors (I argue below that these allegations are overstated) and more with the reactions of self-interested risk creators to the perception that the adjudicative system is loaded against them. Risk producers, concerned about the proplaintiff biases of juries, may attempt to compensate by investing in supraoptimal risk reduction mechanisms that are not justified by the injuries they avoid. This effect may be particularly acute in a system predicated on negligence. Risk producers found not to have acted negligently need pay for none of the injuries their product imposes. Yet a risk producer found to have acted negligently must compensate for all resultant injuries. The (perverse?) consequences of such a system may be demonstrated by the following example.

Assume that a risk producer can make expenditures in accident avoidance only in increments of five units. The more expenditures the risk producer makes, the lower the aggregate expected accident costs due to the underlying activity. Nevertheless, the marginal decrease in expected accident costs becomes smaller with each additional expenditure of five units. Assume further that the risk producer has already invested 990 units in accident avoidance and can reduce expected accident costs with further investment in accident avoidance as shown in Table 7.1.

On these assumptions, how much investment in safety would one wish the risk producer to make? If we desire an optimal level of safety, investment in accident avoidance should stop at 1,000 units. Any increment of five after this point will reduce accidents by less than five units—that is, marginal costs will exceed marginal benefits. (Of course, total benefits may still exceed total costs.) If legal negligence coincided with this calculus (as a strict cost-benefit analysis suggests it should), a risk producer who invested only 1,000 units in accident avoidance would be considered nonnegligent. The risk producer would, therefore, bear none of the 10,000 units of accident costs that materialized, since they did not arise through negligence. If, however, the risk producer believes that proplaintiff juries systematically, if erroneously, overassess risk, it has substantial incentive to overinvest (from a perspective of optimal investment) in risk reduction.

Assume the risk producer believes that juries (imbued with a proplaintiff bias) will find negligence unless 1,005 units of accident avoidance costs are invested. If the risk producer invests the 1,005 units, it will continue to be found nonnegligent, even though the last increment of five units was suboptimal from a societal perspective (i.e., the expenditure of five units only reduced accident costs by two units). Thus, the risk producer will bear none of the liability for the 9,998 units of accident costs that materialize. The risk producer, then, also believes that if it ceases to incur accident avoidance costs after 1,000 units—that is, fails to make the (supraoptimal) investment—juries will find negligence. Should that occur systematically, the risk producer will be liable for the full 10,000 units of accident costs. The marginal investment of five units, under these assumptions, obviously carries a substantial return for the risk producer, notwithstanding its negative sum effect on the rest of us (Shavell 1987; Grady 1983; Cooter 1984; Trebilcock 1987).

The legal system may adjust liability rules to counter incentives for undersupply or misallocation of useful activities. For instance, legal rules may include a series of privileges or immunities for actors who might otherwise be too concerned about personal liability to act in a manner consistent with social welfare. The defenses for defamatory speech, immunizing speakers from liability even for libelous falsehoods, may largely be explained as a means of ensuring that desirable speech is not overdeterred because of fear of liability. Unfortunately, once we confer immunity on an actor, there is less reason for that party to act in socially desirable ways where doing so deviates from self-interest.

Certainly, there is something troublesome about discussing liability exclusively in these quantitative terms (Kennedy 1981; Tribe 1972; Kneese, Ben-David, and Schulze 1983). One may contend that what appears from an economic perspective to be inefficient overinvestment, actually serves competing social objectives (such as those discussed by MacLean and Mills, above), quite well. Thus, imposition of liability may demonstrate a social desire to compensate identifiable victims, even though we know as a matter of naked statistics that we lose more than we gain by such schemes (Schelling 1984).

In a similar way, we explain decisions to make such "inefficient" investments as disrupting traffic patterns on major thoroughfares for several hours and endangering rescuers in order to save a single life.[8] Alternatively, we might explain tort liability as payment to victims whose injuries signal defects in technologies. But for those injuries, useful alterations in the technologies might not be made; because the rest of us benefit from those signals, we owe some debt to the earlier generations who suffered on our behalf.[9] Even if these less quantifiable variables increase the desirability of jury intervention, critics of that system remind us that vindication of our moral sensibilities is not costless. The incentives received by risk producers from the system remind us that among those costs is the irony of more or different risks that we might have to face.

BIASES FOR UNDERASSESSMENT OF RISK IN THE ADJUDICATIVE SYSTEM

It is difficult to argue with those who perceive systematic overassessment of risk in the adjudicative system. The logic of the system suggests that juries are likely to identify more readily with injured victims than with defendant risk producers and are sympathetic to the image of shattered lives. Judges, no less vulnerable to the presence of the injured, and schooled in the notion that optimal risk production requires that defendants internalize all the risks of their enterprises, are similarly willing to entertain novel legal theories on which liability is imposed.

Omitted from this calculus, however, is the understanding that these biases come into play only when cases reach the courts. If victims of risk fail to bring actions for redress, then the incentive signals of liability will never be received by risk producers. Thus, intrinsic biases in the adjudicative system that discourage victims from seeking redress may produce underassessment of the quantum of social risk.[10]

That this is the case may be recognized from the prosaic suggestion that pursuit of redress by victims is a costly enterprise. Not only does it take the plaintiff's time to pursue a case, but litigation costs may themselves be extensive. (I will return shortly to the issue of attorney fees.) These costs will be worth incurring for the individual plaintiff only if they are exceeded by an expected recovery.

Here, a variety of problems arise. Although the damage suffered by the plaintiff may be extensive, other legal prerequisites to recovery, such as demonstration of a causal relationship between the injury and defendant's conduct, may be difficult. Thus, the expected recovery may diminish, as damages are heavily discounted by the lower probability of satisfying the prima facie case. Recent cases concerning the uncertain effects of Bendectin come to mind as examples. Where the damage to any one individual is small, although the affected population is substantial, the expected award may not warrant pursuit of the case by any one victim, even if recovery of damage is certain. Acid rain, which may rust cars or cause defoliage of a property owner's tree, may also serve as an example here.

Unfortunately, modern technological risks tend to have characteristics that exacerbate these problems. Pollutants, drugs, and chemical additives produce adverse effects that have long latency periods and that are diffuse in that the same tortious act injures large numbers of persons. Latency increases substantially the difficulties of proving causal relationships because victims confront various potentially harmful substances between exposure to the injury-causing technology and recognition of the injury.[11] Even if informed about adverse future effects, potential victims may discount the risk during the latency period and overconsume risky technologies or fail to seek legal redress until a relevant statute of limitations has expired.

Diffusion has a more subtle effect. Injuries such as those resulting from medical malpractice are diffuse in that they occur to numerous individuals, but those injuries are also individual and discrete, in that the conditions that produce injury to one plaintiff are typically isolated from all other victims. The diffusion that materializes as a result of risky technologies, on the other hand, typically results when one set of conditions adversely affects numerous individuals. A chemical spill, a defective drug, or a nuclear meltdown are likely to be similar with respect to all those injured by the singular event. Whereas a successful litigant in a medical malpractice case confers little benefit on subsequent litigants (other than the incentive effect of liability that might decrease the probability of a subsequent case arising), the successful litigant in a technological risk case confers substantial benefit on those who come later. The proof of the underlying negligence or defect, of causation, of the type of injury manifested is likely to be similar in all cases. Novel theories of recovery, once accepted, will more readily be employed in subsequent cases.

In our precedential legal system, each of these prior cases constitutes a public good, available for use by those who have contributed nothing to its production. As is also the case with public goods, however, potential users have little incentive to contribute to their creation. Instead, individual "rational" behavior requires withholding contributions until some other party who values the good enough to incur all production costs decides to make it available to all. Where expected recoveries are small, as may be the case with latent, diffuse risks, this rationale affects each victim, so that all are engaged in an n-player Chicken Game. A case worth bringing (in the sense that the costs of avoiding the accident would have been justified by commensurate benefits) may not come to fruition, because the payoff to each of several potential litigants will be higher if some other potential litigant brings the initial lawsuit.

The ironic conclusion of such rational, self-interested behavior is that risk litigation is not oversupplied, as the critics of tort law usually protest. Rather, it is equally likely to be undersupplied, as victims—charged by the theory of adjudicative risk assessment with enforcement of the public welfare—fail to adjudicate.[12]

One adjustment to this "threat" is to compensate for the diffuse effects of risk by giving one individual a stake in the aggregate of harms. That individual would have the incentive to consider *all* costs of a technology and to pursue a recovery where those costs exceed benefits. This deus ex machina theoretically arrives in the guise of the class action attorney. Since the class attorney represents all victims, the theory assumes, he or she will internalize all injuries and will make decisions predicated on a comparison of all relevant data. Were the bar composed of altruists who thoroughly defined their personal interests in terms of the welfare of their clients, the class action would serve as a complete response to the threat of undersupplied litigation. Benevolence, however, has rarely been a primary feature imputed to the plaintiffs' bar. In the absence of benevolent actors, class attorneys' interests can clearly diverge from those of their clients—a tension that infects all principal/agent relationships (Jensen and Meckling 1976). Put most crudely, the class action attorney is likely to consider only his or her personal stake in the litigation, perhaps 25 percent of the total recovery.

As Coffee has illustrated in another context, the fee structure leads to two effects that coincide with a theory of undersupply of litigation (Coffee 1986). First, some socially valuable litigation will remain dormant. The class attorney will perform the same calculus of personal costs and benefits that individual clients perform outside the class action. If a case should require the expenditure of $250,000 in attorney time and expenses (including opportunity costs), a class attorney with an expected recovery rate of 25 percent would accept the case only if expected damages (total plaintiff damages discounted by probability of recovery) exceeded $1 million.

Given that complex class actions are likely to entail difficult legal issues that lower the probability of recovery, the case is likely to be accepted only where injuries attributed to defendants are extremely high.

Even where the class attorney accepts the case, the divergence between attorney and class interests may produce socially perverse behavior. Assume an attorney is considering whether to accept a case with a $1 million expected jury verdict of which he or she will keep 25 percent, or $250,000. Assume further that the attorney expects to incur $100,000 in time and costs for the case prior to trial and expects to incur another $100,000 in opportunity costs during the course of the trial. That is, but for the trial, the attorney could engage in alternative work for an expected fee of $100,000. Thus, the attorney expects to net $50,000 by pursuing this case rather than another one and will take the case.

Now assume that the attorney incurs the initial $100,000 expenditure, but defendants offer to settle prior to trial for $800,000. The class attorney may be entitled to a lesser percentage of the settlement than if the case went to trial. Let us assume a fee of 20 percent, or $160,000, from the settlement. But now our attorney avoids the $100,000 opportunity costs that would have been incurred during a trial. The settlement permits the attorney to accept the alternative work, for a total recovery during the same time period of $260,000. In short, he or she comes out ahead by accepting a settlement, even though the class is compensated less than would be expected if the case went to trial. Here again, the incentive structure of the adjudicative system suggests that risk cases will be undersupplied, or underprosecuted, and not oversupplied.

Again, some counterbalancing mechanisms are at work. Even self-interested attorneys may have incentives not to take their clients' interests so lightly. If the attorney believes that a trial will receive public attention and enhance his or her reputation, he or she might refuse the settlement. Indeed, the attorney might refuse a settlement that served a client's interests in order to achieve the greater notoriety of a public trial. Alternatively, a self-interested attorney might proceed to trial in order to pursue novel legal theories that are frequently involved in complex class litigation.[13] Success in such an endeavor might bring the attorney fame as well as additional business. Even if the effort fails, the reputation value of the effort within the legal community may prove the attempt to be a "loss leader."

In addition, protective devices in the system exist to prevent blatant abuses of client's rights—that is, requirements that settlements be judicially approved.[14] Nevertheless, unless we believe that these internal checks and external protective devices work perfectly, we cannot expect class attorneys to serve as perfect surrogates for the vindication of a socially optimal level of risk.

THE REGULATORY RESPONSE

The typical response to threats of undersupply in risk litigation is to rely on regulation. As noted at the outset, regulation proceeds largely from the premise that many of the incentives for private parties to pursue the public good will not be sufficient. Although most of the literature of regulation speaks of these gaps in terms of information or high administrative costs of using the tort system, the same result obtains where the undersupply is due to the biases of narrow self-interest, latency, and diffusion that I have discussed (Shavell 1987). From this gap arises the publicly spirited regulator, capable of accumulating information at relatively low cost, empowered with the ability to prevent operation of risky technologies ex ante as well as recover for the consequences of their defects ex post, and motivated to issue regulations wherever justified. The problem with this story is that it omits the very same biases of self-interest that render regulation necessary in the first place.

James Krier and I have seized on more contemporary (less naive) conceptions of regulation to suggest there is little reason to imagine that regulation will sufficiently compensate for the failures of market-based (e.g., adjudicative) risk assessment (Krier and Gillette 1985; Barry 1982: 53–56). The argument proceeds from the proposition that regulation is undertaken by officials who are not motivated solely by public interest. Instead, they seek to maximize more personal objectives. In the views of different writers, the goals to be maximized take various forms: personal advancement, agency budgets, votes (Diver 1983: 101–2). The effect of this distortion is that regulators trade in the political marketplace in the same way that private actors trade in the private marketplace. The currency is different—purchases are made through expressions of influence and promises of electoral support, rather than with cold cash. But the effect is the same: scarce goods, be they private goods or governmental services, are allocated to those individuals willing to pay the price.

In the regulatory context, this dynamic suggests that regulation will often be undersupplied or supplied in a manner that deviates from public interest. The explanation again has its origins in the incentive effects of self-interest. Obtaining or deterring regulation is, like litigation, a costly enterprise. Thus, it will come into existence only if someone is willing to bear the costs. Notwithstanding the benefits of a given regulation, it is not clear that someone will. If a regulation would benefit the public at large, it is conceivable that no single individual will gain sufficiently to justify incurring the costs (lobbying, petitioning the support of others) that attend promulgation or passage of the regulation. The cooperation of numerous beneficiaries would be required to secure the regulation. Since each potential cooperator would have to invest more in the political effort than he or she is likely to receive (in reduced pollution, for instance) and will be able to obtain the same benefit should others undertake the political task, cooperation simply does not arise. Rather, free riding on the efforts of others is the order of the day.

Here, the destructive game is not the Chicken Game of litigation, but the redoubtable Prisoners' Dilemma (Hardin 1982). Each situation is characterized by a preference by each player for selfish behavior while some other party engages in cooperative behavior. In the former, however, the payoff from cooperative conduct (bringing the precedent-making lawsuit) is sufficiently great that some self-interested actor may ultimately act if it appears that no one else will. Even though the payoff to that actor will be less than would have been the case had some other actor taken the first step, it is greater than would be the case if there were universal inaction.

In Prisoners' Dilemma, however, there is no positive utility in individual action. The good that is sought can be attained only if several persons contribute to its production. Thus, if one believes that others are unlikely to act cooperatively, individual resources expended in the effort to attain the good will produce no payoff. Regulation of environmental hazards appears readily (too readily, if we are concerned about materialization of those hazards) to fit this model. Since the benefits of regulation are widespread, numerous persons could receive them even if they made no contribution to securing the regulation. Thus, the benefits are unlikely to be sufficiently substantial in any given case to warrant the individual cost that would have to be incurred by those few who are motivated to contribute to collective action. Those who oppose the regulation, on the other hand, are likely to suffer substantial harm should the regulatory effort prevail. In terms of social choice theory, the opponents may constitute a privileged group, small enough to overcome obstacles to cooperation and to induce its members to engage in the political efforts necessary to secure regulatory sympathy.[15]

None of this is to say that regulations will not materialize; the legal landscape is too crowded with administrative intervention to make any such claim. Nor does collective action theory predict a total absence of regulation that serves public interest. Public interest may be vindicated by the presence of altruists, by political entrepreneurs who seek to galvanize support under the rubric of public interest, or by the use of by-products that permit special interest groups to secure the support of large numbers of the public and thus increase their influence with political leaders (Hardin 1982: 33–37; Elliott, Ackerman, and Millian 1985).

The collective action explanation for regulation, however, does postulate that the regulations that emerge will be predicated on the interests of groups that are able to express their view to political leaders, rather than the interests of the public at large. At times, the result may be underregulation, as when an industry group convinces an agency that further governmental intervention is unnecessary. At times, the result may be increased governmental intervention, as when defense contractors persuade agencies of the need for additional armaments. In each case, however, the institutional bias causes results that deviate from the optimum that would result from simple consideration of the ambiguous "public interest." The divergence will rarely be total. An industry that secures a regulation mandating a less than optimal level of pollution may still have to reduce emissions below what it would prefer from a purely self-interested perspective. The aggregation of numerous small divergencies, however, culminates in substantial deviation from an optimal level of social risk.

While these characteristics infect all regulatory efforts, they are of particular moment for modern technological risks for reasons that should now be familiar. Here, again, latency combines with diffusion to misdirect regulatory efforts. Political decision-makers are likely to have a limited time horizon—that is, the next election—to which they refer in deciding the merits of an action or proceeding along a given route. Those who will incur costs as a result of minimizing technological risk—that is, risk producers—will likely incur those costs in the short term. They therefore are motivated to influence decisions by demonstrating how substantial those costs will be in the short term during which the decision-maker is seeking electoral support.

Benefits of such regulation, on the other hand, often appear only in the long term. The environment will not become clean quickly, cancer rates will not show marked decreases immediately. Not only does this delayed reward reduce the incentives for beneficiaries to lobby for governmental intervention (as they may discount the benefits of their activities to present value); the existence of long-term benefits also reduces the politicians' incentives to become involved, as they are unlikely to be in office to accept credit when the perceived benefits materialize.

Other biases serve to augment or counter the political incentives to over- or underregulate risk. A need for bureaucrats to justify their positions may generate the ubiquitous discovery of undue risk. The zeal of agencies such as the Consumer Product Safety Commission may indicate that something along these lines is occurring.[16] Faith in quantifiable variables may lead bureaucrats to underassess social dread of catastrophic events and thus not regulate activities that society perceives as the most risky (Slovic, Fischhoff, and Lichtenstein 1980: 181; 1985: 239). The honest belief that solutions will be found before risks materialize may lead regulators to discount future risk.[17] Regardless of the source, each of these biases sends the same message: our regulatory system can scarcely be considered a compensatory mechanism for the failures of alternative risk assessment procedures.

A PARTIAL INQUIRY INTO WHAT IS TO BE DONE

If we desired to countermand the biases of the legal system that foster incomplete internalization, what governance structure would we create? I want to conclude with an inquiry into some responses to this issue, aimed at a particular source of some biases discussed above.

Many of the problems I have discussed emerge from the fact that the risks we seek to avoid will materialize, if at all, in the distant future. Pollution, resource exhaustion, chemical carcinogens threaten our future selves and our descendants more than they threaten our immediate well-being. Both potential plaintiffs and government regulators appear to respond to the nonimmediacy of technological threats by underassessing their importance. For some of these threats, a narrow view of self-interest may rationally dictate that long-term threats be ignored.

If materialization of the threat is sufficiently distant that it does not even threaten our future selves, one will attend to the threat only on the belief that we owe obligations to future generations.[18] Indeed, even if we have such obligations, it may be that we should be reluctant to engage in political choices that foreclose inhabitants of the future from making their own decisions. (What if it turns out that future generations would prefer that we had done more for ourselves?) Even if harm can be expected to materialize within our own lifetime, we should adjust only if we think that our future preferences are more valuable than our current ones.[19]

The problem is exacerbated by the debate over discounting future effects of current decisions. Full internalization of costs and benefits would appear to require that we recognize the opportunity costs of investing today in the avoidance of injuries that would not otherwise materialize for a substantial period of time. The cost of regulating carcinogens that would have caused disease in ten years includes forgoing the productive and consumption uses that could have been made of those same dollars during the interim period.[20] Nevertheless, discounting future effects may lead to results that seem troublesome, if not insidious. If risks are truly latent over a substantial period of time, the application of even a modest discount rate—that is, less than 5 percent—requires ignoring those effects totally. Assume, for instance, that we are trying to decide whether to site a nuclear power plant on a tract where construction of a facility would immediately impede nearby residents' views of pristine vistas (and thus reduce their property values) or on a fault line that is not expected to cause an earthquake for two hundred years but would then threaten the integrity of the plant's nuclear core. Although the earthquake could ultimately produce catastrophic results, the present value of those effects would be sufficiently minuscule to justify siting the plant on the fault line.

Notwithstanding both the complexity and intrigue of these issues, I want for the moment to grant that it is appropriate to consider future adverse effects in deciding what level of risk to accept today. Assuming further (although this debate, too, is far from over) that it is appropriate for government to intervene in order to ensure that we abide by these moral tenets, it might be worth considering how to implement obligations to the future. Certainly there are constitutional and political limits on what democratic systems would be willing to accept. But here, too, let us relax all constraints and imagine what kind of systems would best internalize the costs of present actions to the future if that were our primary objective.

If we take self-interest as our operative motivation, the easiest way to induce government to take future effects into account is to give officials a personal stake in the future. To some extent, we provide just that incentive by preserving our leaders' places in history. That we speak of "good" presidents and "bad" presidents indicates that current leaders retain a stake in how they are perceived in the future. If they make shortsighted decisions that adversely affect the future, they cannot expect to have favorable reputations in history books. Reputation, however, is important only for a select number of leaders. It is doubtful that current administrators of federal agencies will believe that history will remember them regardless of the positive or negative effects of their short reigns. Instead, their decisions are likely to be attributed to the administration in which they serve.

We might alternatively extend the terms of office of public officials. Those in administrations of four years or congressional terms of two or six years can respond only to short-term interests if they are to expect electoral support in subsequent bids for office. In any event, terms that would ensure that decision-makers remain in office to reap the long-term effects of earlier decisions (fifteen to twenty years) would pose problems of personal longevity. More radical solutions might then be considered. Perhaps even those who dismiss any moral obligation to future generations would feel a special affinity for their own bloodline or gene pool. On this theory, we might restrict public office to those who had children under a certain age. Alternatively, we might explicitly hold the descendants of decision-makers responsible for the unreasonable long-term effects imposed on future generations.

Less frivolous (more mundane) suggestions might rely on the benefits of education as a way to overcome bias or self-interest. If self-interest is socially, rather than genetically, mandated, we might attempt to retrain at least a segment of society in a manner that induces altruistic or benevolent consideration of social welfare. Perhaps enhancing the professionalism of the civil service, requiring those who would serve the public either within a bureaucracy or as elected officials to undergo formal training, might provide opportunities to inculcate a sense of obligation to the future. Indeed, we might consider professional juries for cases that deal with technological risk, so that they might more readily comprehend and consider the implications of their decisions for future risk.

Obviously, any such suggestion creates substantial tension with our nonelitist conception of democracy. Further, it ignores the nontechnical components of risk—that is, dread of particular types of deaths—and ignores the relative capacity of nonexperts to make decisions under conditions of uncertainty, where technical proficiency is less important in reaching rational solutions.

Finally, we might attempt to incorporate concerns for the future into adjudication. Where we know that technologies create hazards for the unborn, we might attach to damage awards a sum to be held in trust for future generations. While we may be unable to save them from risk, if we can predict both the types and numbers of injuries that they will suffer as a result of current practices, a trust fund might at least serve as some offset that simultaneously forces risk creators to consider the long-term effects of their conduct.[21] Indeed, the recent litigation involving Dalkon Shield intrauterine devices has employed just such a mechanism for awarding damages to those not yet determined to have suffered injury.

Consideration of future effects might similarly be strengthened if we could provide some representation for subsequent generations in decisions about whether and how to permit risky technologies. Our legal system frequently utilizes representatives of those who cannot be present to advocate their own views. The class action attorney (ideally) plays this role where plaintiffs are too numerous to represent themselves; similarly, guardians for the incompetent are also frequent players in the litigation game.

While it would require some level of altruism by the representative, there seems little institutional reason to preclude the appointment of trustees for the unborn who are obligated to advocate the position that would advance the interests of the future, even at the expense of the present generation. Those ultimately making the decision presumably would be induced to take account of these factors, and risk creators subject to such decisions would equally be induced to internalize future effects.

None of this is to say that perfect internalization can be expected in the difficult area of intertemporal costs and benefits. We can say that marginal improvements may be possible. There is, however, a more important lesson to be learned from the biases inherent in a legal system that seeks to harness and respond to self-interested conduct. The growth of technology suggests that these biases will become more salient as risks that share characteristics of latency and diffusion multiply. Thus, the divergence between the ideal and actual conduct induced by the legal system is similarly likely to increase. If we are to continue using the legal system as a primary mechanism for monitoring socially acceptable levels of risk, we must at least think about ways to alleviate these biases before we are lulled into a naive belief that optimum risk is within easy grasp.

NOTES

1. As I hope to make clear, by the phrase "the legal system" I mean procedures both for adjudication of losses that materialize as a result of hazards and for regulation that minimizes the probability that a hazard will materialize.

2. In contemporary jurisprudence, outside the realm of defective products, liability without fault, or strict liability, is typically confined to activities that are deemed "abnormally dangerous" (Prosser and Keeton 1984: 545–49). While the relevant activities defy easy definition, they typically provide benefits in excess of expected loss (so that it is not negligent to engage in them) and present risks not easily contained even with the exercise of due care. Additionally, those who engage in the activities typically have an informational advantage over those who might be adversely affected by the activity, so that the former stand in a superior position to determine the propriety of the activity at a given time and place.

3. We do occasionally act as though avoidance of all risk were our goal. Thus, the Delaney Clause of the Federal Food, Drug, and Cosmetic Act seeks to avoid all carcinogenic food additives, regardless of their offsetting benefits or the degree of their carcinogenicity: see 21 U.S.C. §348 (c) (3) (A). Potential reasons for these constraints are explored in chapter 3, above, by Douglas MacLean and Claudia Mills.

4. This implicit cost-benefit analysis of reasonableness is most often attributed to the law and economics movement (see Posner 1986; Shavell 1987). Nevertheless, it is not necessarily tied to any ideological school. It has its explicit origins in Learned Hand's formula for negligence in United States v. Carroll Towing, 159 F. 2d 169 (2d Cir. 1947). It is difficult to imagine an interpretation of reasonableness, even under deontological, noneconomic conceptions of tort law, that does not require some comparison of the costs and benefits of the activity at issue; see Natural Resources Defense Council v. EPA, 824 F. 2d 1146 (D.C. Cir. 1987) (en banc), rejecting strict cost-benefit tests for defining "ample margin of safety" in federal legislation, but permitting consideration of cost and technological factors in regulation of hazardous substances.

5. See Restatement (2d) of Torts §402A.

6. See Restatement (2d) of Torts §402A, comment k; MacDonald v. Ortho Pharmaceutical Corp., 394 Mass. 131, 475 N.E. 2d 65 (1985); Cochran v. Brooke, 243 Or. 89, 409 P. 2d 904 (1966).

7. One may view these withdrawals with some skepticism. If tort immunity had extended to suppliers of vaccine, is it certain that those who left the market would have remained? Given the inelastic demand for immunization from dread disease, one would imagine that much of the producers' liability exposure could be covered by increased prices. Indeed, that is just what some vaccine manufacturers have done (Huber 1985: 289). Alternatively, one might have expected insurers to continue to write insurance, but to exclude particular risks from coverage—e.g., those not specifically attributable to the insured's negligence. What, then, explains the more radical measure of abandoning the market? A variety of solutions having nothing to do with liability is possible. Manufacturers may have believed that the business was worth retaining only if they could achieve a specific market share that they considered unavailable given current market conditions; manufacturers

may have believed that alternative drugs were even more profitable and limited capacity precluded simultaneous production of both. The structure of the industry might include conditions that favor a monopolistic supply structure. Why, however, would members of the industry contend that they were forced out by increasing tort liability if that were not in fact the case? A threat to leave the market may induce others to immunize the manufacturer and thus shift costs of injuries away from the manufacturer. Indeed, that is exactly what happened, as the federal government intervened to immunize vaccine producers from litigation losses. See Neustadt and Fineberg 1978: 57–62; National Childhood Vaccine Injury Act of 1986.

There is a vast difference, however, between threatening to take action and actually taking it. The threatened action may be irrational, as in the case of abandoning a profitable business. Thus, there is no reason for the threatened party to believe the threat. Short-term irrational action, however, may constitute rational action in the long term. If acting on an irrational threat now ensures some protection—e.g., federal insulation from liability—then the actor can reenter the market in the long term and make substantially greater profits than would otherwise be the case (Regan 1972). Even if reentry into a specific market is difficult, governmentally conferred immunity may cross product lines. Thus, a firm that intends to shift from production of X to production of Y may be able to obtain blanket immunity for all its products if it can persuade the government that the "true" reason for its departure from the market for X was increased liability costs. For an analysis that attributes the "insurance crisis" at least partially to an expansion in tort law, see Priest 1987.

8. "Value of One Life? From \$8.37 to \$10 Million," *New York Times*, June 26, 1985.

9. This is an application of Albert Hirschman's Principle of the Hiding Hand (1982).

10. Cognitive or other psychological biases may also lead to underuse of the adjudication system. For instance, victims of a technology may suffer from dissonance that leads them to deny their injury and thus to eschew means for redress (Akerlof and Dickens 1982).

11. On the legal implications of exposure to multiple causes of injury, see Robinson 1982.

12. For a different perspective leading to the same conclusion, see Abel 1987.

13. For instance, market share liability, in which drug manufacturers who could not be linked to specific plaintiffs were required to pay damages based on their share of the market for a specific product, was introduced in the DES cases. See Sindell v. Abbott Laboratories, 26 Cal. 3d 588, 607 P. 2d 924, 163 Cal. Rptr. 132 (1980). Novel efforts to avoid the government contractor defense were undertaken in the Agent Orange litigation: see in re "Agent Orange" Product Liability Litigation, 818 F. 2d 187 (2d Cir. 1987).

14. See Fed. R. Civ. P. 23(e).

15. The label is from the classic work on the failure of collective action to materialize (Olson 1971: 48–52). For an argument that the capacity to overcome obstacles to collective action does not necessarily depend on group size, see Taylor 1987: 9–13.

16. A study commissioned by the Consumer Product Safety Commission has recently found undue risk in permitting children to play baseball without use of chest protectors by pitchers, catchers, and batters. See Prod. and Liab. Rep. 3, Jan. 2, 1987.

17. Hence a willingness to proceed with nuclear power before solving the difficult issue of storing nuclear waste (Douglas and Wildavsky 1982).

18. Two extremely helpful collections on this issue are MacLean and Brown 1983, and Sikora and Barry 1978. In addition, helpful essays include Hubin 1976; Barry 1977; Parfit 1986.

19. On the prudence of considering our future preferences in making current decisions, see Nagel 1970; Regan 1983.

20. See, e.g., Executive Office of the President, Office of Management and Budget, Regulatory Program of the United States Government, April 1, 1987– March 31, 1987, at xxi–xxii.

21. I am assuming that managers of publicly held risk-creating companies do not perfectly consider long-term risk and that stock prices do not perfectly internalize the failures of managers to signal the market that certain practices are overdiscounting future effects. On the principle of offsetting future effects with some kind of compensation from the present generation, see Barry 1983.

REFERENCES

Abel, Richard L.
    1987   "The Real Tort Crisis—Too *Few* Claims." *Ohio State Law Journal* 48 (2): 443–67.
Akerlof, George A., and Dickens, William T.
    1982   "The Economic Consequences of Cognitive Dissonance." *American Economic Review* 72 (3): 307–19.
Barry, Brian
    1977   "Justice Between Generations," in *Law, Morality and Society: Essays in Honour of H. L. A. Hart*, P.M.S. Hacker and J. Raz, eds., 268. Oxford: Clarendon Press.
    1982   "Political Participation as Rational Action," in *Rational Man and Irrational Society?* B. Barry and R. Hardin, eds., 53–56. Beverly Hills: Sage.
    1983   "Intergenerational Justice in Energy Policy," in *Energy and the*

Future, Douglas MacLean and P. Brown, eds., 15–30. Totowa, N.J.: Rowman and Littlefield.

Coffee, John C., Jr.

1986   "Understanding the Plaintiff's Attorney: The Implications of Economic Theory for Private Enforcement of Law Through Class and Derivative Actions." *Columbia Law Review* 86 (4): 669–727.

Consumer Product Safety Commission

1987   *Product and Liability Report* 3. Jan. 2.

Cooter, Robert

1984   "Prices and Sanctions." *Columbia Law Review* 84 (6): 1523–60.

Diver, Colin S.

1983   "The Optimal Precision of Administrative Rules." *Yale Law Journal* 93 (1): 65–109.

Douglas, Mary, and Wildavsky, Aaron

1982   *Risk and Culture*. Berkeley: University of California Press.

Elliott, E. Donald, Ackerman, Bruce A., and Millian, John C.

1985   "Toward a Theory of Statutory Evolution: The Federalization of Environmental Law." *Journal of Law, Economics, and Organization* 1 (2): 313–40.

Executive Office of the President

1987   Office of Management and Budget, Regulatory Program of the United States Government, April 1, 1987–March 31, 1987: xxi–xxii.

Grady, Mark F.

1983   "A New Positive Economic Theory of Negligence." *Yale Law Journal* 92 (5): 799–829.

Hardin, Russell

1982   *Collective Action*. Baltimore: Johns Hopkins University Press.

Hirschman, Albert O.

1982   *Shifting Involvements: Private Interest and Public Action*. Oxford: M. Robertson.

Huber, Peter

1985   "Safety and the Second Best: The Hazards of Public Risk Management in the Courts." *Columbia Law Review* 85 (2): 277–337.

Hubin, D. Clayton

1976   "Justice and Future Generations." *Philosophy and Public Affairs* 6 (1): 70–83.

Jensen, Michael C., and Meckling, William H.

1976   "Theory of the Firm: Managerial Behavior, Agency Costs and Ownership Structure." *Journal of Financial Economics* 3 (4): 305–60.

Kennedy, Duncan

1981   "Cost-Benefit Analysis of Entitlement Problems: A Critique." *Stanford Law Review* 33: 387–445.

Kneese, Allen V., Ben-David, Shaul, and Schulze, William D.

    1983   "The Ethical Foundations of Benefit-Cost Analysis," in *Energy and the Future*, D. MacLean and P. Brown, eds., 59–74. Totowa, N.J.: Rowman and Littlefield.

Krier, James E., and Gillette, Clayton P.

    1985   "The Un-Easy Case for Technological Optimism." *Michigan Law Review* 84 (3): 405–29.

MacLean, Douglas, and Brown, Peter G.

    1983   *Energy and the Future*. Totowa, N.J.: Rowman and Littlefield.

Nagel, Thomas

    1970   *The Possibility of Altruism*. Oxford: Clarendon Press.

National Childhood Vaccine Injury Act of 1986

    1986   Washington, D.C.: U.S. Government Printing Office.

Neustadt, Richard E., and Fineberg, Harvey V.

    1978   *The Swine Flu Affair: Decision-Making on a Slippery Disease*. Washington, D.C.: U.S. Department of Health, Education, and Welfare.

New York Times

    1985   "Value of One Life? From $8.37 to $10." I, 1:2. June 26.

Olson, Mancur

    1971   *The Logic of Collective Action: Public Goods and the Theory of Groups*. Cambridge: Harvard University Press.

Parfit, Derek

    1986   *Reasons and Persons*. New York: Oxford University Press.

Posner, Richard A.

    1986   *Economic Analysis of Law* (3d ed.). Boston: Little, Brown.

Priest, George L.

    1987   "The Current Insurance Crisis and Modern Tort Law." *Yale Law Journal* 96 (7): 1521–90.

Prosser, William, and Keeton, P.

    1984   *Torts* (5th edition).

Regan, Donald H.

    1972   "The Problem of Social Cost Revisited." *Journal of Law and Economics* 15 (2): 427–37.

    1983   "Paternalism, Freedom, Identity, and Commitment," in *Paternalism*, R. Sartorius, ed., 113.

Robinson, Glen O.

    1982   "Multiple Causation in Tort Law: Reflections on the *DES* Cases." *Virginia Law Review* 68 (4): 713–69.

Sartorius, Rolf E., ed.

    1983   *Paternalism*. Minneapolis: University of Minnesota Press.

Schelling, Thomas C.

    1984   *Choice and Consequence*. Cambridge: Harvard University Press.

Shavell, Steven
  1984   "Liability for Harm Versus Regulation of Safety." *Journal of Legal Studies* 13 (2): 357–74.
  1987   *Economic Analysis of Accident Law*. Cambridge: Harvard University Press.
Sikora, R.I., and Barry, Brian
  1978   *Obligations to Future Generations*. Philadelphia: Temple University Press.
Slovic, Paul, Fischhoff, Baruch, and Lichtenstein, Sarah
  1980   "Facts and Fears: Understanding Perceived Risk," in *Societal Risk Assessment: How Safe is Safe Enough?* Richard C. Schwing and Walter A. Albers, eds., 181–216. New York: Plenum Press.
  1985   "Regulation of Risk: A Psychological Perspective," in *Regulatory Policy and the Social Sciences*, Roger G. Noll, ed., 239–78. Berkeley: University of California Press.
Taylor, Michael
  1987   *The Possibility of Cooperation*. Cambridge: Cambridge University Press.
Trebilcock, A.
  1987   "The Social Insurance-Deterrence Dilemma of Modern North American Tort Law: A Canadian Perspective on the Liability Insurance Crisis." *San Diego Law Review* 24: 929.
Tribe, Laurence H.
  1972   "Policy Science: Analysis or Ideology." *Philosophy and Public Affairs* 2: 66–110.

CHAPTER 8

On Risk Communication as Interorganizational Control

The Case of the Aviation Safety Reporting System

Phillip K. Tompkins

The tragedy occurred on a Sunday morning, December 1, 1974, at 11:09. Trans World Airlines (TWA) Flight 514 was headed toward Dulles Airport in turbulent weather. The aircraft descended below the minimum safe altitude and slammed into a Virginia mountaintop. One hundred persons were killed.

As required by law, the National Transportation Safety Board (NTSB) investigated the accident. Two significant facts emerged from the investigation. The first was that a United Airlines crew had narrowly escaped the same tragic fate in the same approach only six weeks before the crash of TWA 514. Had the incident involving the United flight taken place one year earlier, the result would have probably been only a troublesome memory for the crew; there would have been no *institutional memory* of the event. In January 1974, however, United had created an internal reporting system called the "Flight Safety Awareness Program." Crew members were strongly encouraged to report anonymously any incident they felt was a potential threat to safety. The United pilots reported the incident at Dulles, and other United pilots were informed of the trap. Unfortunately, no established channels of communication were available for spreading the word to other airlines. Thus, the crew of TWA 514 was unable to benefit from the report filed by their United counterparts.

The second fact revealed by the NTSB investigation is not as important to the origin of the Aviation Safety Reporting System (ASRS) as it is to the subject of this paper. It was determined that both incidents were caused by the "ambiguous nature of the charted approach procedure and the differences in its interpretation between pilots and controllers" (Reynard et al. 1986: 3). The two incidents giving rise to the creation of the ASRS, one a tragedy and the other having a happier outcome, were found to be the result of two different meanings for the word "clearance"—one intended by the Dulles controllers and the second assigned by the pilots—in short, a breakdown in human communication. The drama of the TWA and United flights illustrates the potential importance of communication in both creating risks and hazards and mitigating or removing them. It also illustrates the crucial role of organizations in risks and hazards.

The starting place for any essay on communication, organization, and technological hazards must be Charles Perrow's *Normal Accidents* (1984). It is necessary, however, to reveal my perspectives on these phenomena before proceeding with the analysis. First, I introduce my terminological and epistemological articles of faith. Second, I examine Perrow's *Normal Accidents* (1984) by means of constructive critique. Third, I consider in some detail the case of the NASA Aviation Safety Reporting System (ASRS) in making my case for communication. Fourth, and finally, I offer a summarizing statement and some recommendations for research and for policy.

TERMINOLOGICAL ARTICLES OF FAITH

I have a long-term interest in organizations-as-communication-systems as demonstrated by studies of labor unions (Tompkins 1962), universities (Tompkins and Anderson 1971), NASA during the Apollo and Apollo Applications era (Tompkins 1977; 1978), as well as theoretical and empirical work on organizational identification and decision-making (Tompkins et al. 1975), and organizational control processes (Tompkins and Cheney 1985). Trained in both quantitative and qualitative methods, I have done both kinds of research, sometimes at the same time, and have participated in the interpretive, rhetorical, or symbolic "turn" in organizational studies (e.g., Tompkins 1985; 1986; in press). This turn, for which I have been an advocate, can be summarized in the following way. Organizational theory is an extension of the classical and modern concerns of rhetorical theory, the study of "the use of language as a symbolic means of inducing co-operation in beings that by nature respond to symbols" (Burke 1969: 43).

Instead of merely *privileging* symbolism over substance, the rhetorical-symbolic turn accepts Kenneth Burke's deconstruction of substance:

> Any attempt to define substance must proceed by means of symbols, unmistakably *not* the thing being defined; substance thus designates a thing in terms of what it is *not*—that is, something intrinsic to a thing is outside or extrinsic to it, as suggested etymologically by *sub*stance, a foundation or a standing under. The paradox of substance thus desta-bilizes the very meaning of the term. [Tompkins in press]

The symbolic turn also embraces Richard Rorty's capitulation in philoso-phy that "words take their meaning from other words rather than by virtue of their representative character, and the corollary that vocabularies acquire their privileges from the men who use them rather than from their transparency to the real" (Rorty 1979: 368).

The symbolic turn does not entail the denial of what is normally called "the real world." Rather, it would acknowledge its existence not as "sub-stance," but as the nonsymbolic or the extrasymbolic. In a methodological extension of this position it is claimed that the " 'text' is the locus of (social) inquiry," both as the "subject" and the product of investigation:

> There is nothing outside the text if we are to conduct research and do criticism; textual production is required to discuss even things which *we commonly treat as outside the domain of the symbolic*; when we imagine, for example, that we are making *direct representation* of physi-cal phenomena like the architecture and environment of a workplace in our reports. [Cheney and Tompkins in press]

Accepting Burke's "logology" as epistemology, and extending his theory of "indexing" literary works to social inquiry in general, Cheney and Tompkins enumerate seven propositions or techniques for analyzing texts in terms of equations, implications, and transformations. The method holds the analyst to the "text," while allowing for the development of inferences and the construction of "proof." The method may as well "be placed within Burke's overarching ontological framework, 'Dramatism,' because it helps us understand *what people are doing* (or *saying*) when they quite literally act" (Cheney and Tompkins in press).

Cheney and Dionisopoulos have recently considered the ramifications of this approach for organizations:

> Now, what are the implications of these views for rhetorical and organizational theory in general, and corporate communications in particular? First, as Phillip Tompkins puts it, symbolism must be considered as the "substance" of organization. . . . This point attends to the rhetorical turn in philosophy and how it was, in fact, anticipated by Kenneth Burke (e.g., 1966; 1969). *The organization is at least words and other symbols*, to deepen the communicative definition offered by Barnard (1968: 65): "a system of consciously coordinated activities or forces of two or more persons." Though we are prone to reify, instantiate, or otherwise make concrete the notion of organization . . . it is better thought of as a "text" or as a thing, an entity, or a monolith. A symbolic, rhetorical, textual conception of organization gives us—individual participants, clients, analysts, consumers, or observers—more direct access to the workings of an organization *qua* an organization. [Cheney and Dionisopoulos 1987: 5–6]

Double Interact of Control

The symbolic or textual approach illuminates patterns of symbolic action between and among beings who by nature respond to symbols. One such pattern is the double interact. First labeled by Hollander and Willis (1967), the double interact was taken over by Weick as the organizational "unit of analysis" (1979: 89). Tompkins and Cheney saw one double interact as more important than others: "*the double interact of control*. Supervisor A gives *directions* to subordinate B; subordinate B complies (or fails to comply) and the 'messages' concerning compliance and goal attainment are *monitored* through feedback loops leading back to A; supervisor A assesses the results of B's performance and accordingly dispenses *rewards* and *punishments* to B. This double interact of control—directing, monitoring, and rewarding/punishing—simultaneously provides us with the basic act of organizing and demonstrates why communicating and organizing are nearly synonymous" (Tompkins and Cheney 1985: 195), and why the double interact of control is the "building block" of organizational life that must be seen "intertextually."

NORMAL ACCIDENTS

Perrow's influential book, *Normal Accidents: Living with High-Risk Technologies* (1984), places organizations at the center of risk-analysis. There is a good reason. Perrow is an organizational theorist. His earlier book, *Complex Organizations: A Critical Essay* (1979), established his reputation, at least in part, through a devastating critique of the psychological approach to organizations and a spirited defense of Weber's ideal type of bureaucracy. Since that earlier book, however, Perrow appears to have been persuaded that modern technology is too much for Weber's rational, calculating, and efficient bureaucracy to handle. The problem is the unanticipated complexity of the technologies that modern bureaucracies must try to master before those technologies master the globe: nuclear power production; nuclear weapons production; petrochemical production; air and marine transportation; and genetic engineering.

Perrow submits these organizations and their technologies to a two-by-two analysis (the same kind of analysis, incidentally, that Weber used to analyze rationality) in which the horizontal oppositions are linear/complex interaction and the vertical oppositions are loose/tight coupling. The dichotomous terms are only vaguely defined and allow for enough "casuistic stretching" (Burke 1984) to make the examples placed in the four quadrants sound plausible. Perrow says of his variables that they are "based entirely on subjective judgments on my part; at present there is no reliable way to measure these two variables, interaction and coupling" (Perrow 1984: 96).

The title of his book is a trope or rhetorical figure, called "perspective by incongruity" by Burke (1984), and directing attention to his conclusion that in complex, tightly coupled systems, the inevitable failures that one expects will one day interact with each other in ways that are incomprehensible to the operators. The result is catastrophe, the "normal" or expected accident; it is normal because it is inevitable and is anticipated by Perrow's analysis. In fact, some have said that Perrow's book "predicted" the disasters we identify today as Challenger, Chernobyl, and Bhopal. I doubt that a close reading of his text would support that claim. For example, his chapter on petrochemical plants (written before the Bhopal catastrophe) says the industry is "quite safe" (Perrow 1984: 101). (In fact, Perrow's meaning for high-risk seems to be radically different from the meaning intended in the risk/hazards literature, and this issue should be debated. Whether relevant or not, Perrow does take a dim view of risk assessors, calling them "a new breed of shamans" [12]. If his charge is true—that the assessors seek to exclude the public from participating in decisions about technology—Perrow has misspoken; they require a stronger epithet.)

My general evaluation of the book is that it is admirable, too important to be ignored. It is a contentious, well-written volume that can be called neither true nor false. It is an argument, based on probabilities, that arrives at a certainty. I happen to think the probabilities are on his side, but at the same time there are deformities in the analysis. One is that he regards human workers in these organizations as components little different from the machines they watch. In fact, when component failures interact to produce "system" errors, the human components of the system, like so many robots, inevitably find the situation incomprehensible. This criticism could be dismissed as a kind of quaint romanticism if it were not for the fact that Perrow's human components seem to be unable to communicate with each other. His variable called interaction does not, from context, mean conversation, dialogue, communication; it seems to have a physical or chemical connotation.

Perrow's operators almost seem speechless; the word "communication" appears in neither his extensive index nor his two-by-two analysis. Communication neither causes nor solves problems at any level of analysis, with one remarkable exception: on pages 168–69 is a note on the Aviation Safety Reporting System. This, as we shall soon see, is a communication system par excellence. After briefly explaining the system, Perrow piles high the praise: the fruits of the program seem to be substantial. Reports pour in about unsafe airport conditions, which are then quickly corrected: changes in Air Traffic Control (ATC) and other types of procedures have been made on the basis of analysis of the ASRS reports (Perrow 1984: 169).

Curiously, Perrow gives communication only 1-½ pages in his long book, although in that brief note its effect is judged to be "substantial." Why is it, then, that communication does not otherwise enter his analysis? If the analysis is correct, the ASRS should *not* matter. If his praise for the ASRS is appropriate, his analysis has not taken into account a major factor, thus leaving us with room to question the inevitability of his predictions. For this reason alone the ASRS should be examined in detail in order to determine what kind of error Perrow might have made. But the motivation for study is not merely academic; there is a more important reason.

In his final chapter, Perrow composes an essay on policy, recommending that the USA abandon nuclear weapons and nuclear power plants, restrict marine transportation and genetic engineering, tolerate and improve the rest of his high-risk technologies. Suppose that I am persuaded by his analysis and support his policy recommendations, or suppose I am persuaded by his policy recommendations for reasons different from those supplied by his analysis. What is to be done if I also doubt the likelihood that nuclear power plants will soon be abandoned?

There is no middle ground, no short-range recommendation in Perrow's policy. Has he forgotten the possibilities inscribed in the final sentence of his note on the ASRS: "It would be extremely beneficial if such a virtually anonymous system were in operation for the nuclear power industry and the marine transport industry" (Perrow 1984: 169)? This forgotten policy option thus supplies an additional motive for the following examination of the Aviation Safety Reporting System.

AVIATION SAFETY REPORTING SYSTEM (ASRS) ORIGINS

Individuals within the U.S. aviation system had long felt the need for a system of incident reporting that would accumulate a data base by which hazardous situations could be analyzed for root causes. It took a tragic drama, however, to provide the impetus for creating the new system. In response to the investigation of the TWA 514 accident and the discovery of the report generated within United's "Flight Safety Awareness Program," the Federal Aviation Administration (FAA) implemented, in May 1975, the Aviation Safety Reporting Program (ASRP), "whose purpose was to improve the flow of information of possible significance to air safety research" (Reynard 1987: 2). To encourage participation in the reporting program, the FAA offered a limited waiver of disciplinary action to those who provided timely reports about critical incidents (except for criminal activities, accidents, reckless operation, willful misconduct, or gross negligence).

The ASRP did not work. That conclusion was reached in a hurry. Members of the aviation community failed to report incidents to any significant degree. The cause of failure was one of the most durable assumptions and findings produced by the young field of organizational communication: upward-directed communication in any organization or institution is inhibited by the fear of punishment (Tompkins 1967). The truth of that proposition is corroborated by the lay maxim that good news goes up the line and bad news comes down, and by the rhetorical question, "Didn't the Romans kill messengers who brought bad news?"

"Rightly or wrongly, the FAA, both the maker of the law and its enforcer, was not generally viewed as a properly disinterested referee" (Reynard et al. 1986: 5). Out of the failure of the ASRP, the ASRS—the current system—was created. The FAA asked the National Aeronautics and Space Administration (NASA), respected by all members of the aviation community, to serve as a third party in the system, as a trusted and disinterested referee. NASA did, of course, have an interest in creating for the first time a systematic data base involving human error. NASA accepted the FAA proposal. The Aviation Safety Reporting System (ASRS) began operations on April 15, 1976. The actual operations have since been handled by a contractor, the Battelle Memorial Institute office at Mountain View, California.

Characteristics of ASRS

The objectives of the ASRS are:

- To make available a confidential reporting system which can be used by any person in the national aviation system.
- To operate a computer-based system for storage and retrieval of processed data.
- To provide an interactive analytical system for routine and special studies of the data.
- To maintain a responsive system for communication of data and analyses to those responsible for aviation safety. [Reynard 1987: 3]

The ASRS is truly a communication system. Input is provided by controllers, pilots, other crew members, and occasionally by passengers and other observers. These reports are filed with an identification strip that is removed by Battelle's analysts when they have analyzed and coded the reports. (The analysts sometimes need to call back the reporter for clarification of the report's text; once the analysts feel they understand the incident well enough to code and store it in the computer, the identification strip is removed and mailed to the reporter, thus guaranteeing anonymity and immunity.) The analysts are experienced pilots and controllers who "have been there." Their analyses—admittedly inferential—are checked independently by other analysts, but no reliability studies have ever been conducted. The total input for the system as of the summer of 1987 was staggering: 70,000 reports concerning 50,000 incidents (a single incident may elicit two or more reports). All of these 70,000 reports have been handled without a single breach of identity.

The output of ASRS since 1976 has been voluminous, and has taken several forms:

1) More than 835 Alert Bulletins—time-critical notices about ongoing hazards such as overgrown trees blocking an approach to a runway, faulty navigational lights and runway markings—have been issued.

2) Over 900 special data requests from the FAA, NTSB, and other organizations have been honored by ASRS. These involve searches of the computerized data base for incidents related to recurring problems and hazards.

3) Fifteen program reports, originally issued quarterly and now issued on a periodic but irregular basis, have been released. These contain sample texts of the anonymous reports thought to be instructive, analytic trends, and the responses to Alert Bulletins.

4) ASRS has produced thirty-four research reports and technical papers dealing with aviation safety. These primarily address human factors: fatigue, cockpit distraction, altitude deviations, and, as we shall see, human communication problems.

5) *Callback*, a highly readable, one-page newsletter devoted to timely safety issues, is available to every member of the aviation community and is mailed on a monthly basis (Reynard 1987: 9–10).

Effectiveness

There can be no quantitative measure of the ASRS impact on the nation's record of aviation safety, for as Reynard says, "It is impossible to document a nonevent" (1987: 11). Nonetheless, it is also impossible to study the record for those eleven years without being convinced that the ASRS has saved countless lives, reduced risks, and eliminated hazards. Reading the Alert Bulletins published in the quarterly reports alone will convince the reader of this conclusion; paired with the bulletins are actions taken in response by the FAA, airport administrators, and other interested parties.

Trees were cut down, lights replaced, code letters and numbers changed, and in one case new procedures were adopted to avoid routing planes through an army artillery range while weapons were being fired.

In addition, the ASRS has improved communication between and among all elements of the aviation community. Its data base has been used to reach a better understanding of hazards and ways to eliminate them. ASRS materials are being used by flight instructors, flight schools, and by both the military and carrier training facilities. ASRS data are used as the basis of "moral suasion" to support a legitimate safety improvement. The act of composing a report is in itself a valuable learning experience; reporters often go beyond the recitation of brute facts to probe their own levels of competence, knowledge, and even motivation.

The ASRS, then, is a successful, industry-wide system of communication that has convincingly demonstrated its beneficial effects on the aviation system. The potential applicability of this communication system to other industries faced with catastrophic risks and hazards will be considered below.

Early ASRS Operation

A chronological reading of the ASRS output provides insight into the doubts with which the analysts approached the initiation of the program. ASRP, the forerunner to ASRS, had failed because pilots and controllers did not file reports, no doubt because of a lack of trust in the FAA promise of immunity. The first quarterly report issued by ASRS (for the period of April 15, 1976, to July 14, 1976) stated with some pride that 1,407 reports relevant to the aims of the program had been received during the first three months of ASRS existence. The identification strip was filled out by 99 percent of the reporters, indicating that the promise of anonymity and immunity was perceived as credible. The quality and detail of the reports were praised by the ASRS analysts. The report indicated that this high quality had led to the release of 130 Alert Bulletins, and action was taken in response to 70 of these. The system seemed to have had a good start.

The third quarterly report (for the period of October 15, 1976, to January 14, 1977) evaluated the effect of the system's incentives on the quality of the reports:

> There is little question that at least some ASRS reports are submitted in order to take advantage of the FAA's limited waiver of disciplinary

action. How many are submitted for this reason alone is impossible to determine. The large number of reports containing detailed analyses and carefully thought-out recommendations would suggest that most ASRS reporters, regardless of their interest in avoiding disciplinary action, are also motivated by the higher purposes of the program. [NASA Technical Memorandum X-3546, 1977: 3]

The fourth quarterly report (for the period of January 15, 1977, to April 14, 1977) coped with epistemological issues. What did the system's operators know from the texts submitted by pilots and controllers? How much confidence should they have in the reports? "It should be pointed out again that because the ASRS is a voluntary system, it is not possible to draw any conclusions concerning the incidence or prevalence of any problems in the national aviation system from the ASRS reports. Reports submitted to ASRS represent simply the reporter's perception of a particular event, occurrence, or situation" (NASA Technical Memorandum 78433, 1977: 7).

The analysts had probably never confronted such thorny problems before. The "because" clause in the preceding quotation is puzzling. What could the voluntary nature of the reports have to do with validity?

The following paragraph of the report sets aside the question of validity by adopting a phenomenological stance:

What can be gained from such reports is an indication of how certain factors in the aviation system are perceived by the persons within that system, and often how those persons respond to such factors. It is not possible, for instance, to determine from these data how prevalent a particular airport marking problem may be; it is quite possible, however, to determine from a small number of reports that a particular marking configuration is misunderstood, not seen under specific circumstances, or confused for something else. [NASA Technical Memorandum 78433, 1977: 7]

Later in the same quarterly report (the fourth), it is admitted:

It will be argued that at best, ASRS reports, containing the perceptions of but a single person, are an imperfect picture of the real world. This is quite true, but it is also true that these perceptions are what motivate the decisions made by these persons. . . . Thus, in certain respects, perceptions of those working in the aviation system are as important as the reality. [NASA Technical Memorandum 78433, 1977: 37]

This passage makes a different point—that it would be better to have the context of multiple reports on each incident. It also acknowledges a distinction between the "reality" of the real world and the perceptions of that reality, making a strong case that the perceived world is as important as the "real one."

The distinction between perception and reality was difficult for the authors of this quarterly report to maintain. After making a case for the perceived world, the authors then turned to "factors" associated with real-world problems and made this identification: "Another major factor which appeared to be associated with problems in this study was that of airspace configuration. The shape, design and use of airspace appear to influence pilot and even controller behavior in many of the occurrences selected for this study" (NASA Technical Memorandum 78433, 1977: 37).

It is obvious that to speak of "airspace configurations," the "shape" and "design" of airspace, is to speak of a symbolic, textual reality, not a real world. After all, it is the symbol-using, symbol-making animal that makes configurations of airspace. This realization helps one understand that the analysts had previously drawn a faulty bifurcation between perception and reality. In fact, they were not even working with perceptions. Quite literally, they were working with perceptions-encoded-in-texts. In short, the distinction they were making could best be expressed as textual vs. nontextual reality. The only way to talk about reality is to compose a text about it.

The ASRS analysts may have come on their own to a realization that they had no alternative to a logological-textual epistemology. By the time of the next quarterly report (the fifth, for the period of April 1, 1977, to June 30, 1977), the question of epistemology was dealt with in a succinct statement of textual validity. "Readers are reminded that these reports are unverified and that specific information cited in them may not be correct. We believe, however, that the lessons which can be learned from them are valid" (NASA Technical Memorandum 78476, 1977: 2). The "text" is, in this sense, all there is to go on.

During a visit to the Battelle office in Mountain View, during the summer of 1987, I inquired about the epistemological edginess in the early publications and was told that it had disappeared. My observation that there was no way of verifying a report *except by means of another report* was not contested, and perhaps the best evidence of a new symbolic or textual sophistication was produced when I pressed one of the staff members about the "reality" of the "shape" and "design" of airspace. The response was a smile and the narrative of a joke about the pilot who deviated from his flight plan. When asked why he had strayed from the assigned airspace, the pilot explained, "I couldn't see the magenta lines on the ground."

The Air Controllers' Strike

The strike of the air traffic controllers in August 1981 gave the ASRS an opportunity to monitor its effects on aviation safety. About one-third of the controllers stayed at work and the rest were fired by President Reagan. Would the remaining controllers be able to service the entire aviation system? Would the radical reduction in force increase the risk of accidents? What effect would the increased workload have on the strained relationship between controllers and pilots? The aviation community in general anticipated a decline in the effectiveness and efficiency of ATC. ASRS staff anticipated an increase in reports from pilots complaining about deficiencies in ATC performance. The increase did not materialize. Two of the first reports received after the strike commenced set the tone for the ensuing period:

> Flights are going smoother than ever—efficient and courteous control. First six days, delays and disruptions were encountered, but generally this was before departure and the rest of the flight is OK. . . . Eyeballs are out the window for traffic watch, but no conflicts apparent . . . traffic has been smooth and professional and we get direct vectors . . . other pilots report same. [NASA Technical Memorandum 84339, 1983: 2]

Before the ASRS analysts remove identification from reports and mail the strips back to the reporters, they have an opportunity to make "callbacks" in order to get additional information about the incidents. After the strike began they intensified the rate of callbacks in order to monitor more effectively the effects of the strike. The overwhelming majority of these conversations confirmed the reports. What was anticipated to be a period of strife turned out rather to be a period of harmony that the ASRS staffers called a "honeymoon" between controllers and pilots.

The strike and Reagan's firing of the strikers was, it can be argued, followed by the safest period in U.S. aviation history. The reasons? The FAA decreased the volume of traffic and increased the required separation distance between planes. The controllers who remained at work probably had different attitudes toward pilots, management, and the system as a whole than did the controllers who struck. The honeymoon period extended beyond the strike period and may have increased the level of confidence in the system to the point of being a contributing factor in creating the current crisis.

The Current Crisis

In 1988 the mass media are full of reports about pilot errors, equipment failures, and near collisions. Planes have been reported landing at the wrong airports and on the wrong runways. A poll by the Associated Press found:

> Forty-six percent of the 1,348 adult Americans in the nationwide telephone poll believe it is more dangerous to fly today than it was in the 1970s, the last decade before deregulation allowed airlines to set their own schedules and destinations. Twenty-two percent said they thought air travel was safer today than in the 1970s, and 24 percent said there had been no change in safety. [*Boulder Daily Camera*, July 20, 1987: 1]

Perhaps it is not an exaggeration to say there is at the moment a crisis of confidence in the system. Although I have no official statistics on the increase in traffic since the 1970s, in a chance conversation in late May 1988 an airline pilot said he believed that traffic had increased by fifty percent since deregulation. Whether or not this figure is accurate, there is no doubt that there has been a significant increase since 1980. In addition the FAA has not yet hired enough controllers to bring their total work force up to the level reached before the strike in 1981. Thus, there are fewer controllers directing a significantly higher density of traffic.

The trend of reports received by ASRS from 1981 to 1986 reflects this condition. A significant decline in late 1981 reflects the decrease in reports due to the strike. The volume of reports remained steady through 1982 and 1983, followed by a rather sharp increase, which has been maintained ever since. This sharp increase has affected the work load at ASRS in a dramatic way. The increase, from 200 to 250 reports per month in 1982–83 to 1,500 per month at present, is threatening to exceed the cognitive capacity of the analysts. The text of each report is given 2½ readings before being placed, in its entirety, into the computerized data base. In 1982–83 four analysts were making approximately 150 readings per month; by 1987 five analysts were making 500 to 600 readings per month. There is no fear that the quality of analysis is declining with this work load increase, but ASRS is no longer able to pursue one of its earlier objectives. Because the

ASRS staff members must direct all their efforts toward getting the analyzed texts into the computer, there is no time to look at trends and make the special studies that have been so useful in the past (a specific example of which I shall shortly consider).

The increase in reports could also be regarded as symptomatic of problems in the aviation system. Each represents what the reporter regards as a "threat to aviation safety." The reports have increased faster than the traffic itself has increased. The relationship between volume of traffic and number of reports is not linear; it is probably closer to a square. (By analogy, when the number of molecules in a gas is doubled, there are four times as many interactions.) The aviation system seems to be approaching its "saturation capacity." Once that threshold is crossed, as an ASRS staff member said, "things go to hell in a hurry."

The ASRS staff thinks some local systems have reached this capacity; some controllers have "two planes too many" to control. The communication capacity of some radio frequencies has been reached. Crews in different planes "step on each other"; two crews may be speaking to the controller at the same time. More and more messages are "crowded" together on the same frequency. Pilots report they "can't get a word in edgewise": "I'm not certain what I'm supposed to do and can't get through."

At one airport a controller with seventeen planes took off his headset and said he had had enough. Several minutes passed before a relief controller took over. As we shall later see, the process of one controller relieving another is problematic under the best of circumstances; taking over seventeen planes without a careful briefing on the entire sector approaches disaster.

At another large, busy airport the controllers are said to advise against the "readback" or acknowledgment that a message has been received by the flight crew. I do not wish to cause or spread panic; some would argue that this particular airport has proved that "it can be done." However, this is so because of a paradox: some of the most dangerous airports are the safest. It is well known in the aviation system that O'Hare, in Chicago, is a zoo; consequently pilots sent in and out of that airport know they must be more than usually alert, with "eyeballs out the window."

In summary, the ASRS has proved in its eleven-year history that it is an effective and elegant communication system. It has largely overcome the barriers to upward-directed communication in hierarchies by escaping from corporate and agency structures to a transcendent, industry-wide system of communication. Reporters do admit personal errors that would not be reported up a corporate line. The data base is probably the single largest pool of information on human performance error ever assembled.

Information about risks and hazards is fed back to the principals by various channels varying in degree of formality; long-range studies provide insights and materials useful in training. The system also provides a voluntary method by which the performance of the larger system itself can be monitored. The potential applicability of the ASRS to other industries will be considered below; however, before turning to that question it is necessary to examine the contents of ASRS reports to see what they can tell us about the central signifier of this essay—communication.

Communication as a Topic in ASRS Reports

It did not take ASRS analysts long to discover communication as a central term and important factor in the reports filed in the data base. The first two quarterly reports were devoted to an explanation of the system and to statistical summaries of the reports received. The third quarterly report (for the period of October 15, 1976, to January 14, 1977) contained the first two analytic studies carried out using the resources of the ASRS data base. They are presented here to suggest the uses to which this analytic tool may be put. The first study, a compilation of altitude deviations, exemplifies an attempt to discern some of the reasons for this rather common event. The second study of misunderstood communication proceeds from the first, in which it was found that misunderstood clearances were one of the factors associated with altitude deviations (NASA Technical Memorandum X-3546, 1977: 11).

Before sampling these studies and the reports upon which they were based, the reader needs to know the basic objectives and some of the key terms of aviation discourse. Air traffic controllers have one basic aim: to keep airplanes apart. They give "clearance" to airplanes for takeoffs, landings, and assigned flying altitudes. An altitude "bust" or deviation by an airplane is a serious threat to safety and in many countries, not including the USA, is a criminal offense. Two methodological definitions are also necessary because Perrow was incorrect in saying that the ASRS analysts "have mastered social research techniques" (Perrow 1984: 169). They instead invented their own techniques.

The reports were coded to avoid the interpretation that "probable cause," as defined by NTSB, was being determined. ASRS analysts in fact deny that the reports can be used to establish or imply causation. No social science model or theory has ever been articulated in an ASRS study, but a rough analogy to epidemiology was drawn by a medical doctor who was one of the founders of the program. Two "diagnostic fields" were established:

- Enabling Factor: An element that is present in the history of an occurrence and without which the occurrence probably would not have happened.
- Associated Factor: An element that is present in the history of an occurrence and is pertinent to the occurrence under study, but which does not fulfill the requirements of an enabling factor. [NASA Technical Memorandum X-3546, 1977: 9–10]

The reports are entered into the computer in "free-text format" and are automatically "indexed" according to the two factors defined above, as well as by "keywords." The computer program is a complex program employing Boolean algebra. One can search for topics or factors. In the first study completed by ASRS, for example, a search for reports on altitude overshoots, excursions, and undershoots yielded forty-six cases. These cases were then analyzed for enabling and associated factors. One-fourth of these cases involved "misunderstood clearances."

The first incident introduced in the first ASRS study, a study of altitude deviations, is taken from the text of a pilot's report. Notice that it involves a breakdown of the double interact of control:

Airline aircraft planned and cleared to 24,000 ft. Center later changed clearance to 17,000 ft because of other traffic. At approximately 16,000 ft Center pointed out traffic and issued what pilot thought was clearance to 18,000 ft. Pilot acknowledged and Center did not correct readback. Factors: (1) I misread his transmission of traffic; (2) He misunderstood my clearance readback or failed to correct it. [NASA Technical Memorandum X-3546, 1977: 15]

The second incident was interpreted as a misunderstanding promoted by "phraseology":

Original clearance was unrestricted to 23,000 feet. Shortly after take-off an amendment was understood by the crew as "Expedite *through* 5000 feet." We did that and at 6300 were questioned as to our altitude. We were then informed that the clearance was "Expedite *to* 5000 feet." No reason for advisory was given. [NASA Technical Memorandum X-3546, 1977: 15]

The first analytic study ever conducted by ASRS, then, started out as an analysis of altitude deviations and became in large part a study of communication.

The second study proceeded from the first and took the title, "Misunderstanding of Communications Between Pilots and Controllers." A search of the ASRS data base was performed for those texts in which "message confirmation procedures" were coded as either an enabling or associated factor; 143 such cases were turned up. A follow-up search showed that forty of those cases were also coded as involving a "potential conflict." These forty texts involved thirty-eight unique events. A long text written by a controller illustrates the complexity involved in traffic at airports with multiple, parallel, or intersecting runways. Notice that many factors combined to produce a situation in which a simple misunderstanding nearly led to a catastrophic conclusion:

> Aircraft A called Tower and reported ready for takeoff runway 18. I instructed A to taxi into position and hold on runway 18. He was not cleared for takeoff because of aircraft C on short final for runway 23. While this was going on I was told to watch for emergency equipment bringing oxygen to gate 6 for a passenger. . . . As aircraft B (same make as A) called the Tower . . . I replied. . . . He answered "We're ready to go runway 36." I then noticed that aircraft C was past midfield, leaving the way clear for aircraft A, in position on 18. My next transmission was "Aircraft A, runway 18, caution wake turbulence arriving jet, you're cleared for takeoff." I received a double reply with aircraft A coming through saying he was rolling. As I cleared A for takeoff I noticed the emergency equipment coming out with the oxygen and having to cross the runway A was using. My attention was momentarily diverted to what the Ground Controller was doing with the emergency equipment because he had cleared the equipment across runway 18 to gate 6. As I instructed the Ground Controller to hold the emergency equipment because A was rolling on runway 18, aircraft B called the tower and said "We're rolling runway 36." With my attention diverted I thought I heard "We're ready runway 36" and I took no action. Aircraft B took aircraft A's clearance for takeoff and took off on runway 36 as aircraft A was taking off on runway 18. At midfield I saw aircraft A take evasive action to miss aircraft B. [NASA Technical Memorandum X-3546, 1977]

Notice again a breakdown in the double interact of control due to a simple misunderstanding. It is a belief among the ASRS staff that the big hazards have been eliminated from the aviation system and that the remaining hazards will be the multiple occurrence of "small" hazards. Misunderstandings and other forms of communication breakdown are consistently coded as one of those hazards. Faulty communications lead to faulty decisions, and in this case to lack of control.

The next quarterly report, the fourth (for the period of January 15 to April 14, 1977), introduces a new terminology for communication problems: "Information transfer difficulties" (Technical Memorandum 78433, 1977: 1). The new terminology suggests the intrusion of a mechanical or physical model of communication, an engineering metaphor that probably comes naturally, almost imperceptibly, to workers concerned with transferring large machines and cargoes from place to place, from ground to air, air to ground, while at all times trying to maintain a separation between and among the machines. The terms and concepts were not generated by communication theorists; nor were these communication problems "found" or discovered by social scientists sensitized by training and "terministic screens" (Burke 1966) to find them where others could not.

It is all the more convincing to read in the fifth quarterly report that since the brief study of misunderstood communications contained in the third quarterly report, the ASRS reports "have contained more examples of such problems" (NASA Technical Memorandum 78476, 1978: 5). A rather rough attempt to categorize the problems produced such headings as lack of courtesy (hogging a frequency), high communications work loads, and simple misunderstandings.

By 1977, about a year after the system was initiated, the analysts realized that misunderstandings occur not only between controller and pilot, and began to take notice of reports dealing with problems of communication among the crew members within the airplane (e.g., a pilot's report detailed how he discovered that a steward had allowed the passengers to leave the aircraft while the plane was still on the runway!) and problems of communication among controllers that resulted in inadequate coordination.

Subsequent quarterly reports continued to find communication problems in analyses of altitude alert systems, pilot-controller interaction (sixth quarterly report), uncontrolled airports, winter operations (seventh report), runway incursions and skydiving (eighth report), and cockpit distractions (ninth quarterly report). The tenth report contains a major study of the ATC system, a large portion of which is devoted to "communications" with the following subheadings: "The ground-to-air link, or 'Whaddesay?'"; "The ground-to-air link: 'I heard what I expected to hear.'" The twelfth quarterly report contains a study of problems in the briefing of air traffic controllers. The thirteenth report introduced a new diagnostic term: "Similar Sounding Alphanumerics," or misunderstandings arising from code numbers and letters that can be easily confused with each other. For example, the flight numbers 111 and 911 sound enough alike that both crews might assume a controller's instructions are meant for them; the message "runway two zero" is read as "runway two"; and aircraft ABC and aircraft CBA both believe they have been cleared to 11,000 feet. The fourteenth quarterly report, the final one available at the time of this writing, contains the study of pilot-controller reactions to the ATC system after the controllers' strike.

In summary, the ASRS quarterly reports discovered communication problems early, if inadvertently, in a study of altitude deviations, and continued to find manifestations of the problem in many ways. ASRS disseminated discussions of these problems in various publications to aviation system personnel, in the hope of raising their sensitivity to the risk of recurrence. The discovery of the "similar sounding alphanumerics" allowed them to recommend the elimination of ambiguous code numbers and letters.

Information Transfer Problems

A major study of communication in the aviation system, actually seven separate studies devoted to the major categories of communication problems, was released in 1981: *Information Transfer Problems in the Aviation System* (Billings and Cheaney 1981). A full understanding of the magnitude of the communication, or information transfer, problem is captured in the report's opening paragraph: "Problems in the transfer of information within the aviation system were noted in over 70 percent of 28,000 reports submitted by pilots and air traffic controllers to the . . . ASRS . . . during a five-year period 1976–1981. These problems are related primarily to voice communications, although many deficiencies in visual information transfer have also been described" (Billings and Cheaney 1981: 1).

The figure of 70 percent can be compared to a percentage yielded by a more specific definition of communication I used to interrogate the data base in the summer of 1987. After I specified that the incident had to involve a "message sent from one person to another," the computer was able to find this factor in 61 percent of the reports placed in the data base since 1978. The analysts helping me with the search assured me that this was a conservative figure. My conclusion is that 60 to 70 percent of the reports in the data base include a reference to human communication as a factor.

Communication thus has a negative connotation in the ASRS studies; it has the status of a "fault"—that is, that a message or some part of the communication process had something wrong with it. This should be placed in the context of the overwhelming majority of flights in the USA in which communication works properly—at least well enough to avoid accidents and near accidents. But just as each of us experiences misunderstandings every day—at least we interpret facts as evidence of misunderstanding— so do pilots and controllers. The complexities of flight are such that a simple misunderstanding can have profound consequences.

The seven communication studies do advance our understanding of the aviation system and its problems. The first study defines the dimensions of the information transfer problem: message origin, message type (e.g., clearance, advisory, confirmation), message problem (e.g., ambiguity, untimeliness, and the intriguing "absent" category—the judgment that a message that should have been sent was not transmitted), and message medium. This introductory study concludes that "verbal communication is an imperfect method of information transfer" and holds out the controversial (as we shall later see) promise that there may be a technological fix for this problem, a fix called the digital data link (Billings and Reynard 1981: 12).

The second study concentrated on the problems associated with the briefing of relief controllers (BOR). Consider the BOR problem. At the end of a work shift, the controller about to be relieved may have fifteen airplanes to worry about, and will have to give clearances and "vectors" (ad hoc variations in the flight plan) to their pilots while simultaneously briefing the relieving controller. Incomplete or inadequate briefings may lead to serious errors on the part of the relieving controller. In five cases drawn from the data base, no relief briefing was given. In most of the cases the controller being relieved was too busy with a heavy traffic load to provide a briefing.

The third study also concentrated on ATC, this time examining the problems associated with coordination between controllers. As a plane moves from a sector managed by one controller into the sector of another controller, a complex communication process that can fairly be called "negotiation" is required. One controller must communicate to the other a request for coordination as the plane is approaching the jurisdiction of the second controller. Concurrence on the part of the second controller will then lead to the development of a plan, or "hand-off." Finally, the hand-off must be executed. According to this study, the problem of "absent" messages is widespread during the coordination process. "The most frequently reported failure is failure to initiate action to establish coordination; the second most frequently reported is failure to execute the agreed plan" (Grayson 1981: 44). In both cases, the double interact of control is not completed.

The fourth study analyzes communication between ATC and the "flight-crew." A typology of problems was created, relying in part on categories developed in earlier analyses, the most important of which is the *expectation factor*. This important and widespread problem appears to be related to the need for uncertainty reduction. A pilot receives clearance for take-off, a left turn, and a climb to, say, 10,000 feet. The pilot acknowledges by a "readback" that she or he is going to turn left and then promptly turns right. Why? In one hundred takeoffs from this airport the pilot has always been instructed to turn right. Habit may therefore contribute as much or more to such an incident as the need to reduce uncertainty. This is clearly a problem requiring further study:

> ASRS reports indicate that many instances of misunderstanding can be attributed to the expectation factor; that is, the recipient (or listener) perceives that he heard what he expected to hear in the message transmitted. Pilots and controllers alike tend to hear what they expect to hear. Deviations from routine are not noted and the readback is heard as the transmitted message, whether correct or incorrect. [Billings and Cheaney 1981: 48]

Pilots who have heard about my research have shown me another side of the expectation problem: when frequencies are jammed and controllers' words are garbled, the pilot has no recourse but to anticipate directions, and past experience inevitably figures in the planning.

"Intracockpit communications" is the topic of the fifth study, which contains a harrowing narrative of an accident involving an airline vice-president—an experienced pilot, who took over the controls of one of his company's commuter aircraft. The first officer had been with the company for two months and was necessarily on probation. The vice-president (pilot), with over 20,000 hours of flight time, was known to rarely acknowledge the checklist items or any other call outs from his first officer. The first officer later testified that the aircraft was well below the assigned altitude during its final slope and that he had made every required call out to that effect. "The evidence suggests that the captain may have been inca-pacitated, but the first officer could not confirm this" (Foushee and Manos 1981: 63). The pilot's reputation for eschewing acknowledgments of call outs created a nightmarish ambiguity for the first officer; the aircraft hit the ground several miles short of the runway.

Foushee and Manos then introduced a new kind of evidence into the analysis of cockpit communication: observational (quantitative) studies of B-747 crews in simulated, routine airline trips. The simulations followed a scenario in which mechanical and meteorological problems were intro-duced in a way that required the crew to coordinate activities and solve problems at a level of complexity that would not preclude an entirely safe operation. Voice recordings of twelve such simulations were subjected to content coding and were correlated with the observed errors the crew made during the simulated flights. There are impressive findings in this provocative study; I choose to stress three:

> 1) A negative correlation ($r = -0.51$) between crewmember observa-tions (spoken comments) and systems operation errors was obtained. This relationship appears quite logical. When more information re-garding flight status was transferred, there were fewer errors related to system operation (e.g., mishandling of engines, hydraulic and fuel systems; misreading and missetting of instruments; and failure to use ice protection). The relationship should serve as important evidence in support of the concept of cross-checking and redundancy among the cockpit crew. . . . 2) Similarly, there was a strong negative relationship ($r = -0.61$) between systems operational errors and acknowledgments. When crews frequently acknowledged commands, inquiries, and obser-vations, these kinds of errors were less apparent. . . . 3) Most significant, however, is the fact that acknowledgments were strongly negatively associated with total errors ($r = -0.68$). [Foushee and Manos 1981: 66]

Such correlations are rather high in comparison with most social sci-entific research. Moreover, although I have not yet had the opportunity to evaluate the methods of data analysis, the willing suspension of dis-belief until that evaluation requires the conclusion that communication is important to the reduction of risks and the avoidance of hazards. The absence of communication will, under certain conditions, produce errors.

The sixth study concentrated on information transfer during con-tingency operations—emergency air-ground communications. Fifty-two data-base instances were found that satisfied the following criteria: (1) an emergency situation leading to (2) an information transfer problem or dysfunction, and (3) an ensuing safety problem. In 46 percent of the cases, the communication problem following the first emergency led to traffic conflicts. The most common information transfer problem in such situations is a lack of interfacility coordination with the ATC. The second most frequent problem arose from inattention on the part of the controller because of the distraction caused by the original emergency (Porter 1981).

The seventh and final essay in the collection is a summary and interpretation of studies done on the information transfer problem for the aviation system as a whole:

> Over one-third of these problems involved the absence of information transfer in situations in which, in the opinion of the analysts, the transfer of the information could have prevented a potentially hazardous occurrence. In another third, information transfer took place, but it was adjudged incomplete or inaccurate, leading in many cases to incorrect actions in flying or controlling aircraft. One-eighth of the reports involved information transfer that was correct but untimely (usually too late to be of assistance) in forestalling a potentially hazardous chain of events. In one-tenth of the reports, the information was transferred but was not perceived or was misperceived by the intended recipients. The remainder of the reports involved equipment problems and a variety of miscellaneous conditions. [Billings and Cheaney 1981: 85]

The most useful contribution of this essay is not in the summaries, useful though they are; more important is the modeling of the entire system that grew out of a consideration of the implications of the findings, and as Billings and Cheaney make clear, "because of the central role of the air traffic controller, any study of information transfer problems must of necessity be largely a study of controller communication behavior" (1981: 87).

ATC as the Double Interact of Control

It should now be clear why the conceptualization of communication as "information transfer" or the "exchange of information" is inadequate for an understanding of the aviation system. Some twenty years ago it was observed that "every communication has a content and a relationship aspect such that the latter classifies the former and is therefore a metacommunication" (Watzlawick, Beavin, and Jackson 1967: 54). Although that observation was offered at the time as a "tentative axiom," it is widely accepted in the field of communication.

Metacommunication is a message about a message. The content is called the report and the metacommunication about the report is called the command. The problem of communicative control, of giving and receiving orders, commands, and directives, is perhaps the central problem in human organization. In the 1920s, based on a study of British strikes and lockouts, Mary Parker Follett noted that "probably more industrial trouble has been caused by the *manner* in which orders are given than in any other way" (1971: 153, emphasis added).

The air traffic controller provides pilots with information, content, or reports; those messages also carry, explicitly or implicitly, commands. Otherwise, we would call the controller an air traffic *informer*, and the system would be called Air Traffic Information instead of Air Traffic Control. We have already seen that the proponents of the "information transfer" concept acknowledge the central, pivotal role of the controller. Consider this description of the pilot in relation to the controller:

> The role of the pilot receiving ATC services in information management is somewhat different from that of the controller in the present aviation system. His task, except in an emergency, is to *receive* advisory information, accept instructions, and to *act upon them*. He provides an element of redundancy by reading back clearances, announcing altitude on initial callup, etc., but otherwise he provides little information *unless it is asked for*. [Billings and Cheaney 1981: 89, emphasis added]

The pilot's role in the exchange is subordinate to the controller's. Their relationship has characteristics that create more strain than the typical superior-subordinate connection. First, the two actors do not even work for the same organization and their relationship lacks the normal hierarchical dynamics. Second, although controllers are in the "superior" position of giving commands, they have less status than pilots, a reversal of the usual arrangement. Third, the two represent different mythic roles, if not cultures, in historic opposition to each other: the controller stays in one place, the pilot is always on the move, as in the case of burghers vs. gypsies, townsfolk vs. nomads, or farmers vs. cowboys. No wonder, then, that this problematic communicative situation is described with euphemisms such as information "transfer" or "exchange." Euphemisms soften and deflect blows to status.

There is an inherent antagonism between controllers and pilots. Controllers have a territorial orientation and speak of "my airspace." Pilots have a sense of prerogatives and do not enjoy being "vectored," or "jerked around" in the air by controllers. The controller cares mainly about maintaining separation; pilots care about safety and the comfort of their passengers. This antagonism has not, however, been a major theme in the ASRS reports since the controllers' strike in 1981, as indicated above. It appears (and this is conjecture) that many of the controllers who struck were Vietnam veterans whose training and outlook were military and territorial in nature. Since those controllers were purged, there is a better relationship between pilots and controllers. The bonds between the two are stronger today; they are getting to know each other and even recognize each others' voices. Pilots are now more sympathetic to the controller's situation than before. Nonetheless, the natural antipathy between the controlled and the controller will probably continue until technology replaces at least one of them.

Elaboration of the Double Interact of Control

The U.S. aviation system is thus more clearly envisioned as a manifestation of the double interact of control than as a process of mere information transfer. The review of the ASRS data base and analytic studies of communication problems described here allows a greater elaboration of the original double interact of control (Tompkins and Cheney 1985). Even with this elaboration, however, the construct is sufficiently abstract to apply to all kinds of organizations.

Direction. The first step in the process involves any of several forms or categories of messages such as informing, advising, suggesting, even outright ordering, or issuing a statement of purpose, objectives, or core value premises; but the metacommunication must be interpreted as a command.

Monitoring. The second step of the double interact is the familiar feedback loop, a deviation-counteracting loop, which may be broken into two temporal or media stages. The first stage is the *confirmation* that the message has been received and acknowledged. Acknowledgments may be nonverbal in the case of simple tasks—a nod or a gesture—or, in more complex tasks, may be written or oral, and can include read-backs. If the controller perceives that the message has been interpreted as intended, the execution of the directions can go forward with or without acknowledgment and confirmation. Some persons in some situations may regard acknowledgments (e.g., read-backs) as demeaning or redundant, but this stage is omitted, according to the empirical research reviewed, at the *risk of increasing serious errors in the system*. In a relatively safe industry, such a risk will often be seen as inconsequential. In a nuclear power plant or the air traffic control system, it should not be regarded as such. The costs, in time and money, associated with such errors will be important criteria in deciding whether or not to require acknowledgments.

The second stage of the monitoring step may be called *evaluation* of performance of the task. (Performance begins between the first and second stages of monitoring.) The evaluation feedback loop manifests in diverse ways and via different media. The foreman may stand and watch the laborers digging the ditch; he will no doubt hear reports about the progress of the digging and inspect the finished product. The supervisor on an assembly line may read a computer printout or receive an oral report from quality control. The air traffic controller will watch the radar for evidence that the pilot has properly executed a "vector" (an ad hoc variation in the flight plan) ordered by the controller. The professor will carefully evaluate the student's term paper and examinations. The professor's dean will carefully evaluate her total productivity at the end of her first six years on the job.

Deviation elimination.   The third step normally takes place after the original directions have been performed and an evaluation has been completed. There are circumstances, however, when it becomes immediately evident that there is a misunderstanding, as when the foreman sees that the laborers have begun to dig the ditch in the wrong direction, or when the controller sees that the pilot has turned left instead of right. The deviation can in many tasks be eliminated early in the performance. A pilot's early error may, however, create an emergency situation that can be resolved only by an ad hoc revision of the original directions. There will almost always be a long-range deviation elimination process, such as performance appraisal (or tenure review). Dismissal is the ultimate organizational solution to consistent deviations. Praise and promotion constitute the positive side of the process.

In all these steps, to echo Mary Follett, the *manner* of giving direction, monitoring, and deviation elimination is extremely important. Most persons do not enjoy being ordered around, evaluated, and corrected by a boss. Being "jerked around" by a boss, particularly in the presence of one's peers, is a serious threat to one's dignity. The modern trend, in fact, is toward unobtrusive control exercised in what Tompkins and Cheney call the "concertive" mode of control (1985), in which members of the unit organization are committed to core values or decisional premises; they exercise self-control individually *and* collectively. Nonetheless, it appears that in certain kinds of tasks—where uncorrected deviations can rapidly deteriorate into catastrophic consequences—the more centralized exercise of control is the most acceptable approach.

Application of ASRS to Other Industries

In his discussion of the ASRS, Perrow concludes that "it would be extremely beneficial if such a virtually anonymous system were in operation for the nuclear power industry and the marine transport industry" (1984: 169). These possibilities were being considered at the time Perrow wrote those words, and other applications have been attempted since. The most comprehensive description of ASRS discusses extrapolation of the concept as "technology transfer" and reports that similar systems are either in place or are being pursued in Great Britain, Canada, Ireland, and Japan (Reynard et al. 1986: 79). It is also reported that interdisciplinary technology transfers are being considered in a variety of activities that are "labor intensive and rely heavily on humans interacting with increasingly sophisticated automation" (79). The interdisciplinary examples reported include:

- The U.S. Nuclear Regulatory Commission (NRC). This organization is actively pursuing an ASRS-type system for use in monitoring the activities of operators of nuclear power facilities.
- Institute of Nuclear Power Operators (INPO). As with the NRC, this industry group is investigating the possibility of an incident reporting system for operators of nuclear power plants; the INPO concept envisions a system managed by industry as opposed to a government program.
- Electric Power Research Institute (EPRI). The EPRI interest in an ASRS-type system is similar to those of the NRC and INPO. The major difference would be the scope of operator involvement; the EPRI plan would extend the incident reporting system to all power plant operators, not just nuclear facilities.
- Nassau County (New York) Criminal Justice Commission. This investigatory body is interested in patterning an anonymous witness program after the ASRS program.
- University of Washington/U.S. Coast Guard. The university, as part

of a study for the Coast Guard, is pursuing the possibility of using an ASRS-type system to permit operators of vessels on Puget Sound to report conflict situations and related marine hazards.

- Swedish Department of Labor. In a circumstance that fits both the international and interdisciplinary categories, this government agency is planning to institute incident reporting capabilities in several labor-intensive industries (e.g., mining and fishing) in an effort to reduce the number of job-related injuries in those occupations. [Reynard et al. 1986: 79–80]

In a lengthy interview with Battelle's project manager, I learned more about these technology transfers or "spin-offs." The results are at best mixed. The Department of Transportation and Battelle, who tried to initiate the ASRS concept in the marine transport industry, were beset with problems from the beginning. The potential reporters, Captains and Masters, have a distrust of government that inhibits reporting. The marine unions did not endorse the concept. At the moment when a critical mass of participants was persuaded to participate, the Office of Management and Budget cut the program. Note that the marine program did not include the provision of transactional immunity.

The application to the nuclear energy industry faces a different problem. It advanced, as indicated in the list above, on two fronts. The NRC was on the brink of adopting the ASRS concept when the Institute of Nuclear Power Operators (INPO) announced that it was implementing a program. The problem is that an industry association does not have the distance from the industry being monitored that NASA-Battelle has from the aviation system, and, again, the concept of transactional immunity was not adopted. This represents a problem both theoretical and practical that must be addressed in the nuclear power industry: if a serious problem develops in a plant and a report to that effect is received, how could an Alert Bulletin concerning that specific plant be issued without identifying the source of the report?

At this point, I am convinced that the ASRS concept has not yet been fairly tested in the nuclear power industry because of the absence of two factors—transactional immunity and a third party to serve as an honest broker—and the concept may, certainly should be, fairly tested in the future. There are additional application prospects. The General Accounting Office has become interested in incident reporting systems for decentralized industries such as pharmaceuticals and medical equipment, and, ironically, the ASRS concept is being imposed on NASA itself. My research on the NASA Marshall Space Flight Center during the Apollo and Apollo Application Programs discovered some upward-directed communication practices that, although not promising immunity in a legal sense, did resemble the ASRS concept. These practices, called "Automatic Responsibility" and the "Monday Notes," seem, unfortunately, to have been abandoned during the space shuttle era (Tompkins 1977; 1978). After the Rogers Commission investigated the Challenger accident, it concluded that NASA had paid insufficient attention to safety. In response to the Commission Report, NASA has appointed a new "guru" for safety and instituted something called the "Protected Reporting System," which is still in trial stage.

Systems and Future Research

I intend to track (and promote) these applications of the ASRS concept and others in the future. I also welcome help. It should be clear that there are at least two aspects of the concept that must be incorporated into a fair test: transactional immunity for the reporter and a third party serving as honest broker. There may be another factor important to the success of the ASRS in the aviation system that may be absent in other industries: the concept of *system* itself.

Chester Barnard was probably the first to define an organization as a system, "something which must be treated as a whole because each part is related to every other part included in it in a significant way" (1968: 77). The notion of system lends itself well to textuality; we may speak about the ASRS intertextualities. In the conceptualization of organizations and whole industries as systems, the perspective of the theorist/researcher has generally been *external* to the system. Of equal importance is subjective understanding, or *Verstehen* (Weber 1978), of the participants *within* the system. It seems clear, particularly since the controllers' strike of 1981, that pilots, controllers, and other actors in the system have *a subjective understanding of interdependence.* They seem to identify with the aviation system at least as much as with their employing organization. It is, for many, a selfish motive to promote safety.

Does a worker in a nuclear power plant have a similar subjective understanding of either the plant or the industry? What of workers in marine transport, medicine, higher education, or defense? This question points toward an area in which empirical research into the subjective understanding of interdependence (or systems thinking) as well as the scope and intensity of identification with a system (see Tompkins and Cheney 1985) is called for in regard to both technological and natural hazards. Such research could lead to the conclusion that there is a need for education about interdependence when it is thought to be present, but the subjective sense of it is found to be absent.

SUMMARY AND RECOMMENDATIONS

The Aviation Safety Reporting System (ASRS) was created out of the ashes of a tragic accident, an accident whose causal factors included a misunderstood message. At the root of the tragedy was ambiguity, two interpretations of the word *clearance* on the part of controller and pilot. In its eleven years of operation, the ASRS has proved to be an effective industry-wide communication system, partly because it transcends the hierarchical inhibitors of organizational communication by means of the incentive of transactional immunity. ASRS has also, no doubt, promoted safety and saved much money and many lives. The sincerest praise of its success, to paraphrase Oscar Wilde, comes from its imitation in several countries.

The content of the reports, in combination with the success of ASRS itself as a communication system, provides support for the claim advanced early in this chapter that Perrow and others have underutilized communication in their analyses of hazardous systems. From 60 to 70 percent of the 70,000 reports received by ASRS have identified communication as either an enabling or associated factor. It is an almost ubiquitous link in the hazardous incident chain of events. The analysis of such events should no longer overlook the problem of communication. The success of the ASRS as a communication *system* has been achieved by a method consistent with the logological-textual understanding advocated above (Cheney and Tompkins in press).

A conceptual shift in the definition of communication could be beneficial to our understanding of the aviation system. By placing the air traffic controller at the hub of the system, by conceiving the interactive process between controller and pilot as one of control rather than as information "transfer" or "exchange," a deeper and more detailed understanding emerges. It also appears that the larger field of risk communication might benefit from the same or a similar shift, the shift away from an emphasis on sheer information to the rhetorical or persuasive function of messages.

If one assumes that every message has a relational as well as a content aspect, any message about risks and hazards should be examined carefully for the metacommunication—the explicit and implicit commands, advice, suggestions, and recommendations. The mere use, or nonuse, of the labels "risk" and "hazard" should be examined as a hortatory act. The elaborated double interact of control should also be considered as an analytic tool in understanding risks, hazards, and the mitigation of death and damage. The suasory nature of discourse itself should be examined for its effect on theory and policy.

The extrapolation of the ASRS concept to other industries has had mixed results at best. It is obvious that other industries are often reluctant to adopt the concept in its entirety, reluctant to build in the incentive of transactional immunity and the organizational sine qua non of the third party or honest broker. Without these aspects the concept will not receive a fair test. In addition, the subjective understanding of the concept of *system*, of interdependence and the degree of identification with the system, could be another factor responsible for the success of ASRS, and thereby relevant to its application to other sectors.

If the premise of this paper is correct, the summary just concluded should be examined for implicit recommendations, if not commands. If so examined, they will be found, and are probably best left in their implicit condition as tacit recognition of what is appropriate in the discourse of the tyro. There are, however, several recommendations that I want to make explicit, even at the risk of impudence.

My first recommendation is also a statement of personal intention. Because the ASRS analysts have been for some time preoccupied with coding and storing the massive flow of texts into the computer, analytic studies of the data have been neglected. It is my intention to undertake systematic study of the reports, in some cases replicating previous studies with a different conceptual approach. This will include the application of the double interact of control in those incidents involving controller-pilot interactions, controller-controller coordination, and intracrew communication. The process of information "transfer" or "exchange" will be redefined to include the suasive nature of discourse and the metacommunicative command. A second recommendation for research is to continue tracking and evaluating the extrapolation of the ASRS concept to other settings and industries.

Three Policy Recommendations

A first policy recommendation is not urged lightly, but grows out of concern that the U.S. aviation system, or at least local systems, is at the moment approaching the saturation point, when increased traffic results in the geometric increase in possible interactions. The Federal Aviation Administration (FAA) should either decrease the amount of traffic in the system or justify the present volume of traffic by directly communicating with the aviation consumers in the USA. If the FAA cannot or will not take one of these two options, the legislative and executive branches should move either to reregulate the industry or tighten their control of the FAA, particularly in reference to the options described above.

A second recommendation is to consider requiring either by law or FAA regulation the acknowledgment by a pilot of the reception of a controller's directive. Misunderstandings will still occur under such a regulation, but empirical research, communication theory, common sense, experience, and intuition all agree that such a procedure would decrease error.

My final recommendation looks to the long-range future of aviation safety. It is the view of some members of the ASRS staff, and also apparently the FAA, that the widespread problem of human communication in the aviation system, particularly in the case of controller-pilot interaction, can be eliminated by a technological "fix." Somewhere around the year 2000, the digital data link will be established for air traffic control. Control will be effected by "error-free" protocols for computer-to-computer communication. Aircraft will then be completely controlled from the ground. Pilots, partly because of their mythic role, can be expected to resist this "fix" for fear of being reduced to the status of passengers.

Error-free communication from ground to air is, needless to say, the ultimate goal of aviation safety. There are valid reasons, however, beyond the pilot's fear of a loss of status, and even beyond the antitechnological reflex, for proceeding very cautiously and carefully with implementation of such a system. After reading a fair number of reports from the ASRS data base, I am convinced there is ample evidence that technological progress in aviation almost always produces unintended side effects that create new hazards.

Altitude alert systems, for example, were introduced as a backup to the crew's direct monitoring of the plane's altitude. Sure enough, crews have become dependent upon these backup systems, relying on them as primary systems. In this technologically induced state of complacency, crews have found themselves in hazardous situations when technology inevitably failed. The reports are replete with stories of risky incidents created by faulty information inserted into computers. And, of course, computers falter. Who will fly the planes when crews become dependent upon the data link fix, and technology fails?

The final reason for caution arises from the question of who will program the computers. As it stands, controllers have an interest in expediting traffic, pilots value safety and comfort, and the air carrier seeks to reduce expenses. Since the optimal choice of an air route can result in the saving of up to $7,000 in fuel costs for a single flight, that interest is strong. Who has control of the decision rules in the computer program will be a contested issue. The choices in the existing system are made in a process of negotiation among the interested parties. As imperfect as the human communication process has been shown to be, the administrators of complex systems should pause before proceeding to eliminate it.

REFERENCES

Barnard, C.
1968   *The Functions of the Executive*. Cambridge: Harvard University Press (first published, 1938).
Billings, C., and Cheaney, E., eds.
1981   *Information Transfer Problems in the Aviation System*. Technical paper 1875. Moffett Field, Calif.: NASA.
Billings, C., and Reynard, W.
1981   "Dimensions of the Information Transfer Problem," in *Information Transfer Problems*, Billings and Cheaney, eds.
Boulder Daily Camera
1987   July 20.
Burke, K.
1966   *Language as Symbolic Action: Essays on Life, Literature, and Method*. Berkeley: University of California Press (originally published, 1945).
1969   *A Rhetoric of Motives*. Berkeley: University of California Press (originally published, 1950).
1984   *Attitudes Toward History*. Berkeley: University of California Press (originally published, 1938).
Cheney, G., and Tompkins, P.
in press "On the Facts of the 'Text' as the Basis of Human Communica-

tion Research," in *Communication Yearbook 11*, J. Anderson, ed. Newbury Park, Calif.: Sage.

Cheney, G., and Dionisopoulos, G.

1987   "Public Relations? No, Relations with Publics." Presented at the Conference of Communication Theory and Public Relations, Illinois State University, Normal, Ill. May.

Covello, V., von Winterfeldt, D., and Slovic, P.

1986   "Risk Communication: A Review of the Literature." *Risk Abstracts* 3: 171–82.

Edwards, R.

1979   *Contested Terrain: The Transformation of the Workplace in the Twentieth Century*. New York: Basic Books.

Follett, Mary Parker

1971   "The Giving of Orders," in *Organization Theory*, D. S. Pugh, ed. Baltimore: Penguin.

Foushee, H., and Manos, K.

1981   "Information Transfer within the Cockpit: Problems in Intracockpit Communications," in *Information Transfer Problems*, Billings and Cheaney, eds.

Gans, H.

1980   *Deciding What's News: A Study of CBS Evening News, NBC Nightly News, Newsweek, and Time*. New York: Vintage.

Grayson, R.

1981   "Information Transfer in the Surface Component of the System: Coordination Problems in Air Traffic Control," in *Information Transfer Problems*, Billings and Cheaney, eds.

Hollander, E., and Willis, R.

1967   "Some Current Issues in the Psychology of Conformity and Nonconformity." *Psychological Bulletin* 68: 62–76.

Kasperson, R., and Pijawka, D.

1985   "Societal Response to Hazards and Major Hazard Events: Comparing Natural and Technological Hazards." *Public Administration Review* 45:7–18.

Miller, G., Burgoon, M., and Burgoon, J.

1984   "The Functions of Human Communication in Changing Attitudes and Gaining Compliance," in *Handbook of Rhetorical and Communication Theory*, C. Arnold and J. Bowers, eds. Boston: Allyn and Bacon.

Miller, G., and Hewgill, M.

1966   "Some Recent Research on Fear-Arousing Message Appeals." *Speech Monographs* 33: 377–91.

Phillip K. Tompkins

U.S. National Aeronautic and Space Administration (NASA)
    1977a   *Third Quarterly Report.* Technical memorandum X-3546. Moffett
              Field, Calif.: NASA.
    1977b   *Fourth Quarterly Report.* Technical memorandum 78433. Moffett
              Field, Calif.: NASA.
    1978   *Fifth Quarterly Report.* Technical memorandum 78476. Moffett
              Field, Calif.: NASA.
    1983   *Report No. 14.* Technical memorandum 84339. Moffett Field, Calif.:
              NASA.

Perrow, C.
    1979   *Complex Organizations: A Critical Essay.* Glenview, Ill.: Scott,
              Foresman.
    1984   *Normal Accidents: Living with High-Risk Technologies.* New York:
              Basic Books.

Porter, R.
    1981   "Information Transfer during Contingency Operations: Emergency
              Air-Ground Communications," in *Information Transfer Problems,*
              Billings and Cheaney, eds.

Reynard, W.
    1987   "The Acquisition and Use of Incident Data," in *An Overview of the
              Aviation Safety Reporting System.* Mountain View, Calif.: Battelle
              Memorial Institute.

Reynard, W., Billings, C., Cheaney, E., and Hardy, R.
    1986   *The Development of the NASA Aviation Safety Reporting System.*
              Reference publication 1114. Moffett Field, Calif.: NASA.

Rogers, E., and Sood, R.
    1981   "Mass Media Operation in a Quick-Onset Natural Disaster: Hurri-
              cane David in Dominica." Working Paper. Los Angeles: University
              of Southern California.

Rorty, R.
    1979   *Philosophy and the Mirror of Nature.* Princeton: Princeton Univer-
              sity Press.

Stohl, C., and Redding, W. C.
    in press "Messages and Message Exchange Processes," in *The Handbook of
              Organizational Communication,* F. Jablin, L. Putnam, K. Roberts,
              and L. Porter, eds. Newbury Park, Calif.: Sage.

Tompkins, P.
    1962   "An Analysis of Communication between Headquarters and Selected
              Units of a National Labor Union." Ph.D. dissertation, Purdue Uni-
              versity.
    1967   "Organizational Communication: A State-of-the-Art Review,"
              in *Proceedings: Conference on Organizational Communication,*
              G. Richetto, ed. Huntsville, Ala.: NASA.

1977   "Management *qua* Communication in Rocket Research and Development." *Communication Monographs* 44:1–26.

1978   "Organizational Metamorphosis in Space Research and Development." *Communication Monographs* 45: 110–18.

1982   *Communication as Action*. Belmont, Calif.: Wadsworth.

1983   "Account Analysis of Organizations: Decision Making and Identification," in *Communication and Organizations: An Interpretive Approach*, L. Putnam and M. Pacanowsky, eds. Newbury Park, Calif.: Sage.

1985   "Symbolism as the Substance of Organization." Paper presented at the annual meeting of the Speech Communication Association, Denver. November.

1986   "Information and its Loss of Innocence." Paper presented at the annual meeting of the Speech Communication Association, Chicago. November.

in press   "Translating Organizational Theory: Symbolism over Substance," *Handbook of Organizational Communication*, F. Jablin, L. Putnam, K. Roberts, and L. Porter, eds.

Tompkins, P., and Anderson, E.

1971   *Communication Crisis at Kent State: A Case Study*. New York: Gorden and Breach.

Tompkins, P., and Cheney, G.

1985   "Communication and Unobtrusive Control in Contemporary Organizations," in *Organizational Communication: Traditional Themes and New Directions*, R. McPhee and P. Tompkins, eds. Newbury Park, Calif.: Sage.

Tompkins, P., Fisher, J., Infante, D., and Tompkins, E.

1975   "Kenneth Burke and the Inherent Characteristics of Formal Organizations: A Field Study." *Speech Monographs* 42: 135–42.

Watzlawick, P., Beavin, J., and Jackson, D.

1967   *Pragmatics of Human Communication: A Study of Interactional Patterns, Pathologies, and Paradoxes*. New York: Norton.

Weber, M.

1978   *Economy and Society*, G. Roth and K. Wittich, trans. and eds. Berkeley: University of California Press.

Weick, K.

1979   *The Social Psychology of Organizing*. Reading, Mass.: Addison-Wesley.

CHAPTER 9

Society and Emergency Preparedness

Looking from the Past into the Future

John H. Sorensen

This chapter explores the general relationship between society and hazards in the context of emergency preparedness. Inasmuch as it is widely recognized that society cannot mitigate or eliminate all hazards, preparedness is a vital component of hazard management. This, however, is not a new insight. As Dynes points out, emergency planning, in concept, dates back to biblical times, and it is likely that early civilizations had strategies to deal with the myriad dangers they encountered (Dynes 1970). Since the 1960s, the trade-offs involved in different strategies to reduce losses from hazards have been explicitly recognized (White 1964).

Today, emergency planning and response touch the lives of millions. Almost daily, some small portion of the population of the United States is warned and evacuated in order to escape the threat of one of a large range of hazards (Mileti and Sorensen 1987). The Superfund Reauthorization Act (SARA) Title III requires *all* communities in the nation to develop emergency response plans for a chemical accident if they house facilities that store certain prescribed amounts of a variety of hazardous materials. Emergency planning and response for technological hazards has become a salient issue at a national as well as on a local level—new technological developments are changing the way society prepares for emergency.

In this chapter, I explore two aspects of emergency planning. First, I examine shifts in the philosophy or strategy of emergency planning in the last decade and the significant events that have shaped the evolution of current emergency practices in the United States. Second, I identify and discuss some major ethical issues associated with emerging preparedness technologies and practices.

SHIFTS IN PREPAREDNESS STRATEGIES

In the past twenty-five years, at least five major developments have occurred that have changed the way the nation deals with emergencies. These are:

1. shifts from single hazard to multihazard planning;
2. shifts from single time phase to multiphase planning;
3. shifts from single protective action to multiprotective action;
4. development of scientific approaches;
5. development of computer aids.

In the remainder of this chapter, these themes are discussed in turn.

Shifts from Single to Multihazard Planning

As of the mid-1960s, planning for emergencies was largely implemented on a hazard-by-hazard basis. Separate plans may have existed at community and state levels for floods, tornadoes, nuclear war, and hurricanes, and plans may have been nonexistent for other hazards such as a release of toxic materials or a radiation accident. Many communities had no strategy until a disaster occurred, and plan development was sporadic and largely unsystematic. Governments treated various hazards as distinctly different problems.

In some cases, there were different agencies at the federal, State, and local levels of government to plan for different events. In Washington, floods were the responsibility of the National Weather Service (NWS), nuclear plants were under the guidance of the Atomic Energy Commission and later the Nuclear Regulatory Commission (NRC), and earthquakes were primarily the responsibility of the U.S. Geological Survey (USGS).

At the State level such differentiation was also in effect. Civil defense was oriented toward nuclear war, not domestic hazards. Radiation threats may have been assigned to State health departments, floods to natural resources departments, and landslides to the State geologist.

The first attempt to pull disparate parts of emergency planning systematically together came in the early 1970s with the passage of the Disaster Relief Acts of 1969 (PL 91-79) and 1970 (PL 91-606: see also chapter 5, above). Prior to this legislation, the main disaster role that the federal government assumed was for repairing local government public facilities (OEP 1972). Major disasters, such as the Alaskan earthquake or Hurricane Betsy, were dealt with by special disaster relief acts. Legislation in 1970 extended the role played by the federal government in a disaster and authorized emergency services such as emergency communications and emergency transportation.

The 1969 act also called for the creation of the Office of Emergency Preparedness (OEP) within the Executive Office of the President. The office was charged with investigating what additional or improved plans, procedures, and facilities were necessary to prevent and minimize casualties and property losses from all natural disasters. The publication of the report *Disaster Preparedness* signified the attempt of the office to bring some overall structure and coordination to emergency planning across a range of natural hazards (OEP 1972). Shortly thereafter, the RANN Program (Research Applied to National Needs) at the National Science Foundation (NSF) funded an interdisciplinary project to integrate knowledge across a wide range of natural events (White and Haas 1975).

The purpose of the study was to investigate how losses from hazards could be reduced by developing new knowledge and investing in different mixes of mitigation strategies. Sixteen natural hazards including volcanoes, urban and rural drought, coastal erosion, snow avalanches, landslides, tsunamis, earthquakes, urban snow, frost, windstorms, hail, lightning, tornadoes, floods, and hurricanes were examined. From these examinations, five common adjustment themes that cut across hazards emerged, including relief and rehabilitation, insurance, warning systems, land use management, and technological aids. This study laid the scientific foundation for multihazard philosophy; however, it was limited to natural hazards.

The major impetus to shift from single hazard to multihazard planning practices came from the efforts of the National Governors Association (NGA 1978). The NGA developed the concept of Comprehensive Emergency Management (CEM) for implementation at the State level. In NGA words, CEM "refers to a State's responsibility and capability for managing all types of emergencies and disasters by coordinating the actions of numerous agencies. . . . It applies to all risks: attack, man-made, and natural."

At the federal level, the creation of FEMA (Federal Emergency Management Agency) to consolidate emergency planning functions further strengthened the multihazard approach. The creation of FEMA initially brought together the following agencies and programs: Dam Safety Coordination, the Earthquake Hazard Reduction Program, Consequences Management of Terrorism, Warning, and Emergency Broadcast, Federal Flood Insurance Program, National Fire Administration, National Weather Service Community Preparedness Program, Defense Civil Preparedness Agency, National Preparedness Agency, and the Federal Disaster Assistance Administration. Major programs added to FEMA included parts of the Radiological Emergency Preparedness Program and, most recently, portions of the hazardous chemical emergency preparedness initiative.

Finally, the development within FEMA of the Integrated Emergency Management System (IEMS) to be implemented at the local level represented an explicit endorsement of the multihazard approach. Although the concept was recast by political opponents to civil defense as a means of fostering crisis relocation programs for nuclear war, the idea has merit. Unfortunately, as rapidly as it was adopted, it was seemingly abandoned. Its quick fall from popularity is indicative of the problems of getting FEMA, as well as the States, to integrate civil defense or nuclear attack planning with planning for all other hazards.

Shifts from Single Phase to Multiphase Planning

As of the 1960s, emergency planning was chiefly segmented into the time phases of a disaster (Barton 1969). Different parties were typically responsible for mitigation, preparedness, warning, emergency response management, and disaster recovery. There was little coordination of such aspects of planning. Again, responsibilities cut across different agencies and levels of government. The lack of coordination created several significant problems, chief of which was the lack of a linkage between relief policies and mitigation. The dominant hazard management policy in the 1960s was to clean up the mess without paying much attention to preventing the mess from occurring again.

The Disaster Relief Act of 1970 brought recognition that preparedness was related to recovery in that it could reduce the burden on the federal government for expenditure of disaster relief funds. *The Assessment of Research on Natural Hazards*, the 1975 White and Haas study, directly confronted the issue of trade-offs in investing in new research in one functional area versus another. The project concluded that a mix of strategies was needed to reduce losses, and that implementation of the mix required coordination. The National Governors Association CEM program also recognized the need for integrating what they defined to be the four phases of disaster: mitigation, preparedness, response, and recovery.

While a life-cycle view of natural hazards emerged in the 1970s, this was not true for all hazards. The lack of coordination between different elements involved in emergency response was perhaps best typified by the Three Mile Island nuclear power plant accident, which is often referred to as an emergency planning—not a nuclear—disaster. Different government and private entities were responsible for developing emergency plans, assessing the hazard, issuing evacuation orders, controlling traffic, monitoring for radiation, and cleaning up. The accident led to broad changes in the way emergency planning for radiological emergencies is done in order to avoid the problems of fragmented organization. Prior to operating, a nuclear power plant must have an emergency plan approved by FEMA and the NRC. The plan must be systematic in its management approach, and consistent for the utility, all local governments, and the State.

First, a plan must contain a predetermined scheme for classifying an accident into one of four categories and establishing initial protective actions based on the classification level. Second, means for prompt notification of public officials and the general population in the Emergency Planning Zone (EPZ) must be established. Third, a means of identifying the accident source terms and projecting the atmospheric dispersion of radioactive particles must be established. These projections are used for recommending an evacuation. Fourth, evacuation routes must be identified. Fifth, evacuation time estimates must be prepared. Sixth, an emergency implementation plan must be prepared.

The plans contain a variety of elements including maps showing evacuation areas, routes, and shelters; maps of the population distribution in the EPZ; the means of notifying the public; the means of protecting the

John H. Sorensen

populace from radiation exposure; projected traffic capacities of evacuation areas; means for controlling access to evacuated areas; identification of and means for dealing with potential traffic impediments; evacuation time estimates; means of registering evacuees; mechanisms for making an evacuation decision; methods for monitoring food and water supplies; and a means of decontaminating evacuees.

The key features of this approach are that it is comprehensive, rigorous, and based on scientific studies of source terms and dispersion potentials. The planning is geared to the whole cycle of the emergency, not a single element. Several more detailed descriptions of the approach (Jaske 1983; Olds 1981) as well as critiques that suggest that integrated planning is still deficient, or even unnecessary, have been written (Cutter 1984; Hull 1981a; 1981b; USGAO 1984).

Shifts from Single to Multiple Protective Actions

For many hazardous situations a single form of response was once considered appropriate. In a tornado one went to a basement shelter; before a hurricane those at risk were evacuated. It is becoming increasingly apparent that in many situations, there is more than one option for protection. In some cases, this may be a choice between two, but in others a choice between many alternatives. The author (1987), for example, has identified a range of actions that could reduce the impacts of exposure to toxic chemicals: evacuation, sheltering, respiratory protection, protective clothing, prophylactic drugs, antidotes, and decontamination.

Evacuation is the movement on foot or by vehicle outside the plume exposure area. Typically one can differentiate precautionary from reactive evacuation. Precautionary evacuation is moving to avoid exposure before a release; reactive evacuation involves moving to avoid or reduce exposure thereafter. Sheltering, the movement into a building or some other structure, has a variety of forms. This may include specialized sheltering such as commercial tents and other structures designed to provide protection in a contaminated environment. Expedient sheltering involves improvising makeshift protection using common materials such as tape or wet towels. Taping doors and windows may cut the infiltration rate of some toxics by half; a wet cloth placed across a door jamb may filter out harmful aerosols.

Pressurized sheltering requires modification of a building with some infiltration reduction and installing a blower to pull in contaminated air and move it through a filter into the building. The pressure prevents infiltra-

246

tion through normal channels in the structure. Enhanced sheltering also includes the reduction of infiltration rates in structures by superweatherproofing. It is feasible to reduce normal infiltration rates by factors of between two to ten.

Respiratory protection is the use of a system to remove aerosols and vapors from the air before they can be inhaled. Some common systems include gas masks with filters, mouthpiece respirators, which are small tubes with filter material inserted into the mouth, and self-contained breathing apparatus including a mask and oxygen tank. More novel systems include hoods, with fan-driven filters, placed over the head and sealed at waist and wrists, and bags that are sealable containers with a fan-driven filter. These are primarily designed for the protection of children and infants. Finally, expedient protection involves improvisation, such as placing a cloth over the nose and mouth.

Protective clothing can be used to prevent skin exposure to chemicals. A variety of clothing has been designed to protect against different chemicals, for use in various types of environments, for doing assorted types of work, and with differing protection levels. Prophylactic drugs, which prevent or block effects before exposure occurs, are not often viewed as a possible form of protective action. The most familiar is potassium iodide, which can be used to block absorption of radioactive iodine by the thyroid gland. Antidotes involve a range of techniques to counter chemical effects after exposure. They include drugs that counteract symptoms or block effects, as well as decontamination procedures such as washing off material or shedding contaminated clothes.

The large range of feasible actions will vary in effectiveness according to the nature and quantity of the hazardous material, the time available to take action, and the protection offered by each action. This creates a fairly complex decision-making problem that is beyond the capabilities of many first responders or local emergency decision-makers. Yet it seems clear, as we face the problem of multiple technological hazards, that the complexities will not disappear. This suggests that emergency planning is shifting from purely an art to a combination of art and science.

Development of a Scientific Approach

Scientific studies have always been an integral part of emergency planning. Until recently, however, the development of scientific information for use in emergency plan development was largely piecemeal and unsystematic.

John H. Sorensen

A systematic approach is best illustrated by the hurricane planning process developed by FEMA in cooperation with the NWS and Army Corps of Engineers (FEMA 1984).

The U.S. coastline has been divided into twenty-two basins for implementation of the planning process. It is at the basin level that technical studies are done to provide data for preparing State and local plans (U.S. Army Corps of Engineers 1984). The quantitative studies include five analyses: hurricane hazard, property and population vulnerability, behavioral analysis, shelter availability, and transportation.

The hurricane hazard analysis involves simulation of hurricanes using computer models. In a study, three hundred to four hundred hypothetical storms are generated by varying hurricane intensity, size, direction, and speed. The National Weather Service had developed two models, SPLASH and SLOSH, for use in these studies. SPLASH is used for open coastlines; SLOSH is used for bays or estuaries, and has the ability to handle unique topographic features and ocean bottom characteristics. Both models have been fine-tuned using historical hurricane run-up data and have an error term of about 20 percent.

Information provided by the SLOSH models includes estimates of the height of water from storm surges, time histories of surges at specified points, wind speeds at specified points, and wind directions at specified points. SPLASH computes only surge heights and durations of an approaching storm. After all the computer simulation runs are made, the outputs are compared and storms with similar impacts are grouped together. Eventually about twelve scenarios are developed, which represent all the storms used in the analysis. When a hurricane threatens, an emergency manager can use estimates of hurricane intensity, speed, and tracks to classify the storm into one of the scenarios and then use the predicted surge and wind speeds to identify areas at risk. Based on the historical model validations, the data used for planning are 20 percent greater than the maximum storm surge depth estimated by the model. The resultant "maximum envelopes of water" (MEOWs) for each scenario define evacuation areas under each scenario.

The vulnerability analysis defines and estimates the population at risk within MEOWs. This represents permanent populations, seasonal, and daily transient populations, and institutionalized populations such as schools, hospitals, nursing homes, jails, and other population concentrations. Behavioral analysis is done to provide data on human response to hurricane warnings. The analysis provides information on hypothetical response to different hurricane scenarios. Information is generated regarding when evacuees think they would leave, how many would leave, the number of vehicles they would use, the need for public transportation, and likely destinations.

The shelter analysis identifies structures outside MEOWs that can be used to shelter evacuees with no other place to go. Using the behavioral data, the demand for shelter is estimated. Based on the estimated demand, the appropriate number and location of shelters is estimated. In addition, the availability of emergency supplies is determined and inventoried. The transportation analysis estimates the time required to evacuate various population zones. The analysis identifies evacuation routes and traffic capacities of those routes. Using data from behavioral studies, assumptions on route demand are made.

Calculations are then made on how long it will take for persons to evacuate to safe areas. This provides the decision-maker with an estimate of when an evacuation decision should be made, based on assumptions about the storm's characteristics. Using the above technical information, evacuation implementation plans are developed at State and local levels. In support of the overall planning effort, a public information program and a property protection and hurricane hazard mitigation plan are developed as well.

The "scientific approach" reflected by the hurricane program does not transfer to all preparedness activities. Preparedness for nuclear attack using such an approach was attempted but bogged down when critics attacked the scientific basis with unrelenting vengeance. For example, when FEMA attempted to establish a technical basis for crisis relocation planning (CRP), a number of critiques attempted to undermine the results of the analyses (Leaning and Keyes 1984), and illustrated that CRP was a political decision and not one that could be easily supported by a scientific rationale.

A different example of the lack of a scientific approach is reflected in Title III requirements. Unlike the nuclear attack situation, in which the approach failed, Title III simply avoids using a systematic planning approach. Instead the effort is oriented toward data dissemination to local government. Chemical companies are required to disclose hazard information (such as the type and quantities of a chemical) to local planning committees during planning and following actual releases. If the hurricane program followed this analogy, the weather service would just be passing weather data to local emergency planners.

John H. Sorensen

Development of Computer Aids

Both the increased complexity of hazard management and the amount of scientific information that goes into planning are becoming overwhelming. Consequently, various prescriptive decision tools or aids have been developed to automate or assist emergency management and decision-making (Carroll 1983; 1985). One type of aid that is being developed is a computerized information system. FEMA has developed the Integrated Emergency Management Information System (IEMIS) for nuclear power plant emergencies and eventual hurricane applications (Jaske 1984; 1986). This system provides the user with information on population, road networks, and environmental features. In addition, through the use of an atmospheric dispersion model, a hazard impact model, a traffic flow model, and a siren sound propagation model, the planner can simulate or model a real emergency. The information outputs can be used to predict needed evacuation zones and locations of potential traffic problems. The system requires considerable input data and computer capacity. A similar system for a microcomputer has also been developed, which incorporates heuristic decision aids (Belardo et al. 1983; Seagle et al. 1985).

Several models have been developed to assist local decision-makers in issuing evacuation recommendations when a hurricane is approaching (Simpson et al. 1985; Ruch 1985; Berke and Ruch 1985; Berke et al. 1985). These systems are designed to produce a recommended action to the user. The Simpson approach is geared to using probabilistic estimates of landfall and confidence intervals to arrive at a decision. The Ruch (1985) model allows the selection of worst case assumptions regarding possible inundation and storm timing to arrive at a decision about when to recommend action based on expected storm arrival. Berke and Ruch (1985) provide a computer simulation model oriented to more general mitigation planning, including evacuation. These systems, however, are largely untested in real applications.

The advent of Title III requirements for hazardous chemicals has led to a host of computer-based information systems serving different requirements and uses. Around fifteen are being marketed at this time, and undoubtedly many more will be available in the future. Many local emergency agencies are in possession of a computer, and some are beginning to explore their use. Pennsylvania is networking counties in a computer-based management system. These innovations will likely have profound effects on the management of emergencies, creating problems and pitfalls as well as providing assistance to managers in areas where rapid decision-making and quick access to information are critical.

Summary: Major Changes in Emergency Planning Policies

The cliché that no one is worried about disasters until one occurs is a basic law behind the evolution of emergency planning. As with changes in mitigation policy, many of the significant changes in emergency planning practices and policies have followed disasters. In addition, change also occurs from a series of close calls or a mismanaged event. Some of the major changes in emergency planning practices are summarized in Table 9.1, along with the events that are believed to have played significant roles in causing the changes.

Although I will not discuss each event in detail, Table 9.1 underscores a central point: as national policies of hazard management evolve, changes are also occurring on a hazard-specific basis. These changes are responses to a perceived need to correct a short-term problem. As a consequence, national policies will continue to be in flux, despite efforts to shift toward more uniform and consistent policies.

Table 9.1. Significant Events and Changes in Emergency Planning

Hazard	Event	Change
Earthquake	1971 San Fernando	1977 Earthquake Reduction Act
Flood	1977 Big Thompson Flood	Program to improve warning systems (interagency)
Dam failure	Series of 1970 failures	Dam Safety Program (interagency)
Hurricane	Close calls by Frederick and David	1981 Tampa Bay Plan; Hurricane Program
Tsunami	1961, Hilo; 1964, Crescent City	Pacific tsunami warning system
Volcano	1980 Mt. St. Helens	Cascade Observatory
Nuclear power	1979 TMI accident	New emergency planning rules
Chemical	1985 Bhopal accident and 1986 Institute accident	1986 Superfund Amendments Reauthorization Act
Nuclear war	1950s cold war	CD Shelter Program
	Soviet Relocation Program revealed	Crisis Relocation

John H. Sorensen

As emergency planning proliferates and becomes increasingly complex, it is likely that more social issues will emerge and become part of the political agenda. The Superfund Amendments and Reauthorization Act requirements for emergency plans have implications for most communities with industrial facilities that use or store toxic materials, and these will result in more widespread public debate of emergency planning proposals. It is anticipated that the issues that may emerge will involve ethical questions regarding the invasion of government into private life, issues concerning costs and benefits and their distribution, issues concerning the provision and withholding of information, and liability issues.

Ethics and Emergency Planning

Emergency plans are meant to serve the public good and enhance the quality of life by reducing the effects of hazardous events. To do so, however, plans require by definition that officials intervene in human lives. By design, warnings are meant to influence and guide behavior. In some cases that guidance is not perfect; in others, it prevents fatalities and injuries. On the one hand, planning and response should ideally not interfere with civil liberties; on the other hand, they cannot help but do so to some degree.

In light of this dilemma, What is the proper role of emergency plans in shaping social behavior and human choice in a disaster? Do warning systems constitute behavior control or are they a form of social services, help, and welfare? The United States is not a police state in which public behavior is completely controlled; yet the ideological danger of sophisticated planning systems is that they do in fact control the behavior of those they are intended to serve. Such control is a two-edged sword, which can be used to benefit or to manipulate individuals. While evidence of deliberate manipulation is lacking, the concern for misuse is real.

Emergency plans should not be viewed as an outcome of an Orwellian world in which information controls behavior, and in which behavior control is the ultimate goal. To use plans in such a manner would ultimately defeat their intended goal. Yet the threat of misuse rises as communication technologies advance, as the social sciences become more and more informed about how to shape human behavior through the manipulation of public information, and as bureaucracies (referred to as "warning systems") emerge to manage information and information technologies. This is not an argument to condemn or even discourage the use or development of emergency plans; it is, however, a caution against the subversion of their intended purpose.

Costs and Benefits of Emergency Planning

Emergency plans cannot be designed or implemented on a benefit/cost basis for two reasons. First, the benefits of planning are not readily quantifiable. Second, even if they were, the benefits are not comparable to the costs of responding or not responding. Establishing a plan is a value-laden activity and is done for humanitarian, not for fiscal, reasons. This is not to imply that plans should be developed for every hazard irrespective of cost. It is clear that some hazards do not warrant a large investment of money in emergency plans, when prevention or mitigation will clearly save more lives. In situations where hazardous systems (particularly ones built or controlled by humans) threaten even one person, the economic issues become cloudy. Is the prevention (or possible prevention) of death "worth" the investment in a warning system, to give one example, beneath a potentially hazardous reservoir? Does the threat of nuclear attack warrant quick communications with each family in the USA?

Ultimately, these are political, not economic, decisions: but too often such decisions are made neither on the basis of benefit/cost nor on humanitarian grounds. All too frequently, plans emerge because of policy decisions based on public outcry after a particular disaster or emergency event. For example, detailed off-site plans for nuclear power plant emergencies in the United States would likely not exist had the Three Mile Island accident not occurred. Conversely, had the Bhopal chemical plant tragedy happened within our borders, the nation would likely have more planning regulations in place for the chemical industry than is now the case. The point is not that the nation's emergency planning guidelines for nuclear power or chemical plants are incorrect—such policy assessment is well beyond the scope of this work. Instead it should be noted that decisions based on benefit/cost analysis, humanitarian concern, and political responsiveness after major emergencies are not necessarily consistent.

Two governmental approaches to dealing with this issue are reflected in the dam safety programs of two federal agencies. Both the Bureau of Reclamation and the Army Corps of Engineers own and regulate dams with downstream populations at risk. Some of these dams may be structurally hazardous. Both agencies are currently making decisions on whether to invest in, and then how much to spend on, emergency planning for dam failure. The basic belief of the Corps of Engineers is that it is a question of economic efficiency; compare the costs and benefits of a warning system with the costs and benefits of improving the structure of the dam to reduce the probability of failure. The decision is based on which plan gives the nation the best benefit for its buck. The Bureau of Reclamation, on the other hand, takes the position that emergency planning is needed when there is a population at risk. Its decision is based on determining the most cost-effective system to provide emergency protection for the downstream population. While this sketch may overstate or oversimplify these two stances, they serve to illustrate differing bureaucratic decisions with regard to the same planning situations.

Withholding Information

The control and timing of hazard information by public officials, private managers, or by other responsible parties will continue to be a thorny issue in emergency management. This is also true regarding the communication of risk information prior to any emergency.

There are several basic reasons for withholding information. First, there seems to be a widespread belief that the public will become unnecessarily alarmed if warned about a low probability but high consequence event. During a potential warning situation, there is reluctance to tell the public until it is absolutely necessary, and even then some warnings are delayed, muddled, or suppressed. While it is suspected that this problem may be greatest for systems containing hazards caused by operations in the private sector, such as chemical plants, many examples from publicly managed natural systems can also be found.

Second, warnings are sometimes withheld because of a perception that their dissemination would have negative social and economic effects on the hazard manager and on society in general. In such cases, only a partial disclosure of information may occur, which can seriously undermine warning effectiveness. In events like this, additional information may well become public, disseminated through the media and from nonofficial sources, creating credibility problems for warning officials. Interestingly, withholding information in a hazardous situation in a free society can, therefore, actually be the cause of the kind of problem it was originally designed to avoid.

The "to tell or not to tell" dilemma, can and will continue to surface in reference to the release of information about hazards to the public. Consider, for example, the dilemma facing scientists with information that a whole town will likely be destroyed from a volcanic eruption that may or may not happen some time during the next twenty years. To which vested interest do geologists bow: the public, who—some think—has the right to know, and who would likely not do anything differently if they did know; the shareholders of a property development corporation, who do not want to know; the owners of the local tourist industry, who may be willing to know but who do not want to tell anyone else; or the State emergency planning bureaucracy, which wants to know in order to plan for the event and legitimate its organizational charter?

In this not-so-hypothetical circumstance, the geologists—if they are like the geologists involved in potential disasters such as the Palmdale Bulge or Mount St. Helens—would likely disclose the information. The dilemma of vested interests, however, will be stronger in the future. Should it happen that hazard information is made public in the future, and that information is designed to maximize a protective response, it will likely be less easy for the public to discount it. Consequently, effective long-term warnings could well elicit the wrath of interest groups not served by the release of believable hazard information.

In one instance, the City of New York discovered in a routine building inspection that sustained winds over fifty miles an hour would lead to the structural failure of a high-rise office building, and that the consequences would be severe. Decision-makers were faced with the choice of whether to "alarm" tenants and workers by developing a plan to evacuate, or to keep quiet while repairs took place to make the building structurally sound. After considerable debate the decision was made to keep silent because the decision-makers believed that telling the public would do more harm than good. In the end the building was repaired, no disaster occurred. Officials had made the "right" decision, at least in their hindsight view.

A parallel situation has developed over the past five years at Mammoth Lakes, California, and remains unresolved. The USGS discovered evidence of renewed volcanism beneath this populated, condominium-laden resort town. Even though they made some bungles in public relations early on, they were not prepared for a "shoot the messenger" response from local political and economic interests. At the current time, the USGS is well prepared for an eruption, with a volcano observatory and a back-up operations center should they be required to move out of the one near Mammoth Lakes. The State built an evacuation route, labeled a "scenic drive" to avoid scaring tourists. The town, however, refuses to plan for an emergency because it does not want to tell the population that the threat is real.

Liability Issues

Liability issues can be a problem for emergency officials in several ways. First, officials may fail to issue warnings to the public, and the event subsequently occurs. Second, they may warn the public but the event does not occur. Third, they may provide warning, but the warning contains wrong information or inadequate information. Fourth, officials may withhold some relevant warning information from the public, either in terms of information content or timing, and the event occurs. The consequences of each of these situations could be litigation against the officials involved in the warning process, or against the organization for which they work. Additionally, officials can make errors in judgment of this sort (or, with hindsight, they can be seen as errors, even though they may have been seen as prudent judgments during the event), and these can be the grounds for successful litigation.

It is possible to discover no more than a few documented cases in which fear of litigation constrained the issuance of public warning. However, this may be due to the infrequency with which the topic has been studied, or testimony to the effectiveness of those engaging in this sort of behavior. Nevertheless, it is important to note that fear of liability can be a constraint to emergency planning. Removal of this fear could be accomplished in one of two ways. First, makers of emergency decisions can be made free of liability for what they do or do not do in a warning situation. This is the case, for example, for the Governor of the State of California regarding earthquake prediction warnings. Second, warning decision-makers can have their decision-making formalized and subject to postevent audits. This is the case, for example, for parts of the warning systems for accidents at nuclear power plants.

Liability fears may also stimulate effort in planning. The current approach of the Superfund Reauthorization Act (SARA III), requiring the development of emergency plans in all communities storing hazardous materials, does not provide any sanctions for noncompliance or incentives to comply. Thus there is no compelling reason for a community to develop the plans. In recent conversations with local officials faced with the task of developing plans, a task they did not greet with enthusiasm, it became apparent that the driving force for compliance was liability. These officials did not want to be faced with litigation for failure to plan if an emergency did occur and damages resulted.

CONCLUSIONS

This chapter has charted some of the major trends in emergency planning over the past twenty-five years. One of the dominant themes that emerges from this review is that emergency planning is becoming more and more complex and more sophisticated in approach. These developments create some uncertainties and distinct problems for the emergency planner. The application of computer technology to deal with these complexities seems inevitable (see also chapter 10, below). To date such technologies are being developed in more or less prototypical forms, but there is little experience as yet with the use of such technologies. It is unclear whether the application of computerized systems will lead to better or worse management.

The social issues that face emergency managers and the public at risk to hazards intertwine with the shifts to automated systems. Will such systems create controls that infringe on human rights? Who will receive the benefits of the most advanced technologies, given the use of cost-benefit models of investment in emergency planning? Will such systems foster free and open disclosure of information and warnings, or be used to regulate risk communications tightly? Who is liable when a computer makes a poor evacuation or other protective action decision? Such questions will help shape the social agenda regarding emergency preparedness policy into the next century.

Emergency planning has extended from civil defense and natural hazards to include technological hazards such as nuclear power, chemicals, and hazardous waste. The existence of such planning will become more of an issue in technology choice and public acceptance of hazardous technology. Will publics be more likely to accept a waste disposal plant if the state-of-the-art planning for an accident is part of the proposed project? Will existing chemical facilities, in the context of the Bhopal accident, be viewed as better members of the community if they participate openly in such schemes? Can the public be convinced that planning can prevent losses in a catastrophic accident?

A final, cross-cutting issue concerns the effects of emergency planning on society as a whole and whether planning increases or decreases societal risks and benefits. Critics of emergency planning for nuclear attack argue that plans increase the likelihood of war because they create the image that such wars are survivable and winnable (Leaning and Keyes 1984). In a similar way opponents of nuclear power argue that emergency plans increase the risk of accidents because they are one of the regulatory requirements that allow plants to operate. Without plans, the public around the plants would not be exposed to the incremental risks posed by plant operations. Indeed, the contested issue of emergency planning at several nuclear sites is being used as a means to prevent plants from operating. Plausible arguments could also be shaped that would suggest that emergency planning for hurricanes could lead to laxity in the enforcement of building codes because the buildings do not need to protect persons who evacuate from a hurricane.

In each of these three cases, arguments can be developed to support or reject the contentions, although we should note that the planning activities do modify the system that they are designed to mitigate. Empirical data do not exist—nor are they likely ever to exist—to help us to prove whether or not emergency planning increases, or decreases, risk.

NOTE

The research reported in this chapter was partially supported by the Technology Utilization Research Program, Energy Division, Oak Ridge National Laboratory.

REFERENCES

Barton, A.
  1969   *Communities in Disaster*. Garden City, N.Y.: Doubleday.
Belardo, S., Howell, A., Ryan, R., and Wallace, W.
  1983   "A Microcomputer-based Emergency Response System." *Disasters* 7:215–20.
Berke, P., and Ruch, C.
  1985   "Application of Computer System for Hurricane Emergency Re-

sponse and Land Use Planning." *Journal of Environmental Manage-ment* 21: 117–34.

Berke, P., Ruch, C., and Rials, D.

1985   "A Computer Simulation System for Assessment of Hurricane Haz-ard Impacts on Land Development," in *Emergency Planning* (vol. 15, no. 1), J. Carroll, ed., 149–54. La Jolla, Calif.: Society for Computer Simulation.

Carroll, J. M., ed.

1983   *Emergency Planning* 11 (2). La Jolla, Calif.: Society for Computer Simulation.

1985   *Emergency Planning* 15 (1). La Jolla, Calif.: Society for Computer Simulation.

Cutter, Susan

1984   "Emergency Preparedness and Planning for Nuclear Power Plant Accidents." *Applied Geography* 4: 235–45.

Dynes, R.

1970   *Organized Behavior in Disasters.* Lexington, Mass.: D. C. Heath.

Federal Emergency Management Agency

1984   *A Guide to Hurricane Preparedness Planning for State and Local Officials.* CPG2–16. Washington, D.C.: FEMA.

Hull, A. P.

1981a   "Emergency Planning for What?" *Nuclear News* (April): 61–67.

1981b   "Critical Evaluation of Radiological Measurements and of the Need for Evacuation of the Nearby Public during the Three Mile Island Incident," in *Current Nuclear Power Plant Safety Issues* (vol. 2), 81–96. Vienna: International Atomic Energy Agency.

Jaske, R.

1983   "Emergency Preparedness: Status and Outlook." *Nuclear Safety* 24 (1): 1–11.

1984   *FEMA's Integrated Emergency Management Information System* (draft). Washington, D.C.: FEMA.

1986   "FEMA's Computerized Aids for Accident Assessment." *Proceed-ings, International Symposium on Emergency Planning and Pre-paredness for Nuclear Facilities.* Rome, 4–8 November. Vienna: International Atomic Energy Agency.

Leaning, J., and Keyes, L.

1984   *The Counterfeit Ark: Crisis Relocation Planning for Nuclear War.* New York: Ballinger.

Mileti, Dennis, and Sorensen, John

1987   "Warning Systems." Draft report to FEMA, unpublished.

National Governors Association (NGA)

1978   *Comprehensive Emergency Management.* Washington, D.C.: National Governors Association.

John H. Sorensen

Office of Emergency Preparedness (OEP)

    1972   *Disaster Preparedness—A Report to the President.* Washington, D.C.: Office of Emergency Preparedness.

Olds, F. C.

    1981   "Emergency Planning for Nuclear Plants." *Power Engineering* (August): 48–56.

Ruch, C.

    1985   *ESTED.* Paper presented at the National Hurricane Conference, New Orleans. April.

Seagle, J., Duchessi, P., and Belardo, S.

    1985   "Simulation Using Geographical Data Bases: An Application in Emergency Management," in *Emergency Planning* 15(1), J. Carroll, ed., 66–68. La Jolla, Calif.: Society for Computer Simulation.

Simpson, R. H., Hayden, B., Garstang, M., and Massie, H.

    1985   "Timing of Hurricane Emergency Actions." *Environmental Management* 9: 61–70.

Sorensen, John

    1987   *Evaluation of Protective Action Implementation Time for Chemical Weapons Accidents.* ORNL TM-10437. Oak Ridge, Tenn.: Oak Ridge National Laboratory.

U.S. Army Corps of Engineers

    1984   *Technical Guidelines for Hurricane Evacuation Studies.* Jacksonville, Fla.: Corps of Engineers District Office.

United States General Accounting Office (USGAO)

    1984   *Further Action Needed to Improve Emergency Preparedness around Nuclear Power Plants.* GAO/RCED–84–43. Washington, D.C.: U.S. Government Printing Office.

White, Gilbert F.

    1964   *Choice of Adjustment to Floods.* Department of Geography Research Paper #93. Chicago: University of Chicago Press.

White, Gilbert F., and Haas, J.

    1975   *Assessment of Research on Natural Hazards.* Cambridge: MIT Press.

CHAPTER 10

On Managing Disasters

The Use of Decision-Aid Technologies

William A. Wallace

Recent advances in information technology, computing, and communications have not gone unnoticed by the disaster management community (Congressional Research Service 1984). Although practitioners may have misgivings about its potential benefits, there is little disagreement that assessing the impacts of this new technology is an important item on the agenda for research in disaster management (Drabek 1986).

This chapter first briefly reviews recent assessments of the technological trends in computing and telecommunications, emphasizing areas that should have the greatest impact on disaster management. It then focuses on the components of information technology that are designed specifically to support the decision-making activities of a disaster manager, the human-computer interface, and the models employed to summarize data. Finally, I propose some items for future research.

TRENDS IN COMPUTING

Recent discussions about the future of computers—in the next ten years at least—concluded:

- the progress in the next decade will be much like the progress of the last ten years, and
- we will continue to "make everything a little bit smaller every year" (Gomory 1986: 330).

Ongoing research is showing that the only real limits to the size at which we can record information are at the molecular level. We should be able to place the equivalent of a million transistors on a chip by 1990; the following years will be spent making the technology commercially available.

This reduction in size will enable us to have central processing units (CPUs) that can process 10–20 MIPS (millions of instructions per second) in the very near future. For comparison, the present MacIntosh runs at 1–2 MIPS, while the IBM AT runs in the 0.4–0.75 MIPS range. We will also have 32-bit processors as opposed to the present 8- or 16-bit machines. While the 32-bit processor will enable us to do more accurate calculations, it will also be able to address approximately 4 billion bytes—four gigabytes—as opposed to the current 1 million bytes for 16-bit processors and 64 thousand for 8-bit devices. These advances will result in very powerful individual work stations that will have the computing power of our present mainframes. However, these advances also mean that we will construct larger machines with parallel CPUs wherein each chip will run 100 MIPS.

Advances in storage technology will mimic these advances in processing, but with one important difference. As we decrease the size and concomitantly increase the density of stored data, it will be progressively more difficult to locate the data on the storage medium, typically a disk. This problem is equivalent to flying a B-1 bomber at "full speed six inches off the ground" (Gomory 1986: 333).

In all likelihood, optical technology will replace the present magnetic technology as the storage medium. Present optical technology is only write-once, read-many (WORM) technology. However, in the near future, we will have erasable laser disks. For comparison, an IBM AT typically has a 20-megabyte disk drive, while a MacIntosh has 0.8 megabytes of storage; in the same space, we will have a 400-megabyte laser disk. Software will continue to influence the application of these technological advances. What are needed (and being studied intensively at Carnegie-Mellon University and MIT, among other institutions) are systems software independent of both the hardware and the applications software being used. Such a "floating" operating system is still a long way off but represents a very commercially attractive research goal (Crecine 1986).

Major advances will be made in applications software, particularly in the context of individual work stations. These will be easy to use, and will connect unobtrusively to large mainframe systems. In fact, the data to be used can reside in the work station, on a centralized mainframe or, more likely, as part of a distributed network. The software will employ concepts of logic programing that give the system the capability of separating the "knowledge" or "model" components from the data. This modularization will permit the user to communicate in queries—by asking a question and letting the machine do the searching. The input/output (I/O) devices will provide the user with a variety of ways to do the asking and to receive the answer. I elaborate on the I/O components and models below.

These advances mean that we will have computing power to spare at a low cost. Therefore, our concerns in computing will shift from efficient use of the computer to effective use in supporting the cognitive processes of humans.

TELECOMMUNICATIONS: A FUZZY FUTURE

Although we can make some educated guesses about trends in computing based upon technological advances, we cannot predict trends in telecommunications with equivalent precision. The reason is not lack of knowledge about advances in technology but rather our inability to "guess" at changes in the marketplace. The controlled introduction of technology under a governmental monopoly has resulted in an untapped reservoir of technology, while worldwide deregulation at various levels has resulted in a flow of new products into the marketplace (Singleton 1986). Progress in telecommunications in the next ten years should at least track that of computing, but the influence of governmental policies and international cooperation will play a more important role than technological advances. Major investments in this industry must follow, or at least be concurrent with, changes in the regulatory environment.

In long-distance communications, the advent of satellites and optical fiber cable has increased our capacity for information flow—probably beyond our needs. For example, Bell Labs recently constructed a 50-kilometer length of one optical fiber cable and transmitted twenty gigabytes—twenty billion bits of information. This technology, coupled with the digitalization of switching, has resulted in the possibility of fully integrated, worldwide communications. This system, presently called Integrated Services Digital Network (ISDN), can increase the capacity of a typical phone line fifteen times and permit the simultaneous transmission of voice, video, and high-speed data. However, the need for the world's major telecommunications companies—some of them nationalized—to agree upon standards or protocols ensures that ISDN is definitely in the future. The lack of standardization is also hindering progress in developing in-house or local-area networks (LANs). The manufacturers and suppliers of LANs have not agreed on common standards, which has kept large corporations and other organizations from investing in this technology.

Of the plethora of products, two technologies could play an important role in emergency management: teleconferencing with high-definition television (HDTV); and portable telecommunications—cellular mobile and radio paging. Teleconferencing has been installed to facilitate communications in emergencies (Hougel, El Sawy, and Donovan 1984). However, the addition of HDTV is necessary to match the quality of the visual displays presently used in emergency operating centers. For comparison, U.S. television uses 525 lines for display and the West European system a noticeably better 625. In 1981 the Japanese demonstrated a system with 1,125 lines that, when projected onto a large screen, had the "clarity of 35mm slides . . . [and was described as] 'more than 100 percent better'; 'sensational'; . . . 'almost three dimensional'" (Singleton 1986: 113). This technology will enable emergency managers to view on-site scenes via hand-held video cameras as well as to share data that can be portrayed graphically and projected onto a large screen.

Mobile phone and paging services will provide the technology for instant voice and data services to anyone—possibly everywhere. Car phones, for example, will soon be available for less than $500. Digital technology will enable users of paging systems to transmit 500-word messages. Two-way message service will be available nationally and perhaps internationally. It is also anticipated that a digital device that can accept, store, and transmit messages will soon be the size of a hand-held calculator, and that the transmissions from and to such a device will be sent via satellite and received via cable (or vice versa). Worldwide communications will enable disaster response to be coordinated instantly, with video teleconferencing to follow.

DECISION-AID TECHNOLOGIES

We can conclude from the foregoing discussion that in the next ten years we will have a tenfold increase in computing power, and we will be able to communicate in voice, video, and data, worldwide and instantaneously.

However, these capabilities do not ensure more effective decision-making, particularly in disaster management. In fact, they seem to ensure the delivery of more data than can be processed effectively in crisis situations. We need to utilize this technology to help alleviate the potential for information overload and, in addition, provide support for the cognitive processes of both individuals and groups involved in disaster management.

For example, a decision-aid that is designed for use in disaster response might be employed as noted in Figure 10.1 (Belardo, Karwan, and Wallace 1984a). In this conceptual model of the disaster-response decision process and the role of a decision-aid, decision quality (Box I) depends on the quality of the information inputs (Box H), the correctness of the objective articulation and evaluation (Box G) (assisted by the decision-aid—Box F), and the cognitive abilities of the decision-maker (Box A). The quality of the information depends upon how well the "system" (Boxes A-E, assisted by the decision-aid) can manage information overloads.

The major differences between a disaster management situation and most other decision situations are the effects of surprise and stress (highlighted by the "loop" in Figure 10.1, from Box A to Box E). The "closed system" nature of the conceptual model indicates the large degree of dependency among the factors—specifically, the damage that surprise and stress can do to information processing abilities. Decision-aids can "dampen" this feedback by helping decision-makers to process information and thereby reduce (or seemingly reduce) their information overload. Decreasing the information overload reduces stress and improves information gathering and processing. This, in turn, enhances the decision-maker's ability to use his or her cognitive processes.

Two components of decision-aid technology that will capitalize on increased computer power and new communications technology are human-computer interface and decision-support models. Before discussing these technologies and their potential contribution, I offer a framework for studying the activities inherent in disaster management.

"Managing" a disaster represents an undertaking that requires infor-

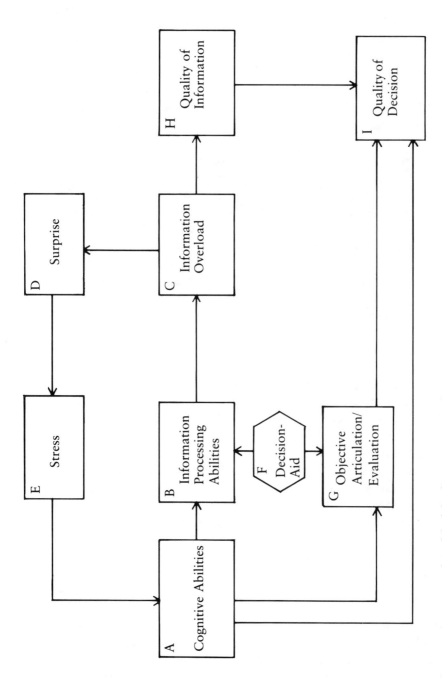

Fig. 10.1. A conceptual model of the disaster response decision process.

mation—not about the anticipated but about the unanticipated. The information must enable the manager to assess the potential impact of these catastrophic events and initiate activities that lessen the impact and ensure survival and recovery. Moreover, the information must be readily available and current, even though it is unused in day-to-day activities.

Various frameworks for understanding and discussing disasters or hazards have been developed (Baisuck and Wallace 1979; Kates 1971). While these frameworks are useful, and I will borrow from them, their orientation is not managerial. One representation that is managerial is the Comprehensive Emergency Management (CEM) system used by the Federal Emergency Management Agency (FEMA). It identifies three interrelated phases of disasters and their management:

Prevention/Mitigation. Prevention refers to activities that seek to eliminate disasters or reduce their numbers. Mitigation refers to activities that reduce the effects of disasters that do occur. The latter also includes such preparedness measures as the development of plans and the conduct of training to save lives and minimize disaster damage.

Response. Response activities follow the occurrence of the potentially disastrous event. Generally they are designed to minimize casualties and protect property to the extent possible through emergency assistance. They also seek to reduce secondary damage and to speed recovery operations.

Recovery. Recovery activities continue until all systems return to previous levels (or better). Short-term recovery returns vital support systems to minimum operating standards. Long-term recovery may continue for many years after a disaster. Recovery activities should include measures to prevent or mitigate a recurrence.

The actions taken in each of these phases can further be delineated as preevent—in which the effect is felt before the event occurs; and postevent—those actions that influence the impact of the event only. Combining the CEM model with this dichotomy results in Figure 10.2. Mitigation is shown as those actions that take place before as well as during the response and recovery phases. Anthony's framework for analysis of planning and control systems (Anthony 1965) can also be used to characterize the activities involved in disaster or hazard management. The levels of this framework—operational, managerial, and strategic—differ according to such characteristics as time horizon, mental activity, nature of structure, and the like. Juxtaposing these levels with the preevent/postevent dichotomy results in the framework shown in Table 10.1. Some of the

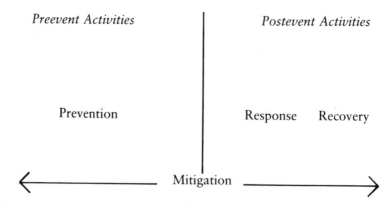

Fig. 10.2. Stages in the management of disaster.

Table 10.1. Level of Disaster Management Activities

Type	Operational control[a]	Managerial control[b]	Strategic planning[c]
Preevent activities	Inspection of facilities; Meteorological assessment	Training and education; Development of emergency response plans	Securing budgetary and legislative support; Enforcement of regulations
Postevent activities	Notification of public; Evacuation of residents	Deployment of relief forces; Request for aid	Administration of aid; Development of zoning and regulatory standards

[a] Less than 1 month.
[b] Less than 1 year.
[c] More than 1 year.

tasks normally associated with emergency management are shown in the appropriate cells.

One major deficiency in this framework is that it does not delineate the degree of risk or uncertainty associated with the management tasks and decisions. While decision-making in a crisis involves tasks that are certain in nature and hence can be structured, it also involves tasks that are uncertain and therefore defy structuring (Anthony 1965). This does not mean that tasks involved in hazard management should be characterized as totally unstructured.

Plans and procedures can be and have been developed for responding to various potential disasters; insurance programs have been developed and implemented. Table 10.2 (Belardo and Wallace 1981) is a proposed

Table 10.2. A Framework for Analysis of Disaster Management Activities

Operational Control[a]	Management Control[b]	Strategic Planning[c]
	Structured Tasks	
Preevent: Inspection; Inventory of resources	Preevent: Assessment of resources; Development of reporting formats	Preevent: Securing budgetary and legislative support for programs
Postevent: Damage assessment; Epidemiological surveillance	Postevent: Treatment of injured; Deployment of relief forces	Postevent: Allocation of scarce resources; Development of zoning and regulatory standards
	Semi-Structured Tasks	
Preevent: Warning and alerting; Meteorological data assessment	Preevent: Development of procedures for conducting post-event damage and loss assessment; Training and education	Preevent: Enforcement of zoning and similar standards; Tests and exercises
Postevent: Notification of responsible officials; Evacuation plan implementation	Postevent: Declaration of state of emergency; Set up of triage/reception centers	Postevent: Administration of disaster relief; Determination of priorities of needs
	Unstructured Tasks	
Preevent: Unanticipated personnel problems; Exacerbating events	Preevent: Replacement for loss of key personnel and equipment	Preevent: Actions to be considered in light of unexpected findings (i.e., geological fault under a nuclear facility)
Postevent: Equipment malfunction; Impacts not foreseen	Postevent: Coping with secondary effects such as epidemics; Search and rescue	Postevent: Decisions to relocate populace; Major recovery expenditures

[a] Less than 1 month.
[b] Less than 1 year.
[c] More than 1 year.

framework that combines decision levels, the structure of tasks, and the preevent/postevent dichotomy. It also provides examples of tasks and decisions encountered in a disaster-management setting. The ability to capture and store large amounts of data does not ensure its usefulness in support of the managerial activities categorized in Table 10.2. These data must be processed and presented in a form meaningful to the disaster manager and of value in his or her decision process. Effective human-computer interfaces and models are the appropriate technologies.

Human-Computer Interface Technology

Technological advances in the next decade will result in a dramatic increase in the possibilities for human-computer interaction (Thomas 1986). We will be able to mimic all our senses (to varying degrees) with these technologies. Optical readers, touch screens, and mouse input are now commonplace. Of particular importance for disaster management is voice and handwritten input. The increased computer power will make the algorithms for speech recognition and natural language processing available in disaster-management work stations.

It may be necessary, initially, to use standard phrases and formats to facilitate processing—jargon similar to military terminology, perhaps. Voice output is now a reality (note food market checkout counters, for example) but its usefulness has yet to be demonstrated (DeHaemer and Wallace 1988). One possible use is in alerting or warning systems, replacing or reinforcing the present bells and sirens.

Another major advance will be in visual displays. In addition to high definition television, we will have enhanced computer graphics. At present, the MacIntosh, considered to be the industry standard, has a screen with 512 by 342 pixels or points of reference. The IBM PC has 80 columns by 25 rows. In the near future, our screens will have 1,000 by 800+ pixels (Crecine 1986). Noting that every pixel needs to be "managed," we see the need for computing power in order to provide a variety of visual displays. For example, 3-D displays could be commonplace; again, we must question their usefulness (Lee, MacLachlan, and Wallace 1986).

Such technologies will enable the disaster manager to replace, by extensive detail transmitted by satellite, the wall chart and grease pen or the unwieldy map with an interactive system. Locating hazard regions, mitigation measures, response resources, health facilities, and so forth, can be done by preprogramed plans or interactively in an analysis or operational setting. Animation can be used to present and evaluate disaster scenarios for the purpose of analysis or group gaming sessions. However, these technologies can be misused and may not take into account the limitations of humans as information processors (Broadherst 1958). Decision-support models are designed to help overcome these limitations.

Decision-Support Models

Recent advances in information technology have resulted in "user friendly" software for employing analytical techniques to develop models. These models, or abstractions of reality, are used to summarize data and, coupled with display technology, to present the results in a form meaningful to the user. The decision-support models themselves, however, are not "competent" to make the decisions. That process cannot be automated. Rather, the decision-making process requires interaction between the model and the user via the interface, as depicted in Figure 10.1, for disaster response.

As technology advances, we will have a greater capability for modeling detail and then aggregating and summarizing for presentation. We will also be able to have the results in "real time," as required to support the decision processes of an individual or group. Although models can be verbal as well as analytic, implicit or explicit or some combination, I focus here on abstractions that can be formalized into a language that can be processed by a computer. Note that this definition covers electronic spread-sheets as well as artificial intelligence. More particularly, I discuss three decision-aid technologies: statistics, operations research, and expert systems. These technologies represent three views of a decision situation: descriptive, prescriptive, and rescriptive (Carrier and Wallace 1989).

Statistics. I use a statistical model to develop a description of reality. The process is one of categorization of data by developing taxonomies, partitioning variation, and showing whether differences are significant. The approach is then extended to make predictions about events outside the data—that is, forecasting. Statistics uses inference with a series of experimental or a priori observations in order to model reality.

With the advent of more powerful mainframes, we will be able to develop very complex statistical models. For example, models used for long-term (and, to some extent, short-range) weather forecasting describe the earth's surface as a series of grids. Micromodels of the conditions within a grid (e.g., heat transfer) are then run and aggregated to describe and predict weather conditions. The accuracy of the forecast is directly dependent on the scale of the grids: the finer the detail, the more accurate the forecast. Large computers will enable us not only to develop these complex models but also to conduct sensitivity analyses to assess their limitations.

To further illustrate the type of analysis that could be commonplace, let us consider the prediction of large-volume oil spills into the marine environment, as happened off the Alaskan coast in 1989 (Paulson, Schumaker, and Wallace 1975). With reference to Table 10.2, more accurate predictions should facilitate the decision process concerned with such operational activities as harbor patrols and monitoring of transfer operations; managerial control tasks such as placement of response equipment; and strategic plans concerning, for example, the budget for the development and staffing of national response teams.

In order to develop a statistical model of such events, data on oil spills were taken from the U.S. Coast Guard Pollution Incident Reporting System (PIRS). The frequency of spills by volume (or magnitude) was then plotted to ascertain a probability distribution or model that would represent the data. Figure 10.3 shows that distributions that have long tails, are extremely skewed, and admit of very large coefficients of variation are prerequisites for a spill-volume distribution function, where the total number of spills [$S(X)$] is a function of individual probabilities [P]:

$$S(X) = P \text{ (individual spill volume} \leq x).$$

Commonly used statistical densities and, therefore, software facilitating statistical model building are not appropriate for representing data such as those exhibited in Figure 10.3. A methodology employing the stable laws, a class of probability distribution functions, was used; software that uses the new computing power is becoming available.

Operations Research. Operations research as a decision-aid technology is employed a priori, to tell how reality can be improved. These models employ a predominantly deductive logic in their approach to reality. Techniques such as linear programing and decision analysis take a normative view and provide answers or solutions.

Let us take the case of managing the response to a major chemical spill in close waters—a harbor—as an example (Harrald and Wallace 1988). Water transportation of chemicals is common and safe despite the large quantities carried in individual ships. Tankers having a cargo-carrying capacity of 40,000 tons are not uncommon. Chemical parcel tankers are often subdivided into forty or more separate tanks and may carry a variety of chemicals simultaneously. Large-volume spills of hazardous chemicals

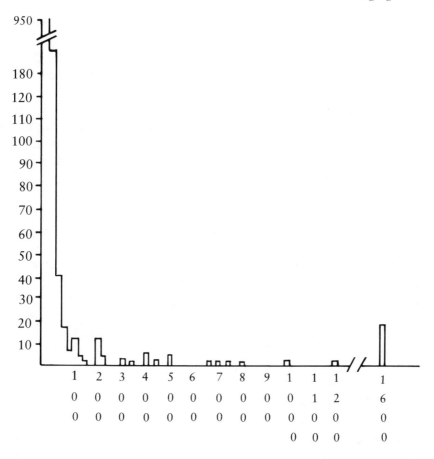

Fig. 10.3. Frequency of spills of given magnitude, District 13, 1970–1972.

from such vessels are relatively infrequent, but when they do occur, they create a major health and safety threat. Response to an accident involving these vessels requires presited response equipment and trained personnel deployable within a very short time. Typical strategic and tactical considerations would involve determining the type and amount of response resources and their location. These decisions would be made in the context of budgetary constraints.

A model that was proposed to address these issues employs a discrete mathematical programing "covering" approach with multiple objectives. The model formalizes the trade-off inherent in the resource allocation decision, in particular, the impact a major chemical spill would have on the surrounding environs. It also relates the type and amount of equipment to the budgetary constraint. Such a model demonstrates that the decision situation can be modeled normatively—without regard to the actual decision process—and can provide support in arriving at decisions concerning the localization of response equipment.

In addition, models of this type can be run on machines the size of the IBM AT, and their output can be presented graphically. In this example, the location of the equipment, time to arrive at an accident, or extent of damage can be shown on a map—over time if desired. The user can then analyze—with the results displayed graphically—the impact of changes in the probabilities of an accident, unavailability of equipment, reduction in the budget, and so forth. Increases in computer power will permit individual work stations to use the software running large-scale operations-research models with graphical output.

Expert Systems. Expert systems are designed to manipulate and solve problems expressed symbolically (Mick and Wallace 1985). These systems attempt to gather and express human experience and judgments in machine-readable form. In applying this decision-aid technology, a decision situation is specified, experts identified, and their knowledge elicited. The goal of the system is to achieve rescription—a rewriting of experts' knowledge in algorithmic form. Expert systems are consultative; they rely on interaction and communication between the builder and the expert. Unlike the induction used by statistical models or the deductive nature of operations research, expert systems attempt to capture the intangible inferences of the expert.

Martha Grabowski and I have completed a prototype expert system for the U.S. Department of Transportation, Maritime Administration (Grabowski and Wallace, in press). The system is designed to support the decision processes of maritime pilots aboard merchant ships in congested waterways, where the potential for accidents is great. It captures the decision-making expertise of the local pilot and provides the operator with information on local environment (platform, port, weather, visibility, handling, traffic, navigation, etc.) and the particular ship's piloting recommendations.

The knowledge base for the Piloting Expert System consisted of twenty rules and 152 objects organized into hierarchical classes and rule sets. The piloting knowledge base contains hierarchically arranged domain *objects* that are "reasoned about" (SHIPS, SHIPPING CHANNELS, etc.) in the *rules* (POWER DRIVEN VESSEL CROSSING RULE).

A menu-driven user interface was developed because it was unreasonable to expect ships' pilots, ships' captains, and deck officers to use a keyboard in order to interact with the system. New technology will permit voice input or, if desired, bypass the human by direct connections with the various sensors for speed, location and meteorological conditions. This integration will free the user to focus on the exceptional and unusual, interacting via voice when necessary. The output is also presented in a form familiar to the user, a combination of text and marine charts. Again, available and anticipated technology will permit video disc map display, overlain with both animation and text.

With these examples, I have tried to illustrate the logical differences in these three decision-aid technologies. These differences are reflected in their approach to modeling: statistics uses (past) data to build a descriptive model, operations research postulates deductively in order to prescribe courses of action, and expert systems capture human experience in order to make recommendations. The result is three decision-aid technologies. However, advances in the technology for human-computer interaction will mask these differences from the user.

CONCLUDING COMMENTS

The advent of more powerful computers and a myriad of telecommunications systems will focus attention on the need to process data in a form meaningful and useful to decision makers. In order to resolve this need, we should consider that information is communicated at three levels:

- technical (the accuracy of the information)
- semantic (the precision of the symbols in conveying information)
- effectiveness (the extent to which the message is effective in motivating actions).

Technology will address the technical problems and will provide the means to transmit data, voice, or video accurately and reliably. Technology for human-computer interaction and decision models will focus on providing assistance in interpretation of the data by appropriate processing and display. The question of effectiveness—Does the user take the appropriate action?—is definitely a research issue.

One way of addressing this research question is to conduct rigorous experimentation. Past research in disaster management has resulted in various conceptual frameworks, taxonomies, typologies, and even "check lists" based upon inductive syntheses of cases (see Drabek 1986; Kreps 1986; Baisuck and Wallace 1979; Kates 1971). These frameworks—an example is found in Table 10.2—can be reconstituted into models that should provide hypotheses that can be tested using reproducible experimentation. This approach is not foreign to disaster management (see Drabek and Haas 1969).

The model of the disaster decision process shown in Figure 10.1 can be used as an experimental vehicle. This methodology has been used to study crisis management situations (Cooper 1978) and the impact of decision-aids on decision-making in a disaster-response setting (Belardo, Karwan, and Wallace 1984b).

In one case, a training exercise for the GYNNA nuclear power generating facility near Rochester, New York, was followed four days later by an actual incident. In both situations, emergency operating centers at State, county, and local levels were activated. We were able to collect logged data on both events as well as to conduct postevent interviews with a sample of the participants (Belardo et al. 1983). We found a similarity between the simulation exercise and actual accident in terms of stress perception, frequency of communication, and the quantity of communication descriptions. These findings suggest that the realism of the disaster environment *can* be replicated using simulation (see also Drabek and Haas 1969; Comfort 1985).

In addition to more experimental research in decision-aid technology, we should also consider a different methodological focus—the use of deduction to build models of disaster management phenomena. I realize that the logical consistency required of deductive models is at times at the expense of realism. However, the realism of today's models may be relatively unimportant; they can, nevertheless, serve as "building blocks" toward models that will provide hypotheses suitable for empirical verification (Camerer 1985). This evolutionary process is possible because the use of mathematics requires a precision in expression that results in commonly agreed upon definitions and processes.

Another area of research that will provide immediate benefits in terms of planning for disaster response is an assessment of the computing and telecommunications technology we can expect in the next century's home, hospital, and office building. Home security systems that are linked by cable, an office building with satellite reception and transmission, or a hospital that has extensive data on the characteristics of its clientele are all potential response resources. Determining the extent and usefulness of this technology in emergency situations where emergent organizations are anticipated should prove very valuable to those responsible for organized response.

An even more futuristic area that will require extensive research is robotics; the development of machines to deal with hazardous situations is just beginning. Obviously, the evolution of such machines will involve questions of mobility and vision that are only beginning to be addressed. Use of this technology will require new disaster management systems that, in turn, will need advanced information technology.

I should like to conclude by suggesting that information technology itself will more and more be viewed as a hazard and that research will increasingly study the concomitant disasters that such technology could produce. This chapter notes one such possible hazard: the new modeling and display technologies that will mask the differences in philosophy or "worldview" inherent in analytical methodologies like statistics, operations research, and expert systems. "User friendliness" may result in inappropriate use of the technology with very misleading results. Finally, another potential hazard is the effect that massive personal data banks will have on individual freedoms. These data banks will permit organizations to compare each of us to some model person and deviations from that norm will be viewed with concern. The "small town" impact of this information technology may inhibit the freedom of personal experimentation that is part of our national character.

REFERENCES

Anthony, R. N.
    1965   *Planning and Control Systems.* Cambridge: Harvard University Press.
Baisuck, A., and Wallace, William A.
    1979   "A Framework for Analyzing Marine Accidents." *Marine Technology Society Journal* 13 (5): 8–14.
Belardo, S., Danko, W. D., Pazer, H. L., and Wallace, William A.
    1983   "Simulation of a Crisis Management Information Network: A Serendipitous Evaluation." *Decision Sciences* 14 (4): 588–606.
Belardo, S., Karwan, K., and Wallace, William A.
    1984a   "Managing the Response to Disasters Using Microcomputers." *Interfaces* 14 (2): 30–39.

William A. Wallace

1984b   "An Investigation of System Design Considerations for Emergency Management Decision Support." *IEEE Transactions on Systems, Man, and Cybernetics* SMC-14 (6): 795–804.

Belardo, S., and Wallace, William A.

1981   "The Design and Test of a Microcomputer-Based Decision-Support System for Disaster Management," in *DSS '81 Transactions*, D. Young and P. G. W. Keen, eds., 152–64. Atlanta: Executom.

Broadherst, D. E.

1958   *Perception and Communication*. London: Pergamon.

Camerer, C.

1985   "Redirecting Research in Business Policy and Strategy." *Strategic Management Journal* 28: 1–15.

Carrier, H. D., and Wallace, William A.

1989   "An Epistemological View of Decision-Aid Technology with Emphasis on Expert Systems." *IEEE Transactions on Systems, Man and Cybernetics* 19(5): 1021–1029.

Comfort, Louise K.

1985   "Action Research: A Model for Organizational Learning." *Journal of Policy Analysis and Management* 15 (1): 100–118.

Congressional Research Service

1984   *Information Technology for Emergency Management*. Washington, D.C.: U.S. Government Printing Office.

Cooper, D. F.

1978   "On the Design and Control of Crisis Games." *Omega* 6: 460–61.

Crecine, J. P.

1986   "The Next Generation of Personal Computers." *Science* 231: 935–43.

DeHaemer, M. J., and Wallace, William A.

in press   "The Effect on Decision Task Performance of Computer Voice Output." *International Journal of Man-Machine Studies*.

Drabek, Thomas E.

1986   *Human System Responses to Disaster: An Inventory of Sociological Findings*. New York: Springer-Verlag.

Drabek, Thomas E. and Haas, J.E.

1969   "Laboratory Simulation of Organizational Stress." *American Sociological Review* 34: 223–38.

Gomory, R. E.

1986   "Trends in Computing." *The European Journal of Operational Research* 26: 330–40.

Grabowski, Martha R., and Wallace, William A.

in press   "An Expert System for Maritime Pilots: its Design and Assessment Using Gaming." *Management Science*.

Harrald, J., and Wallace, William A.
   1988   "An Analytic Approach to Planning the Response to Technological
           Disasters." *Industrial Crisis Quarterly* 2: 257–70.
Hougel, T. J., El Sawy, O. A., and Donovan, P. F.
   1984   "Information Systems for Crisis Management: Lessons from South-
           ern California Edison." *MIS Quarterly* 10 (4): 389–400.
Kates, Robert W.
   1971   "Natural Hazard in Human Ecological Perspective: Hypotheses and
           Models." *Economic Geography* 47: 430–51.
Kreps, Gary A.
   1986   "Future Directions in Disaster Research: What Should We Be
           Doing?" in *Italy-United States Conference on Preparation for Re-
           sponse to and Recovery from Major Community Disasters*. Dover:
           University of Delaware.
Lee, J., MacLachlan, J., and Wallace, William A.
   1986   "The Effect of 3D Imagery on Managerial Data Interpretation." *MIS
           Quarterly* 10 (3): 257–69.
McCall, M. W., Jr., and Lombardo, M. M.
   1982   "Using Simulation for Leadership and Management Research:
           Through the Looking Glass." *Management Science* 28: 533–49.
Mick, S., and Wallace, William A.
   1985   "Expert Systems as Decision Aids for Disaster Management." *Dis-
           asters* 19 (2): 98–101.
Paulson, A. S., Schumaker, A. D., and Wallace, William A.
   1975   "Risk Analytic Approach to Control of Large-Volume Oil Spills," in
           *1975 Conference on Prevention and Control of Oil Pollution: Pro-
           ceedings*, 301–6. Washington, D.C.: American Petroleum Institute.
Simon, Herbert A.
   1960   *The New Science of Management Decisions*. New York: Harper and
           Row.
Singleton, Loya
   1986   *Telecommunications in the Information Age* (second edition). Cam-
           bridge, Mass.: Ballinger.
Thomas, J.
   1986   Abstract for panel on "Human-Computer Interaction for the Year
           2000." *Computer Human Interface '86 Proceedings*. New York:
           Association for Computing Machinery.

Toward a New
Risk Analysis

Andrew Kirby

In this last chapter, it is my intention to build on some inferences taken from the material laid out in the preceding chapters. There is, predictably enough, some dissonance within the volume, much of which can be traced to disagreements between those who see risk as an academic challenge, and those who see it as a managerial responsibility. In consequence, not all the authors would go equally far in welcoming some research alternatives that have already appeared, for instance (cf. chapter 6). Yet the contributions do inexorably point toward a realignment of risk analysis (using that phrase in its broadest sense), to take into account both scholarly attitudes and technical inventions, and these concluding remarks will amplify and extend those insights.

The argument is divided into three main sections; in the first part, I take up again the issue of personal versus private understandings of risk. In the second I discuss the importance of developing our understanding of the society-nature relation. In the third I reintroduce the vexed question of control.

THE PUBLIC AND
PRIVATE UNDERSTANDING OF RISK

As J. M. Baldwin observed several decades ago, knowledge is public property, not a private possession.[1] In consequence, the individual's perception
of risk is usually dependent upon a *social representation*, which can be
defined as a culturally conditioned way of viewing the world and the
events that take place there. Such representations are much more likely to
cover the local environment than remote locations; or to put it another
way, they are apt to focus upon the immediate sphere of everyday life. In
the process, they become a part of what Geertz terms "local knowledge,"
a concept that can be applied as readily to residents as to planners and
disaster managers, as is shown in chapters 9 and 10 (Geertz 1983).

Social representations can be interpreted in various ways. They do not
emerge ready formed, but are a product of interactions within a locality. In
consequence, the process can be seen to be linked to what Harré identifies
as a collective discourse, or what Shotter terms a *common* sense (Harré
1984; Shotter 1986). Both these concepts (which were developed at length
in chapter 1), show how human behavior can be linked back through interpretations of risk and in turn to the discourse that surrounds the issue
in question. Of particular interest is our ability to connect very different—
even discrepant—modes of behavior to extant discourses within the community: such a contradictory example is the firearms owner who weighs
the risk of domestic attack or theft to be greater than the risk of an acci-
dental shooting, a domestic dispute, or suicide in the home. In reality,
the risks are very clearly stacked in favor of such a bloody outcome for
gun owners, which is masked by the political debate over the *rights* of
possession.[2]

In this way, it becomes possible to unravel why the same issue can
lead to very different human responses, and the way in which otherwise
rational persons may hold dissonant views about risks.[3] This kind of perspective is based in the literature of social psychology, which is not the
source of inspiration for many risk analyses. Rather, the latter begin, as
we have seen, with a conventional grounding in behavioral science and an
emphasis upon the individual's interpretation of the world and the actions
that result. As Mitchell indicated in chapter 6, this literature is a large
one and has spawned a number of related fields: that of natural hazards
(based particularly within geography), that of disasters (emerging from

sociology), and that of risk and technology (associated with engineering). While these fields have divergent assumptions and their own journals (such as *Disasters*, *International Journal of Mass Emergencies and Disasters*, or *Risk Analysis*), they are united in two ways. The first is the frequent focus upon the individual, as has been noted. The second is the invocation of an objective risk calculus, against which human acts can be measured.

Risk and Probability

Any epistemology based upon individualism must rest on an assumed basis of rationality, which we can illustrate as follows. Consider these activities, which expose the individual to harm: living close to earthquake fault lines, smoking cigarettes, driving while drunk. Efforts to discover why individuals do these things must begin with the premise that it is possible to compare such actions against objective measures of risk, and to compare these actions one with another. Without such comparisons, it is hardly possible to identify them as risky—and thus perhaps irrational—actions. In consequence, there is a necessity to set up an objective reality against which to compare behavior, often with the stated intention of finding ways "to increase our capacity for dealing with . . . risks in a rational manner" (Covello 1983: 285).

This is not the place to mount a critical analysis of every dimension of risk analysis, but it is important that we separate the various implications of a behavioral approach and a social psychological perspective. There are many instances in which we identify a discrepancy between the results of an objective risk calculus (which points, perhaps, to a high probability of serious accident), and individual action, which ignores this potential. If behavior does not accord with the probabilities, then it is customary to regard the behavior as idiosyncratic (Frisch 1988). As Frisch points out, there is, though, no reason to assume that mathematical rationality is the only rationality available, or even that there is only one route to the latter—a Bayesian calculus will yield very different results in comparison with more traditional methods, for instance. In such situations, we are entitled to ask about the existence of intervening variables that govern behavior, rather than dismissing the latter as idiosyncratic.

To take a simple example, in Australia, a larger proportion of the population smokes than in the USA. An airport lounge in Sydney or Melbourne is filled with tobacco smoke, but smoking is banned entirely on all domestic flights. In the USA, despite the greater collective awareness of the effects of passive smoking (inhaling others' smoke), cigarettes were, until late 1989, permitted on any domestic flight lasting longer than two hours.[4] Clearly, this represented a paradox. The risk calculus is the same—smoking is dangerous, as is its passive counterpart—and yet in the USA smoking was permitted in the air. We might point to the tobacco lobby as one intervening variable in the American case, but we would still be left to ask: Why do Australians expect to smoke freely in the airport, but accept a total prohibition in the aircraft?

The different ways in which the same objective reality is translated into action has little if anything to do with individual interpretations of risk, and almost everything to do with intervening social variables. In Australia the relatively powerful federal government has dictated that flights will be smoke-free, while the much less powerful State and municipal governments have done little to control smoking in airports or restaurants. In the USA smoking is much more of a contested issue; the right to smoke is claimed as a personal freedom and consequently we see more compromises, in the form of no-smoking sections in airports and on airplanes. In both cases, we are able to assert that individuals have similar interpretations of the risks and pleasures of smoking: the important differences lie in the ways in which political conflicts are resolved.

We can go a little further with this; the example reminds us that non-smoking sections in restaurants—even nonsmoking establishments—are much more likely in California than they are in West Virginia or Woolloomooloo. The way in which smoking is enforced or permitted is, in the first instance at least, a function of local practice and local ordinance, as we saw examined by Clay Gillette in chapter 7.[5] Put another way, there is a local discourse that encompasses risks and hazards, and in order to understand individual behavior, we have to understand how such a discourse emerges.

To illuminate this logic, we may turn briefly to a more complex example, that of the Rocky Flats plant site in Colorado, which manufactures plutonium triggers. The safety record of the the plant has been assessed by a number of researchers, including a recent paper by Hohenemser in the journal *Risk Analysis*. What I want to show is the way in which Hohenemser's insights are based very firmly on a traditional view of probabilities and human action that has taken no account of the social representation of risk around the plant; moreover, in depending so heavily upon a rigid risk calculus, the paper goes seriously astray.

Leaving aside for the moment detailed criticisms, we may focus instead on two general issues.[6] First, there is the heroic effort made to distinguish between the production of plutonium triggers for nuclear warheads and the notion of plant safety. Hohenemser sees these as clearly separate realms, and notes with apparent surprise the conflation of the safety of the plant on the one hand, and a fear of nuclear weapons on the other, in the mind of Colorado residents. He seems unable to grasp the logic that many persons have been shown to be very uneasy about the possibilities of nuclear war, and would logically tranfer that unease and suspicion to a weapons factory in close proximity. Second, Hohenemser in turn misses an interesting paradox—namely, that opposition to the weapons plant is in fact dispersed throughout Colorado, while local residents, who are the most likely to be contaminated by ambient radiation or destroyed during an enemy missile attack on strategic targets, are, in relation to Rocky Flats, politically quiescent.

Let us compare his analysis with a study undertaken four years ago (Kirby and Jacob 1986), which involved a questionnaire developed to test political attitudes among residents. The questionnaire was delivered to a stratified sample of households in close proximity to Rocky Flats. As the paper indicates, only 10 percent of respondents regarded the plant as a hazard in their lives; greater attention was paid to issues like air pollution due to automobile emissions, and greater time was spent on political action with regard to zoning and education than on the plant. How should we interpret these results? As a result of ecological sorting and migration, whereby those opposed to the plant leave the area? As proof of rationality, in that the residents come to the same conclusion concerning the low probabilities of accident as does Hohenemser?

We argued that no conclusion is possible concerning *individual* attitudes without first exploring the *collective* risk discourse that exists in the locality. When we attempt this, a number of issues impinge. First, there is the incremental growth of the plant, which, as a result, may no longer be seen as a new or threatening technology. Second, there is the relation between patriotism and weapons production, such that residents feel that opposition to the plant is, in some inchoate way, un-American. Third, and in relation to the second point, there is a high rate of employment in federal enterprise in Denver, and Colorado as a whole, which underlines the importance of continued defense expenditure for local well-being.[7] And fourth, the corporate power of Rockwell, the operator of Rocky Flats until 1989, which stands as a distant and faceless bureaucracy, untouchable by neighborhood concerns.[8] There is no way of knowing, of course, precisely how these issues encroach upon individual attitudes, but there is some necessity to explain why a plant of this type, with a poor safety record, has not generated the conflict found in many other settings.[9] One possibility is to follow Hohenemser's logic, which points inexorably to quiescence as a rational act. The alternative is to address the lack of political efforts to ensure a high quality of life around the plant in terms of broader dampening or inhibiting factors, as we have begun to do here.[10]

The thrust of this example is that any attempt to infer individual *attitudes* from group behavior is problematic, just as is an effort to predict individual *behavior* from those same attitudes. It is also the case that to preserve this duality may be to miscast the problem. A broader—and potentially richer—approach is to examine the uncertainties and contradictions that surround the relations between society and nature, on the grounds that this connection represents the matrix within which many of the phenomena that we call hazards are placed.

This is not to argue though that the society-nature relation is a rubric that can be read easily. Our understanding of it has been fitful, as its complexity justifies, and the documentation of the ways in which scholars have approached society and nature would itself fill a large volume.[11] In the following section, some of the potential for recasting our understanding of society and nature is indicated.

SOCIETY AND NATURE AS A UNIFYING CONCEPT

Crombie points out that our scientific worldview is inextricably linked with the growth of understanding about nature. He writes:

> By deciding . . . that among many possible worlds as envisaged in other cultures, the one world that existed was a world of exclusively self-consistent and discoverable rational causality, the Greek philosophers . . . committed their scientific successors exclusively to this effective direction of thinking. They closed for Western scientific vision the elsewhere open questions of what kind of world people found themselves inhabiting and so of what methods they should use to explore and explain and control it. They introduced in this way the conception of a rational scientific system, a system in which formal reasoning matched natural causation, so that natural events must follow exactly from scientific principles, just as logical and mathematical conclusions must follow from their premises. [Crombie 1988: 1]

In short, Crombie argues that Western science is locked into a view that grounds itself in the supposed predictability of nature. This means that there is a singular scientific method (or so it has come to be believed), and nature must be in turn interpreted through that method. Analysis thus involves the trappings of experimental design, repeatability of experiments, and value-free inference.

Inevitably, representatives of this approach have also reduced the social role in the natural world to little more than a Parsonian black box. On one level, this may be justifiable in terms of streamlined research practice, but the pressing example of hunger shows quite clearly how dangerous such an assumption may be. Climatologists have identified drought as a salient hazard in Africa—an assertion that has become a common currency of television commentary, fund raising, and academic punditry (Glantz 1986). Yet there exists a parallel discourse which would reveal to us the almost infinite complexity of the *malaise paysanne*. Michael Watts, for instance, indicates the way in which an apparent crisis of food *production* may be better read as a massive transformation of the practices of human *consumption* and social reproduction (Watts 1987).

In short, the "problem" facing the African population is less one of producing more food, and much more a recognition of a complex collision between a dynamic global economy and the many layers of local knowledge and peasant practice. Expressed more simply, the attempt to reduce this part of the society-nature relation to a question of drought is akin to the engineer reducing the problem of traffic fatalities to the design of automobiles: better cars might reduce the death toll, but would not deal with drivers' consumption of drugs and alcohol, for example. Similarly, more food may temporarily ease some of the worst manifestations of hunger in Africa (and elsewhere), but in the longer run only increases the consumption-led problems facing many nations.[12]

These types of problems arise because of a mistaken conception of the society-nature relation—one that counterposes society and nature as antithetical. This antithesis has become reified in the ways in which we view (and fund) natural and social science as separate activities. Even three decades ago, C. P. Snow was identifying the existence of "two cultures"— namely, a physical science regime that was unable to maintain a discourse with the humanities (Snow 1955). The problems inherent in maintaining this separation as a normative arrangement require little rehearsal; the problems of trying to maintain a value-free stance have already been indicated with the Hohenemser example, and in research on nuclear accidents, as a result of powerful work by Perrow (Perrow 1984).

In trying to regenerate an understanding of society and nature, we must recognize that there have been shifting relations between the two, which are now frequently obscured. When sociologists Berger and Luckmann write that "man produces himself," they wish away a natural world in a way that is possible only within late capitalism.[13] Indeed, much of human activity can be cast historically as an effort to control nature (Gold 1984; Smith 1984).

City and Countryside as Metaphor

The Western image of nature is most clearly revealed in the dichotomy of city and countryside, which stands as a powerful metaphor for the evolution of our society-nature relation. This theme is explored in depth by Raymond Williams, who shows that the evocation of a lost rural idyll, destroyed by the encroaching city, can be traced back for several centuries (Williams 1973). This image is thus virulent in popular culture, and unsurprisingly it has been powerful too within historical sociology.

Weber developed the notion of the city as a locus of social change, a viewpoint that remains undisturbed. For Giddens, the city in precapitalist (i.e., class-divided) societies played a particular role in terms of the extension of elite mercantile power into backward, feudal rural territories.[14] Given the evolution of views of nature and society, this idealization could not have emerged very differently—although this is not to say that it is an entirely correct interpretation (Braudel 1981: 485).[15]

It was more usual for city and country to assume a reciprocity, in which flows and dependencies moved back and forth. It was, for instance, always the case that the preindustrial city maintained its own agricultural lands, and even nineteenth-century cities had farms within their boundaries. Conversely, some agricultural communities boasted industrial activities more usually thought of as "urban" in character, and it was not unusual to find factories in nonurban settings. As far as economic reciprocity was concerned, it was normal for urban wages to be high, and for surplus generated in the countryside to accumulate in city coffers. At particular periods, however, it was also normal for capital to flow away from cities and out into the countryside, to purchase estates and farms.

To summarize, the city possesses a very specific place within Western thought, regardless of countervailing empirical realities. It constitutes both a powerful image and a symbol of power: it is a representation of the omniscience of society, and the elevation of humankind above nature.

This imagery has maintained, despite the fact that the city is of course dependent on nature (the countryside) for its continued existence. In terms of food, an urban population consumes commodities produced or processed throughout the world; it cannot escape its ties to the environment with respect to water or air resources however.[16] There is a very specific dynamic in the way that society views its immediate physical surroundings, and this has implications for the treatment of nature and the urban development process. Urbanization is something to be achieved at the expense of nature: it is a demonstration of social control rather than an attempt at creating harmony with the physical environment. Even those urban areas that generate some relationship between built form and natural space—I am thinking here of New Towns and Garden Cities—are essentially spurious, insofar as the creation is artificial, and even the natural components have been sculpted. Criticizing Le Corbusier's architectural work in the Indian planned settlement Chandigargh, Bacon comments:

> One of the most decisive consequences of the architectural revolution [is] the cutting off of the building from the land. The mass of the structure is suspended above the land, and the design of each is independent of the other. . . . The effect on the architectural profession was a disaster. No longer was the designer subject to the discipline of land design. Since the design of the building and the design of the land could now be treated separately, and since most architects were interested in buildings and not in land, the result has been concentration on building design independent of its environment, and the thoughtless, arbitrary placing of it on the land, without regard to total design principles. By the great liberation of Le Corbusier, the great surgical amputation of the building from the land, we have a new liberty of design for which we have paid a great price because in the process, the total environment has suffered. [Bacon 1974: 231]

The implications of Bacon's conclusion are twofold. In the first instance, it becomes clear that the city is necessarily superimposed upon whatever the natural environment has to offer. In many instances the latter will be benign: in other instances it will not, and the history of various capital cities indicates that this is no new tendency. From Washington, D.C., and St. Petersburg (Leningrad) to Brasilia, capitals have been constructed de novo in poor locations for very specific reasons: both their creation and their design are symbolic of the vigor of the respective nations, and the poor physical surroundings actually enhance the undertaking.

The second implication is that the city will inevitably fall a victim to its own efforts. Because its inhabitants strive so hard to create a new, specifically urban, environment on the existing physical foundations, we see the deployment of technologies that maintain standards of life, but cannot be closely controlled. Numerous settlements, from Troyes, London, and Constantinople in the seventeenth and eighteenth centuries, to Chicago (1871) and San Francisco (1906), have been destroyed by fire. Air pollution was commonplace in seventeenth-century cities, as was the continual corruption of water supplies: it is no coincidence that early etiological studies on diseases like cholera were undertaken in cities, as Joel Tarr reminded us in chapter 4.

Virtually every technological advance, in either the home or the workplace, has some environmental impact. From the evolution of the urban produce market, with its noxious refuse, through to the horse-drawn tram, which too left its malodorous traces, development has been at a price. This dialectic was noted by de Tocqueville, who wrote of Manchester in 1835, "here humanity attains its most complete development and its most brutish: here civilization makes its miracles, and civilised man is turned back almost into a savage."[17]

Urban development has maintained both a tradition of environmental degradation and an extension into increasingly marginal locations. In examining *individual* perceptions for clues as to why populations live on floodplains, on eroding coastlines, on hillsides experiencing landslides or in areas subject to brushfires, studies start with an assumption that such behavior is irrational. Following on from the line of thought sketched here, such locational decisions are in fact entirely predictable: they are *collective* decisions that reflect the imposition of "urban" values on the countryside without regard to the outcomes (Palm 1990). There is an economic imperative that underlies the extension of urban development into progressively more marginal situations. It is this "spatial fix" in the circulation of capital that constitutes an even more fundamental reason why development on coasts subject to hurricane damage—to take but one example—is predictable (Harvey 1982; 1989). The high exchange value of urban land will always push the developer harder toward the marginal location; it is also the case that the potential resident, immune from a knowledge of the natural world in a home that is landscaped, supplied with water, and fitted with multiple energy sources, is more likely to be persuaded of the safety of almost any location.[18] Put more elegantly, we shall "remain alienated from our own alienation from nature" (Fitzsimmons 1989: 2).

RISK, HAZARDS, AND CONTROL

It is at this point that we confront one of the more complex contradictions in any study of risk—namely, the balance between collective needs and individual wants. To extend the arguments made above concerning risk and probability, we can see that much effort has been expended in the promotion of the ideas that certain hazards are surmountable, and that others are negligible. We thus spend hundreds of millions of dollars in the United States trying to give forewarnings of tornado outbreaks. At the same time there are numerous communities in close proximity to nuclear power plants or to sites where a nuclear waste transport accident might occur not covered by satisfactory evacuation plans—a situation in need of remedy, and not just in terms of fiscal allocations, as John Sorensen indicates in chapter 9.

How this has come about is a complex story, as Popkin revealed in chapter 5. Indeed, the history of disaster legislation in the USA could serve as a concise example of the complexities of the social response to hazards and their aftermath. Congress passed no formal public assistance legislation until 1950; in the five years since 1982, federal aid to communities exceeded $1 billion, spent on 115 declared disasters. The implications of this funding are twofold. In the first case, the large disaster machinery overseen by the Federal Emergency Management Agency (FEMA) serves to legitimate a *lack* of preparedness within communities; if a marginal or downright risky locality is destroyed, FEMA will step in to help once the president has declared an emergency. Some communities have received funds following successive hazard events (hurricanes, earthquakes, etc.), and used them to replace infrastructure in the same location. Of the $1.1 billion spent between 1982 and 1987, 40 percent was channeled to only three territories—California, Virginia, and Puerto Rico. Conversely, FEMA will not pay local communities for their efforts to evacuate residents or to take preventive measures designed to minimize hazard impacts (Moore 1987).

The second issue of importance is the way in which federal agencies employ risk probabilities to dictate spending priorities. A clear example can be used here, relating to the transport of high-level nuclear waste (HLNW), the spent product of nuclear power stations. Such material is dangerous, and is to be shipped to a long-term repository, beginning in the 1990s. But very little public attention has been given to HLNW transport, in part at least because Department of Energy officials have been quite adamant that there are virtually no risks involved in such transport: "the dose to persons near (100 to 2500 feet) the route of a vehicle containing spent fuel would be from 0.0006 to 0.000001 millirem per shipment. If 1000 casks carrying nuclear waste went by the same house every year, the increase in radiation exposure to the inhabitants would be less than 1% of the dose due to natural background radiation" (Kirby and Jacob 1986: 38).

This kind of disclaimer—which involves extrapolating past conditions across a finite future—has been employed extensively in discussions of repository location, in order to minimize political opposition from localities and State governments, nervous about the potential of accidents, radiation exposure, and serious injury. Such local governments may not possess sophisticated equipment and associated software (see chapter 10 by Wallace), and are not consequently in a position to deal effectively with a transportation accident: note once more that such equipment is expensive but cannot be obtained via federal emergency funds.

Paradoxically, entirely different criteria are used in other dimensions of emergency management. While risk analyses are employed to downplay some risks, they are ignored in other settings. Clayton Gillette (this volume, chapter 7) reminds us that rushed corporate reactions to litigation over a product's failures may ignore the majority of consumers who appear satisfied. Equally, the underfunding of the nation's Air Traffic Control system is not based upon a serious estimation of the probabilities of accident, as Phillip Tompkins revealed in chapter 8. Nor is the expanding appropriation of funds for civil defense purposes predicated upon any study that indicates any increased likelihood of nuclear war, a point noted by Sorensen, above. Many commentators argue that FEMA pays great attention to war preparedness, despite an inconsistency between the normative stance of attack planning on the one hand, and reactive disaster relief on the other. FEMA claims that readiness to deal with attack is the best preparedness for "acts of God" as well are undermined by reports of its manifest inability to react effectively to the aftermath of Hurricane Hugo in 1989 (see also Popkin, this volume).

In summary, it becomes clear that in the arena of dealing with disasters past, and disasters yet-to-happen, "the technical concept of risk is too narrow and ambiguous to serve as the crucial yardstick for policy making" (Kasperson et al. 1988: 178). The ways in which we attempt to control risks are inextricably linked to complex political and constitutional struggles within the nation, and to ideologies (relating to war and peace, for example), extending beyond the nation. The implications are clear. It makes little sense to try to understand the place of risk within American society by recourse to behavioral insights. Persons do not display examples of problematic behavior due to their incompetence; rather their actions are to be assessed only within complex historically and culturally determined settings. The same is true of the ways in which efforts are made to reduce risk and deal with the impacts of disaster. Better technologies have a place, but only once we have a clear idea of the legal, political, and institutional conflicts that surround any attempt to take action.

CONCLUSIONS

A reading of the chapters in this book may constitute little more than a glimpse of a new discourse on risk; certainly, they do not claim to encompass fully such a colloquy.[19] Nevertheless, the potential is clearly on show. By moving away from crude behaviorism and confronting the complexity of human and social actions, we immediately get an impression of what a new risk analysis would look like. It would be historically sensitive, and contextually based. It would take as its starting point some of the building blocks that are commonplace elsewhere within the sciences and social sciences: an understanding of our relations with nature, the links between society and the state, the contested development of technology. And most important, it would recognize that risk is a problematic concept, that must be addressed as such and not simplified.

This is perhaps the most controversial thrust. I have tried to lay out the study of risk in a way that draws on the language of critical social thought, rather than the terminology of technology. Put another way, I have tried to show that risk belongs in the domain of social theory, and not solely in the sphere of practice. In order to make progress in the design of our cities, and the ways in which we deal with nature, it is vital that we stand away from the pragmatic demands of the policy process, in favor of the more considered stance of the theorist.

The fact that we have seen so little theorizing in the field of risk and hazards has much to do with the evolution of problems that have come to be seen as public; but it also has a great deal to do with the lamentable state of social theorizing itself. Historians, political scientists, geographers, sociologists, and anthropologists have all made their contributions, but have not chosen to place risk centrally within their concerns. A new risk analysis must face up to this challenge; namely, it must begin at a level of abstraction that will allow us to confront the complexity of the natural world and our roles within it, the evolution of technologies and the development of public policies. Naturally enough, there are dangers here. We do not need yet another single lens through which to view the world. We have already been offered the global economy and the state apparatus; we do not need to set up the exploitation of nature as yet another exclusionary ideal.

The project comes down in the end to this: if we are to make real progress in managing hazards, and this includes complex technologies yet to be designed, we must embrace the difficulties inherent in understanding the social construction of risk. The practice of risk analysis has in the past held out to us the goal of simplifying the problem, of comprehending how persons think, how they behave, and how they can be educated. For the future, we need to address different questions; how social constructions emerge, how they are shaped by social practice, how they are linked to the operation of public institutions. This stance is an abstract one, in the sense that it does not offer immediate policy fixes and palliatives. Yet when we assess what the fixers have achieved, and compare this with the complexity of the next generation of potential problems (notably those of biotechnology), we should be wary of precipitate action. In a humane society, we should never cease our efforts to help those in distress, as Hurricane Hugo and the California earthquake of 1989 remind us. This notwithstanding, it is time to stand back; do, in some situations, less; and think more.

NOTES

1. Quoted in Markova and Wilkie 1987: 390. I am glad to be able to acknowledge the influence of this excellent piece of work.

2. See for instance Kirby 1989 for statistics.

3. For instance, athletes who abhor the risks of smoking, both for themselves and for others, but who enjoy using their bicycles on dangerous public roads.

4. The examples are comparable because both the USA and the continent of Australia are virtually the same size, so that there are the same possibilities for long-distance internal flight.

5. With the caveat that, as noted, more powerful courts or political institu-

tions may then interfere with local ordinances, as has happened in Florida over issues of gun control; see Kirby 1989.

6. While this is not the place to mount an exhaustive criticism of Hohenemser's 1987 paper, the following critical points are nonetheless of importance. First, the plant was not opened in 1951 as claimed; consequently, any comparisons regarding worker safety and health in the plant and outside the plant employ different time periods, to the benefit of the Rocky Flats sample. As we might expect, a numerical analysis may claim great precision, but display fatal flaws. In a similar vein, Hohenemser compares variance in Denver cancer rates with the variance in the U.S. experience, in an effort it seems to suggest that Denver has low cancer rates; one does not of course follow from the other, for the mean cannot be inferred from the variance.

7. Rocky Flats is Colorado's eighth largest employer, with a payroll of $220 million annually.

8. Rockwell's annual corporate report has made no mention of Rocky Flats. Corporate management was passed to EG & G Inc. as a result of DOE investigations of Rockwell's performance, in January 1990.

9. See, for instance, Kirby 1982 for a review of such conflicts.

10. Interestingly, this story has an epilogue. Althugh Hohenemser ends his 1987 paper with the statement "I conclude that Rocky Flats operations are a relative hazard management success" (258), events in 1989 indicate the vacuity of his inferences. The Congressional Energy and Commerce Subcommittee on Oversight and Investigation stated, in June 1989, that "assurances about the adequacy of health and safety at Rocky Flats are simply not true" (quoted *Albuquerque Journal*, 6.23.89, p. B4).

11. There is already an extensive literature on the interpretation of the evolution of society-nature relations, including such benchmark works as Glacken's *Traces on the Rhodian Shore* (1961).

12. Watts points out, for example, how the influx of wheat from food-aid sources into Nigeria led to a massive disruption in the production of idigenous cereals and "traditional" export crops, with the result that the growth of wheat interests, alongside a popular demand for bread, has distorted state agriculture subsidies and prompted the development of expensive irrigation schemes to facilitate wheat production. In short, an intersection of foreign capital penetration and consumer change has resulted in a mix of grain import at the expense of domestic output, and indigenous production of expensive grains: Watts 1987: 215–17.

13. Berger and Luckmann 1967: 49. They also wish away the female half of the human race, which is indicative.

14. Giddens 1981.

15. A reading of Braudel's work indicates that the process of urbanization has proceeded differently in different contexts. It is not the case that harmonious rural

life was always displaced by artificial urban development, and he provides several instances in which *urban* development preceded *rural* development: in Siberia, the New World, and in first-millennium Asia Minor.

16. Interesting statistics are offered by Wolman on these issues: he suggests that an urban dweller consumes 150 gallons of water and 4 pounds of food; these in turn become 120 gallons of sewage. Four pounds of refuse and 1.9 pounds of air pollutants are also generated per inhabitant.

17. De Tocqueville 1835. His phrases could be portentous also. Fitzsimmons reminds us of Ridley Scott's film, *Blade Runner*, in which "nature is universal, but universally the product of capitalism" (1989: 2).

18. The case of global warming is a case in point. The impacts will be greatest in urban areas where airborne pollution has become the standard product of population growth and economic progress. Currently, one-third of the U.S. population lives in regions where the standards of the Clean Air Act (CAA) are not met, due to photochemical smog. High ozone levels present dangers of pulmonary collapse in major cities like Los Angeles and Denver. This problem will become particularly acute as global warming accelerates, as photochemical smog becomes more intense as temperatures rise—in other words, the generic problem will have some explicit, and geographically concentrated, impacts. This example shows the importance of identifying the local effects of large environmental shifts. EPA studies suggest that to bring Los Angeles into compliance with the CAA, draconian regulations would have to be introduced; tripling the cost of gasoline and parking fees, a $1,000 second-car tax, mandatory no-drive days, and a four-day week would reduce the hydrocarbon level by 8 percent from the 1983 base by 2010. Federal intervention may be necessary to achieve the changes that will be required in daily practice; and yet such legislative standards will be irrelevant in Kansas City or Yuba City. We are looking to a near future in which there may have to be federal standards specific to local environmental conditions.

19. See, for instance, the work being undertaken at Clark University on the ways in which certain dimensions of risk are "amplified" within the media on their way to the public: Kasperson et al. 1988.

REFERENCES

Bacon, Edmund N.
    1974   *Design of Cities*. Harmondsworth: Penguin.
Berger, Peter L., and Luckmann, Thomas
    1967   *The Social Construction of Reality*. New York: Doubleday.
Braudel, Fernand
    1981   *Civilization and Capitalism*. New York: Harper and Row.

Covello, Vincent
  1983   "The Perception of Technological Risks." *Technological Forecasting and Social Change* 23: 285–97.
Crombie, Alastair C.
  1988   "Designed in the Mind: Western Visions of Science, Nature and Humankind." *History of Science* 26: 1–12.
Fitzsimmons, Margaret
  1989   "Guest Editorial: reconstructing nature." *Environment and Planning D: Society and Space* 7(1): 1–3.
Frisch, Deborah E.
  1988   "Violations of Probability Theory: What Do They Mean?" *Journal for the Theory of Social Behavior* 18: 137–48.
Geertz, Clifford
  1983   *Local Knowledge.* New York: Basic Books.
Giddens, Anthony
  1981   *A Contemporary Critique of Historical Materialism.* London: Macmillan.
Glacken, Clarence
  1961   *Traces on the Rhodian Shore.* Berkeley: University of California Press.
Glantz, Michael
  1986   *Drought and Hunger in Africa.* New York: Cambridge University Press.
Gold, Mick
  1984   "A History of Nature," in *Geography Matters!*, Doreen Massey and John Allen, eds., 12–32. Cambridge: Cambridge University Press.
Harré, Rom
  1984   *Personal Being: A Theory for Individual Psychology.* Cambridge: Harvard University Press.
Harvey, David
  1982   *The Limits to Capital.* Oxford: Blackwell.
  1989   *The Urban Experience.* Baltimore: Johns Hopkins University Press.
Hohenemser, Chris
  1987   "Public Distrust and Hazard Management Success at the Rocky Flats Nuclear Weapons Plant." *Risk Analysis* 7(2): 243–59.
Kasperson, Roger, Renn, Ortwin, Slovic, Paul, Brown, Halina, Emel, Jacque, Goble, Robert, Kasperson, Jeanne, and Ratick, Samuel
  1988   "The Social Amplification of Risk: A Conceptual Framework." *Risk Analysis* 8(2): 177–87.
Kirby, Andrew
  1982   *The Politics of Location.* New York: Methuen.

1989   "A Smoking Gun: State and Local State Conflicts over Weapons Control." *Policy Studies Journal.*

Kirby, Andrew, and Jacob, Gerald R.

1986   "The Politics of Transportation and Disposal." *Policy and Politics* 14(1): 27–42.

Markova, I., and Wilkie, P.

1987   "Representations, Concepts and Social Change: The Phenomenon of AIDS." *Journal for the Theory of Social Behavior* 17(4): 389–409.

Moore, W. J.

1987   "After the Deluge." *National Journal* 19(16): 932–35.

Palm, Risa I.

1990   *Natural Hazards: An Integrative Theory for Research and Planning.* Baltimore: Johns Hopkins University Press.

Perrow, Charles

1984   *Normal Accidents.* New York: Basic Books.

Shotter, John

1986   "A Sense of Place: Vico and the Social Creation of Social Realities." *British Journal of Social Psychology* 25: 199–211.

Snow, Charles P.

1955   *The Two Cultures.* Cambridge: Cambridge University Press.

Smith, Neil

1984   *Uneven Development.* Oxford: Blackwell.

de Tocqueville, Alexander

1835   *Journeys to England and Ireland.* London.

Watts, Michael D.

1987   "Powers of Production—Geography among the Peasants." *Environment and Planning D: Society and Space* 6(2): 215–30.

Williams, Raymond

1973   *The City and the Countryside.* Cambridge: Cambridge University Press.

Wolman, A.

1965   "The Metabolism of Cities." *Scientific American*, March, 179–90.

Wolpert, Julian

1980   "The Dignity of Risk." *Transactions* of the Institute of British Geographers, ns 5(4): 391–401.

INDEX

ABOUT THE EDITOR

Andrew Kirby is Professor of Geography and Regional Development at the University of Arizona. His interests lie in social theory and urbanism. Recent publications include a special issue of the journal *Cities*, dealing with technological risks in urban areas, and a co-edited book dealing with urban development and public services. Related papers have appeared in *Policy and Politics, Policy Studies Journal, Government and Policy, Urban Affairs Quarterly, Public Administration Review, Society and Space, Urban Geography,* and *Journal for the Theory of Social Behavior.* He is on the editorial boards of both *Cities* and the *Urban Affairs Quarterly,* and is editor of the *Routledge Political Geography* series.